The Dilemma of Freedom
and Foreknowledge

The Dilemma
of Freedom and
Foreknowledge

LINDA TRINKAUS ZAGZEBSKI

New York   Oxford
OXFORD UNIVERSITY PRESS
1991

Dedicated to my father
Walter R. Trinkaus

Oxford University Press

Oxford   New York   Toronto
Delhi   Bombay   Calcutta   Madras   Karachi
Petaling Jaya   Singapore   Hong Kong   Tokyo
Nairobi   Dar es Salaam   Cape Town
Melbourne   Auckland

and associated companies in
Berlin   Ibadan

Published by Oxford University Press, Inc.
200 Madison Avenue, New York, NY 10016

Oxford is a registered trademark of Oxford University Press

Library of Congress Cataloging-in-Publication Data
Zagzebski, Linda Trinkaus, 1946–
The dilemma of freedom and foreknowledge
Linda Trinkaus Zagzebski.
p.   cm.   Includes bibliographical references.
ISBN 0-19-506558-1
1. God—Omniscience.   2. Free will and determinism.
3. Time.5. I. Title.   BT131.Z34   1991
212′.7—dc20   90-35705

1 3 5 7 9 8 6 4 2

Printed in the United States of America
on acid-free paper

ACKNOWLEDGMENTS

Most of this book was written while I was on sabbatical leave from Loyola Marymount University during the academic year 1987–1988. I am grateful to LMU for sabbatical support and for numerous summer research grants, as well as to the many individuals at LMU who have given me constant encouragement in my career, especially Rev. Anthony B. Brzoska, S.J., dean of the College of Liberal Arts, and Dr. David Blake, chair of the Department of Philosophy, 1986–1989. I am also thankful to the Center for Philosophy of Religion at the University of Notre Dame, where I was the recipient of a Distinguished Scholar Fellowship during the fall semester 1987. Participants at the center that semester carefully read Chapter 1 and helped me considerably. They include Philip Quinn, Thomas Flint, George Mavrodes, Toomas Karmo, Robert Audi, Alfred Freddoso, Fred Crosson, David Burrell, and Dewey Houtinga. Alvin Plantinga has been a constant help and inspiration to my work since I first began working on theistic metaphysics.

Many thanks as well to Edward Wierenga for comments on Chapter 1 and parts of Chapters 3 and 4, to William Wainwright for suggestions on Chapters 1 to 4, to Philip Quinn and Norman Kretzmann for comments on Chapter 2, to Robert Adams for Chapter 5, and to Timothy Shanahan for Chapter 6. I am especially grateful to William Alston and Eleonore Stump for detailed comments on the whole manuscript, and to an anonymous Oxford referee. In addition, I wish to thank my devoted research assistant, Daniel E. Deka, who did substantial work on the bibliography.

A portion of Chapter 3 was read at the Pacific Regional Meeting of the Society of Christian Philosophers at Westmont College, Santa Barbara, California, March 1988. The appendix, "A New Foreknowledge Dilemma," was read at the Pacific Division Meeting of the American Philosophical Association in Oakland, California, March 1989, and at the American Catholic Philosophical Association Meeting in New Orleans, Louisiana, March 1989. My thanks to the participants in those discussions.

Finally, I am grateful to my husband Ken and our twin sons Walter and Sander, who put up with my long hours of writing without complaint.

Los Angeles   L. Z.
April 1990

CONTENTS

The Dilemma of Freedom
and Foreknowledge

They therefore as to right belongd,
So were created, nor can justly accuse
Thir maker, or thir making, or thir Fate;
As if Predestination over-rul'd
Thir will, dispos'd by absolute Decree
Or high foreknowledge; they themselves decreed
Thir own revolt, not I: if I foreknew,
Foreknowledge had no influence on their fault,
Which had no less prov'd certain unforeknown.
So without least impulse or shadow of Fate,
Or by me immutablie foreseen,
They trespass, Authors to themselves in all
Both what they judge and what they choose, for so
I formed them free, and free they must remain,
Till they enthrall themselves: I else must change
Their nature, and revoke the high Decree
Unchangeable, Eternal, which Ordain'd
Thir freedom, they themselves ordain'd thir fall.

        MILTON, *Paradise Lost*, Bk. III, 111–128

1

The Foreknowledge Dilemmas

I have a deep desire to know how it can be that God knows all things beforehand and that, nevertheless, we do not sin by necessity. . . . Since God knew that man would sin, that which God foreknew must necessarily come to pass. How then is the will free when there is apparently this unavoidable necessity?

St. Augustine, *On Free Will*, Book III, chap. ii.

1. Introduction

1.1. The Simple Form of the Theological Dilemma

The problem of divine foreknowledge has vexed philosophers as well as ordinary believers in God since at least the third century. In related forms it has bothered philosophers longer than that.[1] It is a fascinating puzzle, and for that reason attracts even nonbelievers. But to the religious person it is not only interesting, it is profoundly important for, if it is not mistaken, it forces the religious person to give up one of a pair of beliefs both of which are central to Christian practice. These beliefs are, first, that God has infallibly true beliefs about everything that will happen in the future, and second, that human beings have free will in a sense of "free" that is incompatible with determinism.

I believe there are strong motivations in the Christian tradition for each of the beliefs that generate the dilemma, although I will not argue extensively for this view. I believe, then, that any putative solution that weakens or denies one of these beliefs should be rejected or, at any rate, accepted only as a last resort. My purpose in this book is to show that we need not fall back on the last resort.

In this chapter I will first present the strongest general form of the dilemma I can devise and will show how it differs from weaker foreknowledge dilemmas and from the problem of future truth. In doing so I will examine the concept of the necessity of the past, an important element in all interesting forms of the dilemma. I will then propose two versions of the dilemma, each threatening human acts with a different sort of necessity. The Accidental Necessity Version has appeared throughout the history of the problem. The Causal Necessity Version has been dismissed as a pseudo-problem since ancient times, but I think current work on the causal relation makes it more threatening now than ever before. I will conclude the chapter by distinguishing negative and positive solutions to the foreknowledge dilemma and will describe what I think we want in a good positive solution.

I have said that the problem of divine foreknowledge arises from an alleged clash between two beliefs. The first is that God has infallibly true beliefs about everything that will happen in the future. This belief is grounded in the conviction that God is essentially omniscient. The second is that some human acts are done freely, in a sense that includes the ability to do otherwise. But these intuitions immediately generate a dilemma, for it seems that the following three states of affairs are inconsistent.

(1) God's being infallible.
(2) God's believing at $t1$ that I will do S at $t3$.
(3) My being free to refrain from doing S at $t3$.

If (1) obtains, then it is impossible that God's beliefs turn out to be false. But if the belief in (2) cannot turn out to be false, and if it is impossible to affect the past, it seems to follow that no matter what I do at $t3$, I cannot make it happen that God did not truthfully believe at $t1$ that I would do S. This seems contrary to (3).

The concept of omniscience is a difficult one, and it raises a number of questions unrelated to the problem of foreknowledge. A strong form of the dilemma of foreknowledge can be generated from just two properties that I take to be consequences of essential omniscience: the property of knowing the future and infallibility.

I will adopt the following definition of "omniscience."

(4) A is *omniscient* $\longleftrightarrow$ A knows the truth value of every proposition.

I do not claim that (4) captures everything that is included in cognitive perfection, but it does seem to me to capture the notion of omniscience, at least to the extent that that notion relates to propositional knowledge. It is compatible with (4) that omniscience be an accidental property. A may acquire the property or lose it. A may have it in one possible world but not others. We should then understand essential omniscience as follows.

(5) *A* is *essentially omniscient* ⟷ It is impossible that *A* exist and fail to know the truth value of any proposition.

(5) says that if *A* is essentially omniscient, then *A* is omniscient at all times in every possible world in which *A* exists. There is no possible world in which *A* exists and fails to know at any time the truth value of every proposition in that world.

Infallibility is a different concept than omniscience, even though the two are clearly related. I suggest we adopt the following definitions.

(6) *A* is *infallible* ⟷ *A* cannot make a mistake in his beliefs. For any proposition *p*, if *A* believes *p* is true, *p* is true. If *A* had believed *p* was true, *p* would have been true.

Even though this definition has modal import, it still permits infallibility to be an accidental property. There is nothing in the definition of "infallible" that prevents the property from being relative to times. The possibility that *A* may acquire infallibility at a time or lose it at a time is left open. Furthermore, infallibility may be relative to certain roles or limited to beliefs of a certain description (e.g., when the Pope speaks *ex cathedra*). Omniscience, in contrast, is never qualified in this way. The definition of essential infallibility is as follows.

(7) *A* is *essentially infallible* ⟷ It is impossible that *A* fail to be infallible. For any proposition *p*, if *A* believes *p* at any time in any world, *p* is true in that world.

On these definitions it follows that a being who is essentially omniscient is infallible and essentially so, and the view that God is infallible no doubt rests on a general belief in his essential omniscience. Simple omniscience does not entail infallibility, however, nor does infallibility or essential infallibility entail omniscience. Simple omniscience does not entail infallibility because omniscience lacks the modal import of infallibility. A being who is omniscient in *w* knows the truth value of all propositions in *w*, but this is not to say it is impossible that he make a mistake. There may be other worlds in which he believes falsehoods. Furthermore, infallibility, even essential infallibility, does not entail omniscience, since all essential infallibility guarantees is the impossibility of a mistake in a belief. There may still be true propositions that an infallible being neither believes nor disbelieves.

All that we need to get a strong general form of the foreknowledge dilemma is the assumption that God is infallible. It must be assumed that if God believed in the past that I would do something in the future, then it is impossible that he be mistaken in that belief. Infallibility is therefore sufficient to support the following premise.

(8) $\Box$ (God believes $p \rightarrow p$).

It is not necessary to assume that he knows the truth value of all propositions, nor that he is infallible at all times in all worlds in which he exists.

What if we *do* assume that God is essentially omniscient? In that case we can support a stronger premise.

(9) $\Box$ (God believes $p \longleftrightarrow p$).

Next consider (2), the state of affairs of God's believing that I will do S at $t3$. Just what state of affairs is this? There is a particular tradition in western philosophy of denying that knowledge entails belief. On this view knowing and believing are mutually exclusive mental states. If this is so, no state of affairs of the form of (2) obtains, although the state of affairs of God's *knowing* my future act does obtain in the past. But no matter how we analyze knowledge and belief, it is still the case that if God knows p than he takes it to be true that p. I wish to formulate the dilemma at the outset in such a way that *believing p* means nothing more than *taking it to be true that p*. This is no more than what Augustine says when he defines belief as *thinking with assent*.[2] At the start of this investigation, then, I wish to remain as neutral as possible with respect to the analysis of such a mental state. In particular, I make no assumptions about whether the object of such a mental state is a proposition or something else, whether the relation between the possessor of that mental state and its object is direct or indirect, whether it is certain or uncertain, fallible or infallible and, indeed, whether upon analysis being in the state of taking something to be true constitutes belief proper.

It is fair to assume, then, that believing is a generic mental state under which the knowing state is subsumed, and that this generic state can be agreed on by all parties to the discussion: Augustine, Boethius, Aquinas, Ockham, and Molina, who all formulated the dilemma in terms of fore*knowledge*, as well as those contemporary philosophers following Nelson Pike, who formulate the dilemma in terms of fore*belief* plus infallibility.[3] In my initial formulation of the dilemma in terms of God's belief about my future act I wish to beg no questions about whether God has beliefs properly speaking, and I leave for a possible future solution the argument that God does not have beliefs.

To get the conclusion that God's foreknowledge entails the necessity of my future act, we need two more assumptions, both of which will be given a great deal of analysis in this book. One is the principle of the necessity of the past, also called "accidental necessity." This kind of necessity has been much discussed in the recent literature, mostly inspired by its use by William of Ockham. Briefly, the idea is that if some event or state of affairs is in the past, there is nothing anyone can do about it now. Nothing an agent can do at $t2$ can affect what happens at $t1$.

The second assumption is the Transfer of Necessity Principle. Two forms of this principle will be discussed in this book.

Transfer of Necessity Principle 1 (TNP 1)

$\Box_w \phi$
$\Box (\phi \rightarrow \psi)$
$\vdash \Box_w \psi$

Transfer of Necessity Principle 2 (TNP 2)

$\Box_w \phi$
$\Box (\phi \longleftrightarrow \psi)$
$\vdash \Box_w \psi$

W-necessity may be any sort of necessity, but accidental necessity (the necessity of the past) is the sort of necessity relevant to our dilemma. The idea behind these two principles is that a necessity weaker than logical necessity can be transferred by strict implication (or strict equivalence) from the antecedent to the consequent of the conditional.

If God is infallible, then (8) is true. So if God's past belief that I will do S in the future now has the necessity of the past, it follows by TNP 1 that my future act is now necessary in the same sense in which the past is necessary. That is, there is nothing we can do about it now. Similarly, if God is essentially omniscient, then (9) is true. So if God's past belief that I will do S in the future now has the necessity of the past, it follows by TNP 2 that my future act is now necessary. Both transfer principles are highly plausible, but TNP 2 is undoubtedly the more plausible of the two. A foreknowledge dilemma that uses TNP 2 might therefore be considered stronger than one using TNP 1. However, the dilemma using TNP 1 requires only the assumption that God is infallible with respect to certain beliefs, while the dilemma using TNP 2 requires the stronger assumption that God is essentially omniscient. I leave it to the reader to decide which of the two forms is the more compelling. Since I believe God is essentially omniscient, I will frequently refer to the version of the dilemma that assumes essential omniscience, even though my purpose in this book is to discuss both versions. In any case, they are very closely related.

We are now ready to construct the general form of the argument for theological fatalism.

Suppose that God believes at $t1$ that I will do S at $t3$ and that God is infallible. It follows from God's infallibility that:

(10) Necessarily, if God believes at $t1$ that I will do S at $t3$, then I do S at $t3$.

From the necessity of the past we know that:

(11) It is accidentally necessary at $t2$ that God believes at $t1$ that I will do S at $t3$.

By TNP 1 we know that:

(12) If (10) and (11), then it is accidentally necessary at $t2$ that I do S at $t3$.

It follows that:

(13) It is accidentally necessary at $t2$ that I do S at $t3$.

But:

(14) If it is accidentally necessary at $t2$ that I do S at $t3$, I do not do S at $t3$ freely.

Therefore:

(15) I do not do S at $t3$ freely.

If we assume that God is essentially omniscient, the argument is exactly similar except that (10) is replaced by the following.

(10') Necessarily, God believes at $t1$ that I will do S at $t3$ if and only if I do S at $t3$.

And (12) follows by TNP 2 instead of TNP 1.

The place of Transfer of Necessity Principles in the strongest formulations of the foreknowledge dilemma shows that it is not guilty of a common modal fallacy. It is sometimes thought that the dilemma has the following form:

It is necessary that if God knows at $t1$ that I will do S at $T3$, then I do S at $t3$. But then if God knows at $t1$ that I will do S at $t3$, it is necessary that I will do S at $t3$.

We can see that this argument fallaciously moves from a proposition of the form

(16) $\Box (Kgp \rightarrow p)$

to a proposition of the form

(17) $Kgp \rightarrow \Box p$

where Kxp: x knows p, and g: God. The truth of (16) is required by the logic of knowledge and is just a special case of the necessary truth.

(18) $\Box [(\exists x) Kxp \rightarrow p]$

(17) is needed for the denial of logical contingency to my act, but it is false.

The distinction in the scope of the modal operator expressed in (16) and (17) was understood by Aquinas and the medieval logicians.[4] It is sufficient to show that the truth of (16) does not make p necessary, and if this was all there is to the foreknowledge dilemma it would not be much of a dilemma. However, as we have just seen, it is not (16) alone that generates the problem, but the combination of (16) and $\Box$ Kgp, where the type of necessity intended in the necessity operator is the necessity of the past.

1.2. Related Foreknowledge Dilemmas

The dilemma of divine foreknowledge should not be confused with other related dilemmas. First, there is the problem of foreknowledge *simpliciter*. If I believe that classes at my university begin on a certain future date and I have very good grounds for my belief, then as long as my belief is true, this is usually thought to entail that I *know* the date classes begin. But I am not infallible; it could turn out that I am wrong. If it does turn out that I am wrong, then we say in retrospect that I did not know the date, whereas if it turns out that I am right, we say that I did know the date. So *if* the world cooperates with my justified beliefs about the future, those beliefs are called cases of knowledge. But God's beliefs about the future have a quite different status from mine. There is no question of waiting to see if the world cooperates with his justified beliefs in order to determine whether they merit the title "knowledge." Unlike the human case, there is no element of epistemic luck in God's knowledge. Since he is infallible, it is impossible for the world *not* to cooperate with his beliefs. And this feature of God's beliefs—their infallibility—makes the problem of divine foreknowledge much more intractable than the more general problem of noninfallible foreknowledge, or foreknowledge *simpliciter*.

What's more, the problem of divine foreknowledge is harder than the problem of the foreknowledge of an infallible, but nondivine, knower. This is because God is assumed to be much more than the passive recipient of the objects of knowledge. If God is the providential creator of everything outside of himself, his relationship to contingent events is not at all like the relationship between other knowers and contingent events. According to Christian doctrine, nothing is brought about, continues to be, or goes on unless God wills or at least permits it to be so. So if we interpret "wills" in a sense that includes "permits," and if we also assume that God is necessarily existent and essentially omniscient, then any proposition of the form *God wills that p* is strictly equivalent to the proposition *p*. But I hope to show by a thought experiment that this creates special problems for a solution to the problem of *divine* foreknowledge. This is because the providence doctrine seems to preclude any solution in which God's will plays no part in making what is true be true. In fact, many Christian philosophers have thought that God knows the future precisely *by* knowing his will.[5]

To see why the dilemma of a divine, infallible foreknower is more difficult than the dilemma of a nondivine infallible foreknower, consider a certain imaginative attempt to get out of the foreknowledge dilemma. Suppose that one day you run across a library of books called "The Story of the World." This amazing collection of books contains volumes giving in chronological order a complete description of the created world as far back as you care to go on into the indefinite future. If it is thought that the world has no beginning and/or no end, we can add the stipulation that no matter how far you walk in either direction, you never reach the end of the collection. Now suppose that you first glance at the books and see that there are sentences written on all the pages for every moment of every day of every year, both for those years in the past and for those years still to come. Sentences do not leap onto blank pages as you read them or anything like that. The books are just like any other books except for the mind-boggling size of the collection. Now I think that most of us are strongly inclined to say that reading the pages of one of these books has no effect on what is written on the pages and, therefore, your knowing what the book says has no bearing on the fact that it says it. You might not have found the book—in fact, it might have happened that nobody ever found the book—but we do not think that that would have made any difference at all to what the book says.

Of course, you might doubt whether such a library is possible. You might say that the future or parts of the future have not been written yet and, if so, you might say that this is because they are not yet true. But that is another problem. The point is just that *if* there could be such books, it seems to make no difference to what the books say that you know what they say. Your knowing seems to create no difficulties that are not there already because of the very existence of the books.

Furthermore, I think we might still maintain this even if your powers of cognition were infallible. Suppose that the books not only contain the whole truth and nothing but the truth, but they have a certain essential power. They cause anyone who reads them to grasp perfectly and come to believe whatever they say and nothing else. So even if the world had been different and the books had therefore said something different, a reader would have believed whatever they said. And suppose that you have the essential property of reading the books at a certain time. If this happened, your beliefs at the time of your reading would be infallible. But even then, it does not look as if either your infallibility or the fact of your knowing some specific contents of the books has anything to do with what the books say. It is tempting to draw a moral from this story, namely, that knowing *p* does not affect the truth of *p*, and this is the case even if the knowing is infallible. Knowing is an act or a state that is logically independent of whatever it is that makes the object of knowledge true.

I will argue that this way out of the dilemma does not work even for the nondivine knower but, even if it did, it cannot work in the case of a God who is the creator of the world and conserves it in existence from moment to moment. This is because God as creator is the metaphysical ground of all truth. On the book analogy he is not just the reader, but the author (or at least coauthor) of the books. The fact that God is the ground of all truth creates tensions with human freedom anyway, but it also puts a constraint on any acceptable solution to the divine foreknowledge problem. An acceptable solution cannot portray God as the passive finder and reader of "The Story of the World." Even if the infallible foreknowledge of a reader of "The Story of the World" does not take away our freedom, such a model cannot be used to explain the foreknowledge of a providential God. We will return to the doctrine of providence in Chapter 5. Here I wish to point out simply that this doctrine creates special restrictions on the type of solution we can permit. I conclude that the problem of a creating and providential God who has infallible foreknowledge of human free acts is harder than the problem of nonprovidential infallible foreknowledge and much harder than the problem of noninfallible foreknowledge.

"The Story of the World" analogy might lead us to conclude that the threat of fatalism brought about by God's foreknowledge is just a special case of the threat of fatalism brought about by future truth. That is, it is sometimes thought that the mere fact that certain propositions about the future are now true makes them or the states of affairs they are about necessary. Several writers on foreknowledge see no difference between the foreknowledge dilemma and the problem of logical fatalism.[6] About "The Story of the World" analogy they would say that the mere existence of such a set of books with the pages for the future filled in is sufficient to take away our freedom. Conversely, if there is nothing fatalistic in the existence of "The Story of the World," there is nothing fatalistic in the act of reading future parts of the story. Theological fatalism is just a special case of logical fatalism, they would say and, if there is no worry about the latter, there is no worry about the former.

This conclusion, however, would be too hasty. I will argue next that the premise of the necessity of the past is much more plausible in the argument for theological fatalism than in the argument for logical fatalism. This means that the problem of infallible foreknowledge is considerably more serious than the problem of future truth.

1.3. Logical Fatalism

There are a number of different versions of the argument for logical fatalism, although each one argues from the truth of a proposition at one point in time to the necessity of it, or to the necessity of a proposition entailed by it, at another point in time. Some commit a common modal fallacy that parallels the fallacious argument I discussed in Section 1.1, and I will not consider any of those here. The more interesting make use of the notion of necessity *per accidens*, or the necessity of the past. This concept appears in the strongest versions of both the argument for logical fatalism and the argument for theological fatalism.

In the following arguments I will assume that propositions are the things that are true or false and that propositions are expressed by sentences. I do not think either of the arguments requires a particular view on the nature of propositions, that is, what sorts of entities they are. It is not even necessary that they be distinguished from sentences, although in that case the arguments would require some minor rewording.

The identity conditions for propositions will not be given, but an assumption about propositional identity must be made in the first argument. In that argument it is assumed that a particular future-tensed sentence about an event at *t3* expresses the same proposition at *t1* as it does at *t2*. This seems to be a reasonable assumption about the identity of this proposition and, again, it does not matter whether the proposition is understood to be the same as the sentence. In the second argument this assumption about the identity of propositions is not needed. Instead, it is assumed that what the sentence "Jones will not do *S* tomorrow" now expresses entails what the sentence "Jones will not do *S* the day after tomorrow" expressed yesterday. It does not matter for that argument whether or not they are the same proposition.

Finally, both arguments assume a certain connection between propositions and states of affairs. Necessarily, if a certain proposition is true, then a certain state of affairs obtains. That state of affairs is said to obtain by the proposition. The notions of necessity and contingency apply both to propositions and to states of affairs. A proposition is necessarily true just in case the state of affairs said to obtain by that proposition obtains necessarily in the same sense of "necessary." A proposition is contingently true just in case the state of affairs said to obtain by that proposition obtains contingently in the same sense of "contingent." The relevant sense of necessity is accidental necessity, which will be explained presently.

Occasionally I will speak of "events" instead of "states of affairs." I assume that events are a subclass of states of affairs, but nothing turns on their being singled out as a special class, and their identity conditions should not be relevant to the arguments I will consider. Some examples simply seem to be more naturally understood as examples about events rather than as examples of the more general category of states of affairs.

The logical fatalist argues that if the past is necessary *per accidens*, so is the future. I will consider first a past-to-future version of the argument for logical fatalism and then a future-to-past *reductio* version. The wording of both arguments is my own; however, the second one comes from Diodorus Cronus and the spirit of the first can be found in many places. I have chosen these two because I think they are strong examples of the case for logical fatalism.

First Argument for Logical Fatalism

Consider the proposition expressed at *t1* by "Jones will do *S* at *t3*," which we will suppose is true at *t1*, and suppose that it is now *t2*. Call that proposition *Sj*. If what *was* the case is now necessarily or

inalterably the case, since *Sj was* true, it is now necessarily or
inalterably the case that *Sj* was true. The fact that it was true is now
necessary *per accidens*. But if it is inalterably the case that *Sj*
was true, and if a proposition cannot change truth value, it is
inalterably the case that *Sj is* true. Since *Sj* is still expressed by
"Jones will do *S* at *t3*", it is now necessarily or inalterably the case
that what "Jones will do *S* at *t3*" now expresses is true. So Jones's
future acts *S* is even now inalterable. By a generalization of the
foregoing argument it follows that the future has the same necessity
as the past.

A *reductio* version that goes from future to past, and which I have
modified from the Master Argument of Diodorus Cronus is an interesting variation.

Second Argument for Logical Fatalism

Assume that it is *not* now inevitable that Jones will do *S* tomorrow,
although he will, as a matter of fact, do *S*. This means that the
proposition expressed today by "Jones will do *S* tomorrow" is true,
but possibly false. So what "Jones will not do *S* tomorrow" now
expresses is possibly true. That proposition entails the proposition
expressed yesterday by "Jones will not do *S* the day after tomorrow." But it was true yesterday and, hence, is now necessary *per
accidens*, that what "Jones will do *S* the day after tomorrow"
expressed was true. But then it is impossible *per accidens* that what
"Jones will not do *S* the day after tomorrow" expressed yesterday
was true. But since a possibility cannot imply an impossibility, the
assumption that the proposition expressed now by "Jones will not
do *S* tomorrow" is now possibly true is false. It must, therefore, be
impossible that it is true, and so it is inevitable that Jones do *S*
tomorrow after all.

Even though I believe the threat of logical fatalism is weaker than the
threat of theological fatalism, this cannot be demonstrated without an
examination of the concept of the necessity of the past, a type of necessity
that both the logical fatalist and the theological fatalist require in their
respective arguments. Section 2 will be devoted to an examination of this
notion. In Section 3 we will return to logical fatalism and will see how the
logical fatalist's appeal to the necessity of the past is weaker than the
analogous appeal of the theological fatalist.

2. Necessity *per accidens*: The Necessity of the Past

2.1. Historical Background

The move from truth to necessity that is at heart of the argument for fatalism is completely implausible without the view that the past has a special kind of necessity, what the thirteenth-century logicians called necessity *per accidens*, and which is associated in the contemporary literature with William of Ockham. In this section I wish to look at the basis of this notion in philosophy and common sense.

In the introduction to the Kretzmann-Adams translation of Ockham's treatise *De Praedestinatione*, Adams says the term "necessity *per accidens*" had already appeared in the work of the thirteenth-century logician William of Sherwood, who introduces the notion as follows.

> Notice, however, that "impossible" is used in two ways. It is used in one way of whatever cannot be true now or in the future or in the past; and this is "impossible *per se*"—e.g., "a man is an ass." It is used in the other way of whatever cannot be true now or in the future although it could have been true in the past, as if I were to say "I have not walked"; and this is "impossible *per accidens*." Similarly, in case something cannot be false now or in the future or in the past it is said to be "necessary *per se*"—e.g., "God is." But it is "necessary *per accidens*" in case something cannot be false now or in the future although it could have been [false] in the past—e.g., "I have walked."[7]

As the notion is used in this passage, necessity *per accidens* is a temporally relative kind of necessity. The salient difference between things that are necessary *per accidens* and those that are necessary *per se* is that there was a time in the past when the former was not necessary, whereas the latter is necessary at all times. It cannot be, then, that anything is necessary *per accidens* at all moments of time. This should immediately alert us to a difficulty in any argument for fatalism that purports to use *this* notion of necessity.

Ockham uses a related concept in his treatise *De Praedestinatione*, where the temporal relativity is connected more closely with the time of the state of affairs the proposition is about.

> Some propositions are about the present as regards both their wording and their subject matter. Where such [propositions] are concerned, it is universally true that every true proposition about the present has [corresponding to it] a necessary one about the past—e.g., "Socrates is seated," "Socrates is walking," "Socrates is just," and the like.

> Other propositions are about the present as regards their wording only and are equivalently about the future. Where such [propositions] are concerned, the rule that every true proposition about the present has [corresponding to it] a necessary one about the past is not true.[8]

Ockham's use of the label "necessity *per accidens*" appears in at least one place: "Many propositions about the past are of this sort. They are necessary *per accidens* because it was contingent that they would be necessary, and they were not always necessary."[9] Ockham, then, like William of Sherwood, uses "accidental necessity" in such a way that it does not apply to propositions that are always necessary.

The concept of the necessity of the past is, however, much older than the thirteenth century, although it did not go under the name "necessity *per accidens*." Aristotle's argument for fatalism in *Metaph.* vi, 3, is explicitly based on the necessity of the past, and Richard Sorabji argues that the famous Sea Battle argument of *De. Int.* 9 implicitly uses it as well.[10] And, of course, we have just looked at a version of the argument of Aristotle's younger contemporary, Diodorus Cronus, that includes the premise that whatever is past is necessary.

Aquinas refers to the necessity of the past in several places. He expresses it in the *Summa Theologiae* as follows.

> Although it is impossible accidentally for the past not to have been, if one considers the past thing itself, as, for instance, the running of Socrates, nevertheless, if the past thing is considered as past, that it should not have been is impossible, not only in itself, but absolutely since it implies a contradiction. . . .
>
> Some things, however, at one time were in the nature of possibility, whilst they were yet to be done, which now fall short of the nature of possibility, when they have been done. So is God said not to be able to do them because they themselves cannot be done.[11]

Notice that like Sherwood and Ockham, Aquinas means by the necessity of the past a kind of necessity that applies to things that at one time were not necessary.

Finally, in contemporary philosophy, David Lewis defines a type of necessity that seems to be very close to the notion of necessity *per accidens*.

> Corresponding to a kind of time-dependent necessity we may call inevitability at time t, and its strict conditional, we assign to each world i as its sphere of accessibility the set of all worlds that are exactly like i at all times up to time t, so $\Box$ ($\phi \rightarrow \psi$) is true at i if and only if ψ is true at all ϕ-worlds that are exactly like i up to t.[12]

It is risky to attribute the same motive for this notion of necessity to philosophers as disparate as Diodorus Cronus, Ockham, and Lewis, but it seems to me likely that the fact that it has appeared so often, at different points in philosophical history, and in philosophers otherwise so different from each other suggests that the root of the notion is something simple, something many people would take to be common sense. The basis for the notion of the necessity of the past, I suggest, is a certain view on the nature of time.

2.2. Temporal Asymmetry

It is usually thought that the past and the future are ontologically asymmetrical, although it is not easy to say just what this asymmetry amounts to. Often it is said that the past is real while the future is not. The future does not exist, so the past is not related to the present as the present is related to the future since the future is not *there* to be related to anything. The present contains traces of the past, but no traces of the future. This difference is reflected in the way we treat past and future individuals and in the way we think of our past and future selves. What I am now is no doubt constituted much more by my past self than by my future self, and generally we think of the present as partially constituted by the past but not at all by the future. We also think that different feelings are appropriate for the future than for the past. We feel regret, guilt, relief, and nostalgia about the past, but not about the future, while we feel fear, dread, excitement or joy about the future, but not about the past. The idea that the future does not exist is connected with the belief that there can be no backward causation, for how could the nonexistent have any causal efficacy?[13] It is also connected with the idea that there is no backward counterfactual dependency, a point that Lewis says is *the* element constituting the asymmetry between past and future.[14]

The intuition that there is an ontological temporal asymmetry is admittedly vague, but nonetheless important. Its significance for the present discussion lies in its connection with the view that the asymmetry is also modal. Most people believe that the past has a necessity that the future lacks. This is perhaps unhappily expressed by the claim that the past is "inalterable," whereas the future is not. There is nothing we can do now about the past, although it is at least arguable that we can do something about the future. In common parlance this is expressed by the aphorism "There is no use crying over spilt milk," which is interesting, not only for what it claims there is no use crying over as for what it implies there *is* some use in crying over, namely, the future.[15] Perhaps the most perspicuous way of putting this is to say that there is only one possible past, but there are many possible futures, each of which, but no more than one of which, can be *the* future. It is now necessary that the actual past be the past and impossible that anything other than the actual past be the past. On the contrary, it is now possible that any one of a number of alternative futures be the future including, perhaps, no future at all. We can easily think of the world going out of existence now, but not of its coming into existence now. We can easily think of the world going in any number of directions after now, but not so easily of its coming to now from any number of directions. So there are possible but nonactual futures, but no possible but nonactual pasts.

The temporal asymmetry I claim is part of common sense is both ontological and modal, and the two asymmetries are probably connected. This connection is expressed by the claim that the past is fixed while the future is open. The terms "fixed" and "open" can be understood in both ontological and modal senses. If the past is fixed in the sense that it is genuinely real and hence ontologically finished, this suggests that it is determinate, untouchable. On the other hand, if the future is not real, it is indeterminate and still to be created, and this leaves open the possibility that we might have a hand in creating it.

As Ockham sees it, the ontological difference between past and future is related to the Aristotelian act/potency distinction. The past has been actualized, but the contingent future, unlike the contingent past, exists merely in potency. If some state of affairs A is causally contingent, then there is a time at which there exists the potency in things both for A and for not A. But once one becomes actual, the potency for the other is lost from that point of time on.[16] Ockham used this picture to explain how it is that the contingent past has a kind of necessity lacking in the contingent future.[17] A true future contingent proposition is about a state of affairs that is not now settled by something actual, whereas a true past contingent proposition *is* settled by something actual. And this is the basis for the claim that the latter has a necessity that the former lacks. The necessity in question is intrinsically related to lacking potency for the opposite.

The *truth* of a proposition p at t, however, does not require that there be no potency in things at t for p's being false. A proposition is true at *every* time as long as there is *some* time at which the potency for its being false is lost. So even though the truth of a future contingent proposition cannot change and the state of affairs expressed by the proposition will obtain, there is still potency for the opposite until such time as it becomes actual, and necessity goes with actuality. This is the reason a true future contingent proposition is not now necessary *per accidens* but a true contingent proposition about the past or present is.

Necessity *per accidens* is therefore meant to be distinct from both logical and causal necessity. An event in the past that is logically and causally contingent can still be accidentally necessary. It seems, then, that the notion of accidental necessity ought to be defined independently of logical and causal necessity. Unfortunately, discussions of it often do not do this, and the resulting confusion makes an analysis of the concept very difficult. For example, causal necessity is often treated as a species of accidental necessity, and it is said that anything that is a causal consequence of something that is accidentally necessary is also accidentally necessary. This would not lead to difficulty if the distinctive element in those states of affairs that are accidentally necessary but not causally necessary were identified. But the only element I know of mentioned by either the medieval or contemporary writers on this topic is simple pastness. This suggests that it is pastness alone that confers accidental necessity. If this were the case, then *all* of the past would be accidentally necessary. As we will see in Chapter 3, some proponents of accidental necessity wish to deny this. But then they must intend there to be a criterion in addition to pastness that must obtain if something is necessary *per accidens*. To my knowledge no such criterion has been satisfactorily identified.

If pastness is the distinguishing element of the accidentally necessary, there is another problem. None of the future could be accidentally necessary. But, it will be objected, it is impossible to isolate necessity *per accidens* to the past because of the Transfer of Necessity Principles. TNP 1 is often claimed to be highly plausible, even undeniable. If a state of affairs *A* is accidentally necessary and *A* strictly implies a state of affairs *B*, then *B* is accidentally necessary, no matter how *B* is temporally related to the present. The Transfer of Necessity Principles will be more thoroughly discussed in Chapter 6 and their denial proposed as a possible solution to the dilemma, but I think it is fair to note at the outset that any such principle requires argument, or at least intuitive justification, and such support must be examined against the content of the concept it is supposed to elucidate. I have claimed that both the philosophical background of the notion of accidental necessity in Aristotelian metaphysics and certain commonsense claims about time produce a notion of a kind of necessity that belongs to the past and not to the future. Of course, as is the case with all preanalytic concepts, once philosophers begin working on them they may need to be modified. So it may turn out that for good philosophical reasons we must say that not all of the past is accidentally necessary while some of the future is. But concepts will bend only so far. It seems to me that the root intuition of the concept of necessity *per accidens* is as strong about what it excludes as about what it includes. The intuition that the past has a special kind of necessity distinct from both logical and causal necessity is no stronger than the intuition that the future does not have such necessity.

In support of this claim, consider the following experiment. Suppose you are asked to make two lists. On the *A* list you are to write down things you can no longer do anything about, and imagine you are instructed to leave out anything logically or causally necessary. On the *B* list you are to write down things you *can* do something about. Now it seems to me that the *A* list will include simple past events and states of affairs, such as your attending a certain university 20 years ago, a car accident you had last week, and your failure to pay your credit card bill by the due date last month. It probably would not include (unless you have thought about this in advance more than you should!) disjunctive states of affairs or such alleged states of affairs as its-being-the-case-last-week-that-in-1999-Smith-will-die-a-violent-death. Your *B* list will include simple logically and causally contingent future events or states of affairs. Some of the items on your *B* list might be just like items on your *A* list except that the latter is past and the former is future, such as visiting-Gary-last-week, as opposed to visiting-Gary-next-week. If you thought of it, you might even put down the past beliefs of persons on your *A* list.

My point in describing this thought experiment is that the way in which you make out the *A* list is not independent of the way in which you make out the *B* list. You may be consciously following a principle such as: Logically and causally contingent past events go on the *A* list; logically and causally contingent future events go on the *B* list. But it might be that you cannot formulate such a principle to your satisfaction at all, and it is very probable that you cannot precisely define what you mean by an event or state of affairs. Nonetheless, I maintain that most people would have no trouble writing down many items on both lists. An account of accidental necessity, I suggest, should be consistent with typical examples of these lists.

It seems, then, that the pastness of some state of affairs *A* gives *A* a special kind of necessity. It is a factor in virtue of which I am unable to do anything about *A*. Just as I am unable to do anything about the logically necessary state of affairs of its being the case that $2 + 2 = 4$, and I am unable to do anything about the causally necessary state of affairs of the sun's rising tomorrow, I am also unable to do anything about even logically and causally contingent events that are now over and done with.

At least, that is what is claimed by the proponents of the concept of accidental necessity.

2.3. Objections to Temporal Asymmetry

I have argued that the concept of accidental necessity relies on an alleged asymmetry between past and future. But some philosophers have denied temporal asymmetry. In a fascinating passage Lukasiewicz makes the claim that we should not think of the past as any different than the future.

> We should not treat the past differently from the future. . . . Facts whose effects have disappeared altogether, and which even an omniscient mind could not infer from those now occurring, belong to the realm of possibility. One cannot say about them that they took place, but only that they were *possible*. It is well that it should be so. There are hard moments of suffering and still harder ones of guilt in everyone's life. We should be glad to be able to erase them not only from our memory but also from existence.[18]

Lukasiewicz is undoubtedly right that we all would be glad to erase some parts of the past from existence, but I doubt that very many of us think that this is an option. However, I am not attempting to refute those who share the view of Lukasiewicz here. Those people have an easy solution to the foreknowledge dilemma and will not be bothered enough by it to read this book anyway. I quote Lukasiewicz since I think most of us find it dramatic precisely because it is directly contrary to our own intuitions.

For quite different reasons Anthony Kenny and A. N. Prior deny temporal asymmetry, arguing that the putative asymmetry is based on a misunderstanding about the concepts of past and future. Sometimes we speak of "the past" as what *did* happen, while "the future" means what *might* happen, and with this way of speaking it seems that although there is a single past, there are many alternative futures. But this, they say, is a mistake.[19] The past just is what *has* happened, given that all the deterministic and indeterministic causes affecting the past were what they were. And, similarly, the future just is what *will* happen, given that all the deterministic and indeterministic causes affecting the future will be what they will be. In other words, the future, like the past, is the outcome of whatever produces events and states of affairs, so there is one future just as much as there is one past. But in this sense of "past" and "future," although we cannot alter the past, we cannot alter the future either.

The notion of accidental necessity is not much threatened by this argument. Even though the terms "the past" and "the future" imply that there is uniquely one of each, the proponent of accidental necessity need not deny this. As stated before, the point of the claim of temporal asymmetry is just that there are many alternative chains of events, each of which now has the status of possibly being *the* future. On the other hand, there is only one chain of events that now has the status of possibly being the past.

Even though this view is supported by common sense, I have not argued that it is perspicuous. Theoreticians from the time of Aristotle to the present have attempted to make it so, but it seems to me that its justifiability is much deeper than that provided by any particular metaphysical theory. For the purposes of this chapter, I am arguing merely that the concept of necessity *per accidens* has time relativity as an essential component. It is supposed to be a kind of necessity that is directly connected to the nature of time. It belongs to the past in a way in which it does not and cannot belong to the future. So even if it becomes necessary to modify the view that necessity *per accidens* applies to all and only past states of affairs, it cannot turn out that all events, past, present, and future, have *this* kind of necessity.

Let us consider one more objection to temporal asymmetry. It might be thought that modern physics has made the concept obsolete. This is because one consequence of Einstein's theory of relativity is that simultaneity is relative. And this seems to mean that past and future are also relative, since the boundary between the past and the future is defined by the set of states of affairs simultaneous with "now." So two observers moving relative to each other at high speed and thinking themselves as at rest will, as they pass each other and say "past" and "future," refer to different things. What is future for one may be past for the other. But how can there be a real modal or ontological difference between past and future if the question of whether some event is past or future depends on my velocity relative to some other observer? It seems that the commonsense view of temporal asymmetry works only if there is a preferred frame of reference. But even though the view that there is such a preferred frame of reference is not inconsistent with Einsteinian physics, it may seem to be somewhat contrary to its spirit.[20]

Richard Sorabji and John Lucas have argued independently that relativity theory does not threaten the commonsense view of temporal asymmetry.[21] Lucas first argues that scientists ought to presuppose the modal asymmetry of past and future, since such asymmetry is a requirement for human agency.

The agent's concept of time is modal. Time is the passage from possibility through actuality to necessity. It clearly has a direction and to that extent coheres with what some physicists are impelled to say, but it clearly goes much further than physicists want to go, both in the uniqueness ascribed to the present and in the different status ascribed to the future and the past. . . .

In our generation scientists have come to recognize their moral responsibilities, and appreciate that although a particular science cannot answer questions of right and wrong, that does not mean that these are questions that scientists can put on one side. In the same way, it would be irrational when thinking about time to put on one side the knowledge gleaned from our own experience of time, either as observers or as agents. We could not be scientists unless we were also agents.[22]

In addition, Lucas argues that there are models in physics for the position that there is a state of absolute rest corresponding to which we can define the "real" relation of simultaneity and hence save the common-sense view of temporal asymmetry.

. . . although the special theory of relativity cannot single out any one of a set of frames of reference that are equivalent to one another under the Lorentz transformation as being at absolute rest, there is no reason why the special theory plus some other theory or some other consideration should not do so. This indeed happens in some versions of the general theory of relativity, where we sometimes distinguish a preferred frame of reference which we regard as being at rest. And we might have reason to do the same if we adjoined to the special theory some version of quantum mechanics or supposed our special relativistic universe peopled by rational agents.[23]

It seems to me that the state of modern physics with respect to the question of the absoluteness of past and future is ambiguous at best. It may succeed in weakening the hold of common sense on our notion of time, but it is nowhere near strong enough to demolish it altogether. The belief that time is asymmetrical in the sense I have described is supported by the enormous combined force of common sense and a metaphysics of time that has been developed over many centuries. It would take quite a bit more to threaten the idea of the necessity of the past used in the arguments for fatalism. If physics gets to such a point that we eventually see that the notion of time explained and indirectly defended here is to be rejected and that the argument against the compatibility of foreknowledge and freedom collapses with it, that is no problem for me, since my purpose is to defend the compatibilist position. But I wish to argue in this book that compatibilism can be defended even without help from modern physics.

3. The Rejection of Logical Fatalism

3.1. Truth in the Past and Accidental Necessity

We are now ready to use the analysis of necessity *per accidens* to show two things: first, that no argument using the concept of necessity *per accidens* can succeed in showing that the future has the same necessity as the past and, second, that aside from this point, the threat of logical fatalism, arising from the truth of future contingents, is not as strong as the threat of theological fatalism, arising from divine foreknowledge.

Notice first that if the intuition generating the concept of accidental necessity is what I have said it is, no argument for fatalism using such a concept can succeed, whether logical or theological. This is because we saw that the distinguishing feature of necessity *per accidens* is that it is a necessity that applies to propositions that were not always necessary. It is a type of necessity that applies to states of affairs for no reason other than their simple pastness. Temporal relativity is built into this notion of necessity. If it is removed, there is nothing left to it. We saw in Section 2.1 that this is a kind of necessity that is supposed to distinguish the logically and causally contingent past from the logically and causally contingent future. No matter how this kind of necessity is analyzed, it is not *accidental* necessity if it does not have this characteristic. Our quotations from William of Sherwood, William of Ockham, and St. Thomas Aquinas showed that in their uses of the notion the one feature that distinguished it from a stronger kind of necessity was the fact that if a proposition has it, it did not always have it. The temporal asymmetry of this type of necessity is central to it; it is what distinguishes it from all others. This means it can be maintained prior to an analysis of the concept. But then any argument that purports to show that such necessity belongs to the future just as well as the past must fail. At best it shows that the concept of accidental necessity is incoherent.

So if the concept of accidental necessity logically leads to the conclusion that there is no significant difference between the past and future with respect to our power to affect it, the concept is incoherent. And if the concept of accidental necessity is incoherent, not only can no argument for fatalism based on it succeed, but the commonsense intuitions about the asymmetry of past and future are false. On the other hand, if these intuitions about time are sound, the concept of accidental necessity as just explained is not empty and, if it is not empty, there must be a difference between the past and future with respect to it. In that case as well, the argument for fatalism must fail. So whether or not necessity *per accidens* is coherent, the argument for fatalism fails.

Let us now turn to the arguments for logical fatalism presented in Section 1.3. There is a vast literature on logical fatalism, and most of it attempts to find fault with fatalistic arguments. My purpose will not be to identify all the mistakes in the two arguments I have given. I wish to make only one point about them. I will argue that even though we know ahead of time that any argument for fatalism based on the necessity of the past must fail for the reasons just given, the argument for theological fatalism is more serious.

In each of the arguments for logical fatalism the past truth of a proposition is said now to be necessary *per accidens*. Both arguments need the assumption that if a certain proposition was true in the past, there is nothing we can do now about the fact that it was true in the past. In addition, the first argument needs the premise that the truth of a proposition cannot change over time, while the second argument needs instead the premise that a certain proposition expressed today entails a certain proposition that was (could have been) expressed yesterday.

Assuming that the concept of accidental necessity is coherent and that the arguments for fatalism are valid, it follows that each must have a false premise. The most direct and plausible escape from both arguments is to deny the first premise. It is false that the proposition expressed at $t1$ by "Jones will do S at $t3$" is accidentally necessary at $t2$. Similarly, it is false that the proposition expressed yesterday by "Jones will do S the day after tomorrow" is accidentally necessary today. There are many ways to justify these claims. One way is to say that propositions are timeless entities and are not literally true at times at all. If not, their truth cannot be accidentally necessary at times either. This move seems plausible to me, but I will not pursue it here. Another way is to say the propositions in question were not *yet* true at $t1$ (day before yesterday). Ockham rejects this move, and I think he was right to do so, even though it permits an easy solution to both kinds of fatalist arguments. A third way is to say that although these propositions were true at $t1$, they are in a class of exceptional cases that are not accidentally necessary at $t2$. This is Ockham's move, and it will be discussed in Chapter 3. Yet another way is to say that the past truth of propositions is not the sort of thing to which accidental necessity applies anyway. I prefer the final option, an option also taken by Sorabji.[24] I will attempt to motivate that choice next.

Both fatalist arguments proceed on the assumption that the truth of a proposition is the sort of thing that is accidentally necessary. The past truth of a proposition counts as something that *was* the case.[25] But it seems to me to be probable that if accidental necessity is anything at all, it is not something that belongs at *t2* to a particular proposition true at *t1*. In fact, I think that to be faithful to the intuition behind the concept of accidental necessity, we must deny that it applies to the truth of propositions at all. That may be surprising, given the fact that Ockham's account of necessity *per accidens* does make it a property of propositions, and virtually all of the recent literature follows him in this. But even apart from the logical fatalist's threat, I believe my interpretation is most faithful to the view of time underlying the notion of necessity *per accidens*. And I believe the defense of this view will show why the argument for theological fatalism is stronger than the argument for logical fatalism.

I have argued that according to the commonsense view of time, there is an asymmetry between past and future, an asymmetry that is both ontological and modal. The past is real; the future is not. The past is fixed; the future is not. Furthermore, I have argued that the notion of necessity *per accidens* as developed by medieval philosophers is closely connected with the Aristotelian distinction between potency and act, a distinction that is temporally relative. But notice that these intuitions are only plausible if the asymmetry in question is between the occurrence of past and future events (or states of affairs), not between the past and future truth of propositions. No one would speak of some propositions as real and others as unreal. And it is unnatural to speak of some propositions as fixed and others as open. Furthermore, the act/potency distinction has no application to propositions except derivatively. The intuition about the necessity of the past is an intuition about what has *happened* in the past, that is, about the events/states of affairs that obtained in the past. It is common, of course, to think that propositions and states of affairs are isomorphic. Every proposition says that some state of affairs obtains and that state of affairs is said to obtain by some proposition. I have no objections to thinking of states of affairs in this way for some purposes. But it seems to me that when we say that the past is necessary, fixed, irrevocable, beyond our control, we mean that the events and states of affairs that occurred in the past have that property, and that we mean this in a narrower sense of "states of affairs" than the one that is isomorphic with propositions.

What sense of state of affairs, then, is the one relevant to the concept of accidental necessity? In Section 2.2 I proposed a thought experiment with which an answer to this question should comply. I claimed that if asked to make two lists—one a list of things we can do nothing about and one a 'ist of things we *can* do something about—the items we would put on the first list would be typical cases of states of affairs in the intended sense. Let us consider an example. Take the founding of the Society of Christian Philosophers (SCP) in 1978. This is an event that took place in that year and the proposition *the SCP was founded in 1978* says that this event occurred. The intuition that the past is fixed is an intuition that events are fixed in the sense in which this event is fixed. Of course, given that this event occurred, it is related to other events and to other moments of time in many ways, and there are true propositions that say that these relationships obtain. For example, in 1948 the proposition *the SCP will be founded in 30 years* was true. But it is not correct to say that *that* proposition asserts the occurrence of an event or state of affairs that took place in 1948 and that thereafter became fixed. If there is any such state of affairs as *its being such that the SCP would be founded in 30 years*, it is not in the sense applicable to the intuition of the fixedness of the past. If we were giving a complete history of the world up to 1950, the things that were "over and done with" in 1950, it would *not* include any such state of affairs. One reason for this comes from the historical genesis of the notion of accidental necessity in the act/potency distinction. It is not reasonable to say that in 1948 the prior potency for its being the case that the SCP would be founded in 30 years became actual. To say that it did become actual is to say that it was really related to the founding of the SCP. However, if the future has no reality, but exists only in potency, the founding of the SCP did not yet have any reality and existed only in potency. Therefore, it could not have been the case that a potency for being 30 years before the founding of the SCP became actual in 1948.

We can borrow a position of William of Ockham to make this point in a different way. According to Ockham, the truth of a proposition at all times is *settled by* something real or actual at some time or other.[26] But this means that the fact that a proposition is true is not itself something real or actual, at least not in the sense related to accidental necessity. Ockham clearly distinguishes between the truth of a proposition and the actuality of something that settles such truth, and it is only the latter that is in the right category for becoming "fixed" and, hence, accidentally necessary.

Propositions and states of affairs have an important difference. A proposition is not tied to moments of time as an event is. Its truth is usually thought to be either timeless or omnitemporal. If omnitemporal, then if true at one time, it is true at all times, and there is no asymmetry between past and future. If timeless, then it is not true at moments of time at all and, again, there is no asymmetry between past and future. So there is not, or at least should not be, a temptation to think of propositions as becoming fixed at some point in time as there is with events. So on either view the proposition expressed by "Jones will do S at $t3$" is not accidentally necessary before $t3$.

I have suggested that the commonsense intuition about the unreality of the future, along with the act/potency distinction used by the medieval proponents of accidental necessity, show that the sense in which states of affairs in the past are accidentally necessary must be a narrower sense of "state of affairs" than the one that is isomorphic with propositions. And this sense excludes alleged states of affairs such as *being 400 years before the murder of Julius Caesar*, although I have given no reason to think it would exclude the beliefs of persons. I think it must be admitted that the intuitions grounding the concept of necessity *per accidens* are too vague to permit a definition of "state of affairs" in the intended sense. For my arguments in this chapter I do not need to give one anyway. My point is that it is reasonable to exclude from the category of past states of affairs that are now accidentally necessary those putative states of affairs that are needed for the argument for logical fatalism. I do not mean to say there is no reason *at all* to fear that the past truth of propositions is now accidentally necessary, but rather that God's past beliefs are not nearly as easy to exclude. And that is why the argument for theological fatalism is more serious.

It seems to me, then, that past truth does not threaten fatalism to the extent threatened by divine foreknowledge. This is because past truth is not an event or state of affairs that becomes "fixed" once it occurs or obtains, or if it *is* an event/state of affairs, it is so only marginally or ambiguously. The argument for logical fatalism, then, does not seriously threaten Jones's act with accidental necessity.

3.2. *Plantinga on Logical and Theological Fatalism*

I believe Alvin Plantinga gives logical fatalism more credit than he should in "On Ockham's Way Out." Here he maintains that the argument for theological fatalism formulated by Jonathan Edwards reduces to the argument for logical fatalism (called "logical determinism" by Plantinga).

> Clearly enough the argument can be transformed into an argument for logical determinism, which would run as follows. It was true, eighty years ago, that I will mow my lawn this afternoon. Since what is past is now necessary, it is now necessary that it was true eighty years ago that I will mow my lawn today. But it is logically necessary that if it was true eighty years ago that I will mow my lawn today, then I will mow my lawn today. It is therefore necessary that I will mow my lawn—necessary in just the sense

in which the past is necessary. But then it is not within my power not to mow; hence I will not mow freely.[27]

But as was noted before, the intuition that the past is necessary is not very convincing when understood as an intuition about the past truth of propositions. It is not plausible to say, as Plantinga does, "Since what is past is now necessary, it is now necessary that it was true eighty years ago that I will mow my lawn today." What *is* plausible is to say that what *happened* 80 years ago is now necessary *per accidens*. But even though it was the case 80 years ago that Plantinga would mow in 80 years, this is not something that happened then. That is not something that went on in the past, and there should be no worry that it now has the property of accidental necessity. There was, of course, a proposition that was true at that time to the effect that Plantinga would mow in 80 years, but I have suggested that there is no asymmetry between past and future truth as there is between the occurrence of past and future events. The logical fatalist, perhaps, does not appreciate this fact, but I suspect Edwards did. It is significant that his argument for theological fatalism seems to attribute accidental necessity to events or states of affairs rather than to propositions. But Plantinga ignores this aspect of it when he claims that it can be transformed into an argument for logical fatalism.

Consider the first part of Plantinga's quotation from Edwards.

1. I observed before, in explaining the nature of necessity, that in things which are past, their past existence is now necessary: having already made sure of existence, 'tis now impossible, that it should be otherwise than true, that that thing has existed.

2. If there be any such thing as a divine foreknowledge of the volitions of free agents, that foreknowledge, by the supposition, is a thing which already has, and long ago had existence; and so, now its existence is necessary; it is now utterly impossible to be otherwise, than that this foreknowledge should be, or should have been.[28]

What could Edwards mean by "things which are past," that have "already made sure of existence," if not events or states of affairs in the past? When he talks about foreknowledge that "is a thing which already has, and long ago had existence," he must mean the actual event/state of affairs of God's foreknowing. Whatever it is that already has existence, even though previously it did not, clearly it is not a proposition. A proposition is not the sort of thing that "makes sure of existence" at some time in the past. It is not one of the "things which are past." Nor is it reasonable to think of the truth of the proposition as one of the things that are past and that have made sure of existence, since the truth of that proposition is made sure of existence by something that happens 80 years future. It is most reasonable, then, to interpret the necessity of the past as used by Edwards in the preceding passage as referring to the events/states of affairs in the past, not to the existence of propositions in the past or to their past truth.

I conclude that if the necessity of the past is primarily an intuition about past events, the argument for theological fatalism is stronger than the argument for logical fatalism. So if Plantinga formulates theological fatalism in terms of past truth rather than the occurrence of past events, he is right that it reduces to logical fatalism, but then it seems to me he has not considered the strongest interpretation of Edwards' argument.

4. Two Versions of the Dilemma of Theological Fatalism

The divine foreknowledge dilemma poses a more serious problem than the problem of future truth. We simply cannot deny the accidental necessity of God's past beliefs as easily as the accidental necessity of the past truth of propositions. God's belief at $t1$ certainly seems to be an event or state of affairs, although we will leave for a possible future solution the position that it is not. On the face of it, then, God's past belief has the same necessity as any other past belief. But given the plausibility of the Transfer of Necessity Principles, aren't we led to the conclusion that my act at $t3$ was accidentally necessary before $t3$? Not quite. We saw in Section 3 that the analysis of the concept of necessity *per accidens* cannot apply to everything in the future, since temporal asymmetry is essential to that concept. So we are justified in concluding that there must be *something* wrong with the argument for theological fatalism. But since there is no point at which the argument clearly goes wrong, as there is in the argument for logical fatalism, it is a much greater threat.

Let us make a simple amendment to the Transfer of Necessity Principles to give theological fatalism as great an advantage as possible. Let us say that accidental necessity* is the kind of necessity (if any) that some state of affairs ψ has when ψ is strictly implied by some accidentally necessary state of affairs ϕ. The fact that the necessity of the *past* cannot be transferred to the future over strict implication does not derail the intuition that *some* kind of necessity is so transferred. Accidental necessity* cannot be identified with the necessity of the past, but the intuitive plausibility of the Transfer of Necessity Principles suggests that there is some kind of necessity transferred by the Transfer of Necessity Principles, a necessity just as strong as the necessity of the past, at least with respect to our lack of power over it. If there is a necessity of this kind, it seems that all human acts have it and hence are not free. Let us call the dilemma that is generated by the conjunction of the accidental necessity of God's past beliefs and TNP 1 or TNP 2 the Accidental Necessity Version of the dilemma, formulated as follows.

Accidental Necessity Version of Foreknowledge Dilemma

The state of affairs

(1) God's being infallible (or essentially omniscient)

and

(2) God's believing at $t1$ that I will do S at $t3$

are jointly inconsistent with

(3') The accidental contingency* of S at $t2$

and hence with

(3) My being free to refrain from doing S at $t3$.

This version of the foreknowledge dilemma has been much discussed in the recent literature, and we will look at responses to it in Chapters 2, 3, 5, and 6.

A second dilemma is suggested by some plausible recent attempts to analyze the causal relation in terms of counterfactuals, in particular, the theory of John Pollock. There is no possible world with our causal laws in which God's belief at $t1$ occurs and in which my act at $t3$ does not occur. My act counterfactually depends on God's previous belief. For this reason it may be tempting to say that God's belief causally necessitates my act. And, as we will see in Chapter 4, that is exactly the conclusion we get from Pollock's theory. But if my act S at $t3$ is causally necessitated by God's belief, this seems to preclude my freedom to refrain from doing S at $t3$, since we have assumed that causal contingency, or lack of causal necessitation, is a precondition for freedom. We may call this the Causal Necessity Version of the dilemma, formulated as follows.

Causal Necessity Version of Foreknowledge Dilemma

The states of affairs

(1) God's being infallible (or essentially omniscient)

and

(2) God's believing at $t1$ that I will do S at $t3$

are jointly inconsistent with

(3″) The causal contingency of S at $t2$

and hence with

(3) My being free to refrain from doing S at $t3$

I know of no one who has seriously proposed this dilemma in the literature, but I will consider it myself in Chapter 4.

5. Solutions to the Theological Dilemma

It is usual to count a demonstration of the consistency of (1)–(3) a solution to the problem of divine foreknowledge. Such a solution is the weakest defense of (1)–(3), however, since it may be possible that some states of affairs jointly obtain, even though it is not plausible that they jointly obtain. It is now widely agreed, for example, that it is logically possible that the following two states of affairs both obtain.

(19) The existence of an omnipotent, omniscient, and wholly good God.
(20) The existence of evil in the world,

although many say, of course, that it is *unlikely* that (19) and (20) both obtain. So even if the disharmony between or among some given states of affairs is not of the worst sort (i.e., logical inconsistency), this is not yet to say there is no disharmony among them and that it is reasonable to conclude that they all obtain.[29]

Let us call an account that shows (1)–(3) to be consistent (copossible) a negative solution to the dilemma, and one that shows (1)–(3) to be coplausible a positive solution. Since the foreknowledge problem is typically discussed in terms of propositions instead of states of affairs, it is usual to attempt to show the propositional equivalents of (1)–(3) consistent. That is, the project is generally understood to be the attempt to show the consistency of the following set of propositions.

(1p) God is essentially omniscient.
(2p) God believes at $t1$ that I will do S at $t3$.
(3p) I am free to refrain from doing S at $t3$.

To show a set of three propositions consistent it is sufficient to find a logically contingent proposition C that is clearly consistent with two of the propositions in the set and that together with these two propositions entails the third. It is not even necessary that *C* be true. It may even be known to be false. But reasonable people expect more than that, and so most well-known attempts to solve the foreknowledge dilemma aim at more than a negative solution. They attempt a resolution of the problem that shows that (1p)–(3p) are coplausible and do so by maintaining only other plausibly held propositions.

To see the difference between a positive and a negative solution, consider a solution defended by Mavrodes. If he is right that backward agent causation is logically possible, then he has successfully provided a negative solution to the dilemma [30] This is because the proposition that my act retroactively causes God's previous belief, together with the proposition that my act occurs, entails the proposition that God has such a belief, and is consistent with the proposition that my act is free in the sense required and that God is essentially omniscient. But even if backward causation is logically possible, *I* think we have very good reason to believe it is false, although I will not defend this claim here. But if it is false, this solution is useless as a way of showing the coplausibility of foreknowledge and free will.

Clearly, a positive solution is a great deal more difficult than a negative solution. Nonetheless, it should be our aim. Unlike negative solutions, which either succeed or do not succeed, the success of a positive solution is a matter of degree. It can go a little way or a long way toward making (1p)–(3p) coplausible. I believe we should aim for a positive solution to the foreknowledge dilemma, and the farther it goes, the better.

I wish to comment on certain "solutions" that weaken or deny one of the propositions (1p)–(3p). Some deny that future contingent propositions have a truth value.[31] Some claim that while future contingents may be true, they are nonetheless unknowable.[32] Others deny that human beings are free in a sense that is incompatible with causal necessitation.[33] None of these is a solution in the sense in which I am using the term, since all of them give up one of the intuitions that generate the dilemma. These proposals typically arise out of a conviction that (1p)–(3p) are not consistent as they stand. But I believe the motivations in Christian theology for (1p)–(3p) are strong enough to make none of these moves desirable except as a last resort.

Consider first the intuition that God is omniscient and infallible. I have defined omniscience as the knowledge of the truth value of all propositions. Christians traditionally have held that God knows all truths and believes no falsehoods and that this includes foreknowledge. Aquinas claims that foreknowledge is in fact the distinguishing mark of divinity in his account of why it is that the angels do not have foreknowledge.

> Whatever is the proper sign of the Divinity does not belong to the angels. But to know future events is the exclusive sign of the Divinity, according to Isa. 41. 23: "Show the things that are to come hereafter, and we shall know that ye are gods." Therefore, the angels do not know future events.[34]

The importance of God's omniscience and infallible foreknowledge is partly due to its association with the power necessary to be worthy of worship. The possession of the maximum possible degree of knowledge may be necessary for the possession of the maximum possible degree of power and, in any case, the former is necessary for the exercise of the latter in an effective way. In the second place, both God's omniscience and his infallibility seem to be necessary for him to be able to exercise the degree of providential care for us that is a central feature of the Christian God, and this applies especially to the knowledge of future contingents. Just how far a divine being can make a mistake about the future and still be worthy of the absolute trust Christians place in him may, of course, be debated, but at least the initial tendency of most such believers is to say that it is not very far. And even if God's knowledge of future contingents is not religiously mandatory, it certainly seems to be religiously preferable. So if a solution to the foreknowledge dilemma can be given that does not involve limiting God's knowledge of the future, so much the better.

Consider next the intuition that human beings have free will in a sense that is incompatible with determinism (hereafter called "incompatibilist free will"). I will suggest an account of the connection between incompatibilist free will and the ability to do or choose otherwise in Chapter 6. Here I am concerned only with the motivation for claiming we have incompatibilist free will. It seems to me to be central to our idea of ourselves as persons that we have this kind of freedom, and that moral responsibility is meaningless without it. Many philosophers, of course, deny that we need this kind of freedom for these purposes, although almost everybody agrees that we must be free in a sense that is compatible both with moral responsibility and our identity as persons. The kind of freedom I am assuming we have is a strong one, and I will try to demonstrate in this book that freedom of this sort is compatible with a strong view of omniscience, and that the plausibility of maintaining the one is not diminished by maintaining the other.

In Chapters 2, 3, 5, and 6 I will examine the three traditional solutions to the Accidental Necessity Version of the dilemma: the Boethian, Ockhamist, and Molinist solutions, as well as three solutions of my own. In addition I will propose a solution to the Causal Necessity Version of the dilemma and will discuss the connection between the causal relation and the typical subjunctive conditionals affirmed by foreknowledge compatibilists. In the appendix I will present a new foreknowledge dilemma that purports to show that the foreknowledge of an essentially omniscient being conflicts with the notion of temporal asymmetry introduced in this chapter quite apart from any consideration of free will. This dilemma is as strong as the foreknowledge/freedom dilemma but with fewer ways out.

2

The Boethian Solution

1. Introduction

In Chapter 1 it was argued that the Accidental Necessity Version of the foreknowledge dilemma is a very strong one.[1] In addition, there is the bothersome problem of the Causal Necessity Version. In this chapter I wish to examine one classic response that would solve both of them. The move comes from Boethius and Aquinas, but it has roots in the writing of Proclus and Ammonius. This is the claim that God does not have beliefs in time at all.

As shown in Chapter 1, the strongest forms of the foreknowledge dilemma make the assumption that in every possible world in which I do some act S, God previously believes that I will do S and the belief is infallible. This assumption, together with the principle of the Necessity of the Past and a Transfer of Necessity Principle, leads to the conclusion that I do not bring about S freely. The infallibility version of the argument is as follows.

(1) God's belief at $t1$ that I will do S at $t3$ is accidentally necessary at $t2$.

(2) If A is accidentally necessary at t and A strictly implies B, then B is accidentally necessary* at t.

(3) God's belief at $t1$ strictly implies my act at $t3$.

(4) So my act at $t3$ is accidentally necessary* at $t2$.

(5) If my act at $t3$ is accidentally necessary* at $t2$, I cannot do otherwise than bring about that act at $t3$.

(6) If when I bring about an act I cannot do otherwise, I do not bring it about freely.

(7) Therefore, I do not bring about my act at $t3$ freely.

The essential omniscience version of the argument differs on lines (2) and (3). (2) is replaced by the even more plausible Transfer of Necessity Principle

(2') If A is accidentally necessary at t and A is strictly equivalent to B, then B is accidentally necessary* at t.

36

(3) is replaced by

> (3') God's belief at *t1* is strictly equivalent to my act at *t3*.

In the rest of this book I will examine reasons for rejecting four premises of this argument. The Boethian solution of this chapter gives us a reason to reject premise (1) on the grounds that God does not have beliefs at moments of time. The Ockhamist solution of Chapter 3 gives us a different reason for rejecting premise (1), this time on the grounds that God's belief at *t1* about a contingent event at *t3* does not have the necessity of the past at *t2*. In Chapter 3 I will present a solution of my own that I call Thomistic Ockhamism. I will argue that if God's state of knowing has the features described by Aquinas, it is so unlike other past events that even if it is in time, both premises (1) and (3) are false. The Molinist solution of Chapter 5 involves the rejection of one of the Transfer of Necessity Principles, premise (2). Molina's reasons for denying this premise are indirect. I will give my own argument for rejecting both transfer principles in my second solution of Chapter 6. In the first solution of that chapter I will give an argument for rejecting premise (6). My own solutions, then, involve reasons for rejecting premises (1), (2), (3), and (6).

In this chapter I will discuss the timelessness solution and will argue that even though the objections commonly given to it are answerable, it generates another dilemma and should not be considered a solution to the foreknowledge problem. However, the dilemma it generates may be easier to solve in some respects than the standard one, so it may still be useful as a partial solution. Each defensible solution has a philosophical price, and this will make certain solutions unacceptable to some people, but I think that there are enough different acceptable solutions that there should be one for almost any philosophical taste.

St. Thomas Aquinas seems to have an argument in mind very close to the one I have just presented. He says:

> But this is a true conditional proposition, *If God knew that this thing will be, it will be*, for the knowledge of God is only of true things. Now the antecedent conditional of this is absolutely necessary, because it is eternal and because it is signified as past. Therefore, the consequent is also absolutely necessary. Therefore, whatever God knows, is necessary, and so the knowledge of God is not of contingent things.[2]

Aquinas has several things to say about this argument, but the answer I want to focus on here is his well-known claim that God exists and has beliefs eternally rather than temporally. On this solution it is not proper to speak of God's knowing or believing at a time, nor is it proper to speak of the object of his knowledge as a proposition expressed by a tensed sentence. There is therefore no state of affairs consisting in God's believing anything at *t1*. The proposition expressed by "God believes at *t1* that I will do *S* at *t3*" is false, not because God is ignorant of what *we* express by the sentence "I will do *S* at *t3*," but because any tensed sentence expressing God's knowledge is ill formed. God is eternally acquainted with all that takes place at every moment of time, but since he himself is outside time, he knows none of these things as having a certain temporal relation to himself. An explanation of this claim and its application to the foreknowledge dilemma will be the task for this chapter.

2. God's Eternity

2.1. Boethius

The classic definition of eternity was given in the sixth century by Boethius, who called it "the complete, simultaneous, and perfect possession of illimitable life."[3] Suppose we understand by a timeless being one which lacks temporal location. Then an eternal being is timeless, but is more than timeless. Boethius says, "Of necessity it [an eternal being] is always present to itself, in full possession of itself, having present the infinity of fleeting time."[4] Such a being, unlike other putatively timeless entities such as numbers and propositions, has both perfect life and the conscious, complete, and immediate apprehension of all temporal occurrences.

The knowledge of an eternal being is explained by Boethius as follows.

> Since, then, all judgment comprehends those things presented to it according to its own nature, and since the state of God is ever that of eternal presence, His knowledge transcends all temporal change and abides in the immediacy of his presence. It embraces the infinite sweep of past and future, and views all things in the immediacy of its knowing as though they are happening in the present. If you wish to consider, then, the foreknowledge or prevision by which He discovers all things, it will be more correct to think of it not as a kind of foreknowledge of the future, but as the knowledge of a never changing present. For this reason divine knowledge is better called providence or "looking forth" than prevision or "seeing beforehand," for it is far removed from matters below and looks forth at all things as though from a lofty peak above them.
>
> Why, then, do you imagine that all that is illuminated by the sight of God is necessary? Men see things but this certainly doesn't make them

necessary. And your seeing them doesn't impose any necessity on the things you see present, does it?[5]

All things, then, are present to God, not in the sense of being temporally present, but in the sense of being "before the mind." The things before God's mind do have the necessity of the present, but Boethius explains this is an innocuous kind of conditional necessity.

> For there are two kinds of necessity: one is simple, as the necessity by which all men are mortal; the other is conditional, as is the case when, if you know that someone is walking, he must be walking. For that which a man knows cannot be other than as it is known; but this conditional necessity does not imply simple necessity, because it does not exist in virtue of its own nature, but in virtue of a condition which is added. No necessity forces the man to walk who is making his way of his own free will, although it is necessary that he walks when he takes a step.[6]

By the same reasoning, no necessity forces the man to walk when he walks of his own free will, although the following is necessary *de dicto*: Given that God eternally knows of his walking, he walks.

Human freedom to alter a course of action is compatible with God's eternal knowledge.

> But, you will reply, if it lies in my power to change a proposed course of action, I will be able to evade Providence, for I will perhaps have altered things which Providence foreknows. My answer will be that you can alter your plan, but that since this is possible, and since the present truth of Providence sees that you can, and whether or not you will, you cannot escape divine foreknowledge any more than you can escape the sight of an eye that is present to watch, though of your own free will you may turn to a variety of actions.[7]

It has been argued that Boethius does not fully appreciate the way in which God's infallible beliefs about the future threaten human free will.[8] As far as I can see, however, it matters not at all whether he appreciates the force of the strongest form of the dilemma, since his theory on God's eternity is applicable to any version of the dilemma in which temporal order is relevant. That would include both the Causal Necessity and Accidental Necessity versions of the dilemma presented in Chapter 1.

2.2. Aquinas

St. Thomas Aquinas develops the Boethian solution, even using some of the same metaphors. In explaining how God knows eternally he says:

Boethius clearly explains how this happens at the end of the *Consolation of Philosophy*, Book V, last prose section. For every cognition exists in the way appropriate to the knower, as was said. Therefore, since God is eternal, His cognition must have the aspect of eternity, which is to be simultaneously whole without succession. Thus, although time is successive, nevertheless, His eternity is present to all times by one and the same indivisible, standing now. Likewise, His cognition intuits all temporal things, even though they succeed one another as present to it. Nor is any of them future with respect to His cognition, but one is future with respect to another. . . .[9]

And in the *Summa Theologiae* Aquinas expresses the way in which God knows using a well-known metaphor already suggested by Boethius.

Things reduced to act in time are known by us successively in time, but by God are known in eternity, which is above time. Whence to us they cannot be certain, since we know future contingent things only as contingent futures; but they are certain to God alone, whose understanding is in eternity above time; just as he who goes along the road does not see those who come after him, although he who sees the whole road from a height sees at once all travelling by the way.[10]

Another well-known metaphor is the circle analogy. This was already used by Boethius,[11] and it appears in *Summa Contra Gentiles* I, chapter 66. Here Aquinas compares the way eternity is present to each and every moment of time to that in which the center of a circle is present to each and every point on the circumference. The points on the circle are spatially ordered in such a way that no point coincides with any other, yet each point is equidistant from and directly opposite the center of the circle. Likewise, although the moments of time are ordered in such a way that they are truly distinct from one another, each is present to eternity.

On the view of Aquinas, God's knowledge is not divided into discrete propositions. If it were, it is hard to avoid the conclusion that God's knowledge that *A* is distinct from his knowledge that *B*, and this conflicts with the doctrine of divine simplicity. Instead, God knows by a direct and perfect intuition of his own nature, but in knowing himself he knows everything else. It is therefore inaccurate to say that God knows *p*, not only because both God's knowing and the object of his knowledge are tenseless. but because the object of God's knowledge is not a proposition in any case.

2.3. Stump and Kretzmann

A very interesting and influential recent account of God's eternity has been given by Eleonore Stump and Norman Kretzmann.[12] They see themselves as explicating Boethius, even though they refine the view considerably. They claim that on Boethius' definition eternity includes not only the elements of life, illimitability, and atemporality, but also duration—an infinitely extended, nonsequential, atemporal duration.[13] It can be argued that duration is entailed by illimitable life; however, some commentators find it inconsistent with atemporality.[14] As far as I can tell, it does not matter for Boethius' solution to the foreknowledge problem whether God's mode of being has duration or not, and I will be neutral on this issue. What does matter is that God has no location in time and yet is able to perfectly grasp every temporal being and every temporal event from his atemporal perspective.[15]

Stump and Kretzmann's discussion of the relation between an eternal being and temporal beings is more relevant to the present topic. They define a species of simultaneity—what they call ET-simultaneity—that holds between the temporal and the eternal. The definition is as follows.

> So we can characterize ET-simultaneity in this way. Let 'x' and 'y' range over entities and events. Then:
> (ET) for every x and for every y, x and y are ET-simultaneous iff
> (i) either x is eternal and y is temporal, or vice versa; and
> (ii) for some observer, A, in the unique eternal reference frame, x and y are both present—i.e., either x is eternally present and y is observed as temporally present, or vice versa; and
> (iii) for some observer, B, in one of the infinitely many temporal reference frames, x and y are both present—i.e., either x is observed as eternally present and y is temporally present, or vice versa.[16]

Notice that according to this definition simultaneity is relative to an observer.[17] The need for this is not clear, although they provide some motivation for conditions (ii) and (iii) in the passage immediately following the one just quoted.

> Given the concept of eternity, condition (ii) provides that a temporal entity or event observed as temporally present by some eternal observer A is ET-simultaneous with every eternal entity or event; and condition (iii) provides that an eternal entity or event observed as eternally present (or simply as eternal) by some temporal observer B is ET-simultaneous with every temporal entity or event.[18]

I find this passage difficult to understand. It can be interpreted in a way that suggests a B-theory of time and, if so, many philosophers would consider this a difficulty. I will discuss this objection in Section 3.2 and will argue that there is no reason to think the timelessness solution is committed to it.

I am treating the theory of God's eternity as presented by Boethius, Aquinas, and Stump and Kretzmann as the same theory; at least, it seems to me to be the same in those aspects of it that bear on the foreknowledge issue. I will sometimes refer to it as the Boethian solution or the timelessness solution.

Stump and Kretzmann's solution to the foreknowledge problem is then given as follows.

> First, the short answer to the question whether God can foreknow contingent events is no. It is impossible that any event occur late than an eternal entity's present state of awareness, since every temporal event is ET-simultaneous with that state, and so an eternal entity cannot foreknow anything. Instead, such an entity considered as omniscient knows—is aware of—all temporal events, including those which are future with respect to our current temporal viewpoint; but, because the times at which those future events will be present events are ET-simultaneous with the whole of eternity, an omniscient eternal entity is aware of them as they are present.[19]

The doctrine of divine eternity permits a simple answer to the argument at the beginning of this chapter. God does not know or believe at moments of time at all, and so the first premise of the argument is false. For this answer it is not necessary that God be actually eternal (i.e., that he fully satisfy the Boethian definition of eternity), but only that he be timeless (i.e., that he have no location in time and that no property can be correctly attributed to him at a time). Notice that this is not, strictly speaking, a solution to the foreknowledge dilemma, since it requires the rejection of the claim that God actually foreknows anything. But if we add to the view that God is timeless the view that God knows everything that goes on at every moment of time, foreknowledge can be reinterpreted as timeless knowledge. If this theory is even possibly true, it constitutes what I have called a negative solution to every version of the foreknowledge dilemma, since it shows that there is no inconsistency between God's knowledge of all temporal events, including ones in our future, and the freedom of human agents.

The Boethian view has the potential to provide much more than a negative solution to the dilemma, however. If the full doctrine of God's eternity can be made plausible, it can be developed as part of a general theory of how God knows and how God relates to temporal beings. Certainly in the case of Aquinas the attribute of eternity gains persuasiveness because of its logical relations to other important attributes such as immateriality and immutability. In addition, Aquinas's theory of divine knowing gains plausibility through detail, and even more detail is given in Stump and Kretzmann's account. The more refined a position is and the more developed its connections with positions on other issues, the greater its explanatory force, and the greater its explanatory force, the greater its plausibility. In the case of the doctrine of eternity there is no question that its part in an elaborate theistic metaphysics gives it an advantage over alternative views. The timelessness solution therefore has the potential for being a positive solution to the foreknowledge problem. If it worked it would be very powerful.

3. Objections to the Timeless Knowledge Solution

The view that God is eternal in the timeless sense has a long and impressive history. Nevertheless, it has recently been attacked on grounds that are independent of the foreknowledge problem. Robert C. Coburn and Nelson Pike have each argued that a timeless being could not be a person.[20] Other philosophers have argued that timelessness is incompatible with other, more central attributes of God, notably omniscience. For example, Kenny and Prior have called the concept of timeless knowledge by an omniscient being "radically incoherent," and Kenny repeats Prior's well-known objection that "it seems an extraordinary way of affirming God's omniscience if a person, when asked what God knows now, must say 'nothing,' and when asked what he knew yesterday, must again say 'nothing,' and must yet again say 'nothing,' when asked what God will know tomorrow."[21] In addition, some philosophers have argued that divine timelessness is incompatible with distinctive Christian beliefs. Nicholas Wolterstorff claims that the God presented in Scripture is a changing, temporal being,[22] while Richard Swinburne argues that if God does such things as warn, punish, and forgive, he cannot be timeless.[23] And timelessness has been called incompatible with divine providence.[24] Furthermore, even when philosophers are satisfied that difficulties of coherence are answerable, they may still balk at accepting the metaphysics that goes with the doctrine of eternity. Such is the case with William Hasker.[25]

I will not attempt to address all of these problems here. I will look only at objections that directly bear on the success or failure of this position as a negative solution to the foreknowledge problem. I will examine five of them. These objections are the most important ones I know of, and I found each of them convincing at one time. I now think I have an adequate answer to each of the first four, and although I still think the fifth objection shows the Boethian move is not sufficient because it generates another dilemma, I will argue in Chapters 3 and 6 that my foreknowledge solutions in those chapters can solve this dilemma as well. This means that for those who find the claim that God is timeless attractive and who can answer the problems raised about its coherence and consistency with other Christian doctrines, the Boethian move may be an acceptable partial solution to God's knowledge of future contingents. However, since it is not my preferred solution, I will not attempt a full-scale defense of it.

3.1. First Objection

The first objection to the timeless knowledge solution has been offered by Alvin Plantinga and is one I mentioned favorably in an earlier paper.[26] According to this objection the timelessness move does not solve the dilemma. The argument arises from a consideration of the proposition expressed by the sentence "God timelessly knows p." According to the Boethian solution this sentence is well formed as long as "knows" is taken in a timeless sense rather than the present tense of the verb, and the proposition p is not such that it can only be expressed by a tensed verb. But this proposition has a truth value. Propositions are either true at times or they are timelessly true. Suppose first that they are true at times. If so, they are either omnitemporally true or they become true at some time or other, presumably the time of the event the proposition is about. But since *God timelessly knows p* is not about something that takes place in time at all, there is no moment of time at which it could plausibly be said to become true. Hence, if it is true at any times, it must be true at all times. But if *God timelessly knows p* is true at all times, it must have been true long before the event described by the proposition p. But then this means that, say, 80 years before that event, the proposition *God timelessly knows p* was true. But, if so, the foreknowledge dilemma is generated again, for the truth of this proposition is accidentally necessary long before the event.

Now suppose instead that propositions are timelessly true. Plantinga argues that this option does not help matters, for we can still ask whether the *sentence* "God timelessly knows p" expressed a true proposition 80 years before. If it did, the foreknowledge dilemma arises again. Quoting Plantinga:

> Concede for a moment that it makes no sense to say of a proposition that it was true at a time; it nonetheless makes good sense, obviously, to say of a

sentence that it expressed a certain proposition at a time. But it also makes good sense to say of a sentence that it expressed a truth at a time. Now eighty years ago the sentence

[(8)] God knows (eternally) that Paul mows in 1995

expressed the proposition that God knows eternally that Paul mows in 1995 (and for simplicity let us suppose that proposition was the only proposition it expressed then). But if in fact Paul will mow in 1995, then [(8)] also expressed a truth eighty years ago. So eighty years ago [(8)] expressed the proposition that Paul will mow in 1995 and expressed a truth; since what is past is now necessary, it is now necessary that eighty years ago [(8)] expressed that proposition and expressed a truth. But it is necessary in the broadly logical sense that if [(8)] then expressed that proposition (and only that proposition) and expressed a truth, then Paul will mow in 1995. It is therefore necessary that Paul will mow then; hence his mowing then is necessary in just the way the past is. Accordingly, the claim that God is outside of time is essentially irrelevant to Edwardsian arguments.[27]

Here Plantinga understands the argument for theological fatalism as essentially identical to the argument for logical fatalism. My objections to this were given in Chapter 1. I argued there that it is a mistake to look at the past truth of propositions rather than the past occurrence of events as the entities to which accidental necessity applies. This is because the concept of the necessity of the past originated in connection with the Aristotelian act/potency distinction. There is not now a potency in things for anything other than the actual past, even though there is a potency in things now for any number of different futures. This is said to give the past a kind of necessity lacked by the future. Accidental necessity is the necessity of lack of potency. On the other hand, truth is not associated with potency and act in the same way. Ockham says that the truth of a proposition is *settled by* something that is in act at some time or other. This suggests that the truth of a proposition is not itself something that is ever either in potency or in act. If so, it would not make sense to speak of the truth of a proposition or something expressing a proposition as having accidental necessity.

Plantinga's argument against the Boethian solution can therefore be blocked at the point at which he says, "since what is past is now necessary, it is now necessary that eighty years ago [(8)] expressed that proposition and expressed a truth." The concept of accidental necessity does not make it now necessary that 80 years ago a certain proposition was true, nor does it make it now necessary that 80 years ago a certain sentence expressed a true proposition. Since accidental necessity is not a property of the proposition *God timelessly knows p* nor of any sentence that expressed it, and since nothing happened 80 years ago that could be called the timeless knowing by God of *p*, the Boethian position is not thereby threatened.

3.2. Second Objection

The second objection is that the timelessness move requires a B-theory of time. This is argued explicitly by William Craig, who treats it as an objection, and also by Marilyn Adams, who does not treat it as an objection.[28] The distinction between the A-theory and the B-theory of time originated with McTaggart. He distinguished between two ways in which we order events in time. First, we order events according to the predicates "is past," "is present," and "is future." This creates an ordering of temporal events that he calls the A-series, a series that goes from the more to less distant past up to the present, followed by the less and then more distant future. This series continually changes, since each event changes position from the distant future down to the present and on to the distant past. Second, we order events according to the relations "is earlier than" and "is later than." This creates an ordering of temporal events that he calls the B-series, the series of moments of time that moves from earlier to later and can be sequentially numbered $t_n, t_{n+1}, t_{n+2}, \ldots$ The B-series, in contrast to the A-series, is unchanging. If some event x is earlier than y and y is earlier than z, these relations among x, y, and z never change; in fact, it is impossible that they change.

There are significant disputes over the relation between these two ways of ordering time and related issues in the ontology of time. B-theorists make a number of claims that may not all be logically interdependent and that are denied by A-theorists:

> (a) At every moment of time t, all events past, present, and future relative to t are equally real.
> (b) The B-series is ontologically basic. The A-series is reducible to the B-series.
> (c) Temporal becoming is purely subjective, since the A-series involves a B-relation to an observer.
> (d) All true propositions can be fully expressed using only the B-series. Tenses and other temporal indexicals are eliminable.

Adams does not mention the B-theory by name, but she says that Aquinas is presupposing an ontology in which everything that has temporal location is timelessly present to God "in its own determinate existence." This implies, she says, that there is no ontological distinction among past, present, and future things.

> Aquinas thus seems to be presupposing not only that God is timeless, but that everything that has any temporal location is also timelessly given "in its own determinate existence." The temporal order is merely a system of before-, after-, and simultaneity relations among such timelessly given things. There is no difference in the ontological statuses of past, present, and future things. And since to say that a thing is past, present, or future is merely to comment on the relational properties that timelessly obtain between it and other things so ordered as timelessly actual, each temporally ordered thing can be timelessly present to God. And since each is timelessly present to Him, He timelessly sees each in its own determinate existence, and so timelessly has certain knowledge of them and their precise location in the temporal order. Nevertheless, some temporalia are contingent because there is, in their temporally prior causes, both a potency for them to be and a potency for them not to be.[29]

Making a similar point, Craig argues that Aquinas's theory requires that from his point of view, all states of the world, past, present, and future, are not just epistemically on a par, but are ontologically on a par. He believes he finds support for this both in the *Summa Contra Gentiles* and in the following passage from the *Summa Theologiae*:

> . . . God knows all contingent events not only as they are in their causes but also as each of them is in actual existence in itself. Now although contingent events come into actual existence successively, God does not, as we do, know them in their actual existence successively, but all at once; because his knowledge is measured by eternity, as is also his existence; and eternity, which exists as a simultaneous whole, takes in the whole of time. . . . Hence all that takes place in time is eternally present to God, not merely, as some hold, in the sense that he has the intelligible natures of things present in himself, but because he eternally surveys all things as they are in their presence to him.[30]

In commenting on this passage Craig says:

> The point here seems to be that this presence is not internal to God, but a real external presence. Since God knows contingents according to their actual existence, it seems undeniable that for God future contingents actually exist. This does not mean that such events always exist, for on this view that would be to exist throughout all time, which they do not. But the whole temporal series would seem to exist timelessly, on the analogy of a spatial extension, and as such is known by God.[31]

But it is not so clear that Aquinas (or Boethius or Stump and Kretzmann) is committed to a B-theory. Let us first consider tenet (a) of the theory. Craig and Adams argue that Aquinas is committed to (a). Craig says Aquinas is committed to (a) on the grounds that *to God* all moments of time and the events that occur at those moments of time are equally present to him. The idea seems to be that something cannot be known even by an omniscient being unless it is *there* to be known. Therefore, all moments of time *really exist* from an eternal perspective, even though from a temporal perspective future events and moments of time do not yet exist.

This argument for Aquinas's commitment to tenet (a) assumes that the timeless point of view is ontologically basic. If a timeless being sees each moment of time as the same as every other, and if a temporal being sees them as different, we are to conclude that all moments of time are *really* the same. This is intuitively plausible, given that a timeless being has a broader perspective, which it is tempting to consider more objective. And, in any case, we think that God's perspective is superior to our own. But tenet (a) does not automatically follow from *that*. The A- and B-theories are competing theories about the status of events in some temporal observer's future. The A-theory maintains that events future relative to *t* are not real *at t*, while the B-theory maintains that events future relative to *t are* real *at t*. Tenet (a) is therefore a claim about the status of events relative to a time *t*. How events are related to a reference point outside of time is no part of either the A- or B-theories of time. The temporal mode of existence is a real mode of existence, but the nature of that mode of existence is in dispute. On the A-theory temporal becoming really occurs. It is really true at *t1* that *t2* does not yet exist, and it is really true that the child who will be conceived at *t3* does not somehow "preexist" at *t1*. The B-theory denies this. But all of this is independent of there being an entity outside of time that is able to grasp all of time at once. If there is an atemporal being that is aware of all temporal objects and events, surely this fact is neutral with respect to the dispute between the A-theory and the B-theory on the relative ontological status of events from a temporal perspective. Since there is no past and future to an eternal being, the question of whether events future relative to *t* are real *at t* does not arise.

On a B-theory, we might picture all temporal events as if they were on a conveyer belt. An observer watches them move past. The point at which they are directly opposite the observer is analogous to the present. Past events are those that have already gone by, while future events are those that have not yet gone by. An ordinary observer can see only those directly opposite her, yet all events, both those that have gone past her view and those that have not, are equally real. That is, they are equally "there" on the conveyer belt. On an A-theory, in contrast, there is nothing on the conveyer belt that has not yet appeared to the observer. Events come into existence when they appear in front of her. Future events, then, are not really there, but past and present ones are.

It should be clear that the observer is herself in time in both of these theories, and is no less in time even if her vision expands so that she sees not only what is directly in front of her, but the entire conveyer belt and everything on it. Let us call such a hypothetical observer of the entire moving belt Big-Viewer. The dispute between the A- and B-theories on tenet (a) is over the problem of what Big-Viewer would see. Would there be anything on the belt that had not yet passed in front of her or not? The dispute therefore involves the relative status of events at the present moment of time, the time at which things are directly in front of Big-Viewer.

But if God is outside of time, he is not like Big-Viewer. He does not observe a moving conveyer belt at all. What God sees does not move past anything, since that would fix a particular point as the (temporal) present and, by hypothesis, there is no such present to God. But if he does not see events moving past anything, he does not see them moving at all. If he is atemporal, there is no "now," so the question of what he knows to be real now does not arise. He, of course, sees everything on the belt that ever moves past Big-Viewer, and he sees their proper order. But what he sees is not what Big-Viewer sees. If the A-theory is right, God timelessly sees there is nothing on the conveyer belt until it passes Big-Viewer, and also timelessly sees what passes Big-Viewer at t_n, $t_n + 1$, $t_n + 2$, and so forth. God therefore sees much more than Big-Viewer sees at any one time. So it is possible for God to know timelessly that the A-theory of time is true and also to know timelessly the future. On the other hand, if the B-theory is right, God timelesssly sees the same events as Big-Viewer sees at any one time, but he does not see them moving past him the way Big-Viewer does. In neither case does God's point of view affect the point of view of Big-Viewer and the dispute between the A- and B-theories on the status of the future. I conclude that Aquinas is not committed to (a), the central tenet of the B-theory.

What about (b)? As we have seen, Marilyn Adams explicity attributes this tenet of the B-theory to Aquinas. According to tenet (b), while the B-series represents a basic feature of time, the A-series does not. What the A-series does represent can be disputed, but the most common view is expressed by tenet (c), which is that the A-series represents the subjective experience of observers in time. So temporal becoming is a psychological fact about the way time is experienced by temporal beings, but such facts are fully expressible in terms of B-relations.

What's more, it may seem that the eternity advocate is committed to something even more radical than (b) or (c). If God does not know an A-series, so that temporal becoming plays no part in the objects of God's knowledge, then it looks as if temporal becoming is not only subjective, it is illusory. As Richard Creel has put it, "In brief, either a thing is changing or it is not. If God does not know it as changing but we know it as changing, then one of us is mistaken, and it surely is not God."[32]

I cannot see that Aquinas or Boethius is committed to either tenets (b) or (c), much less to the view that temporal change is illusory. Craig admits that for Aquinas temporal becoming is not mind dependent.[33] His claim, however, is not that Aquinas consciously accepts a B-theory, but that his position on God's knowledge of temporal events does not make sense without it. But what makes Aquinas committed to (b) or (c)? How does the claim that there is an atemporal being who is acquainted with all of time commit anyone to a view about whether the A-series or the B-series is basic? Again, such a dispute is over the relative ontological status of events *at moments of time*. Temporal becoming may or may not be an objectively basic feature of time. To say one series or the other is basic is to say something about what the temporal mode of existence is like. But that implies nothing about what an atemporal mode of existence is like, nor about what the temporal mode of existence looks like to an atemporal being. If the A-theory is correct, it is an irreducible fact now that the Battle of Hastings is over. That fact cannot be reduced to any fact that refers only to the B-series. But that cannot be an irreducible fact to an atemporal being, since it is not a fact at all to an atemporal being. By hypothesis such a being does not exist now and has nothing in his past. The view that Aquinas is committed to (b) and (c), like the view that he is committed to (a), founders on the assumption that the way temporal events look from an atemporal perspective implies something about the way they *really* are from a temporal perspective. But as far as I can see, there is no reason to believe that this is true or that Aquinas or Boethius thought so.

Likewise, Creel supposes that if events seem different from different perpectives, at most one such perspective can be an awareness of those events as they are in reality; the other must be illusory. If our perspective is different from God's, we must be the ones suffering from an illusion. But this is to make the assumption that reality admits of only one perspective. Either it is really temporal or it is really atemporal. I have argued that there is no reason to think that there cannot be both a real temporal mode of existence and a real atemporal mode of existence.

Stump and Kretzmann seem to deny that the timelessness view is committed to tenets (a), (b), and (c) of the B-theory in the following passage:

> What the concept of eternity implies instead is that there is one objective reality that contains two modes of real existence in which two different sorts of duration are measured by two irreducibly different sorts of measure: time and eternity.[34]

If I understand their view, the point is that there is one objective reality containing two modes of real existence, neither of which is reducible to the other. What this means may not be perfectly clear, but surely it is clear enough to see that they are not committed to the view that the A-series is reducible to the B-series or that temporal becoming is purely subjective or that the future (relative to us now) is just as real as the past. Stump and Kretzmann go to great pains to separate the two modes of existence, temporal and atemporal, and their doing so suggests that in their view a theory about the one has no direct bearing on a theory about the other. The doctrine of eternality is a theory about the atemporal mode of being. It should not in itself have any implications about the nature of the temporal mode of being.[35]

Furthermore, on the Stump-Kretzmann theory of eternity, even though God is ET-simultaneous with each instant of time, ET-simultaneity is not transitive. From the fact that each instant of time is ET-simultaneous with the eternal present, it does not follow that each instant of time is ET-simultaneous with every other instant and that therefore there is no distinction between past and future in time. The relations among temporal events are independent of their relation to the eternal present. To suppose otherwise is to suppose that the relationship that holds between God and instants of time also holds among the instants of time themselves. But this is to assume that ET-simultaneity is transitive, an assumption that Stump and Kretzmann deny.

Now what about tenet (d)? This one is more problematic because it is not a point about ontology, but about truth. The alleged commitment comes not from the eternity doctrine *per se*, but from a combination of the claims that God is eternal and God is omniscient.[36] This is because if God is timeless he cannot know any proposition that includes as part of its propositional content a temporal relation to the knower. If there are propositions that essentially include such temporal relations in the propositional content, an atemporal being could not know such propositions. But if God is omniscient and if omniscience includes knowledge of all true propositions, it follows that no true proposition contains as an essential part of its propositional content a temporal relation to the knower. This point is usually expressed as the claim that tenses are eliminable. Whatever proposition is expressed by tensed sentences or by indexicals representing a temporal relationship to the present using the A-series can be expressed tenselessly using the B-series. So the view that God is both timeless and omniscient seems to be committed to claim (d) of the B-theory. If God is both eternal and omniscient, it does look as if (d) follows. This objection will be taken up next.

3.3. Third Objection

We have just looked at an argument that the Boethian solution is committed to tenet (d) of the B-theory of time, which says that propositions are fully expressible without tenses or indexical expressions relating what the proposition is about to the present. Many philosophers object to this view and, hence, they object to the Boethian solution, which is said to imply it. In this section I will examine this objection.

It has often been argued that tensed propositions cannot be reduced to tenseless ones, and so God is not omniscient on the timeless view.[37] Sorabji, for example, puts the worry this way:

> For if he has not a position in time, he cannot know any tensed propositions such as that there *will* be a sea battle. For someone who has this thought must be thinking of the battle as *later* than his thought, and God's thoughts, on the present view, are not in time. God would at best know the *tenseless* proposition that there is (tenselessly) a sea battle on such and such a date, and that was argued in Chapter Five to be a *different* proposition from the tensed one.[38]

Sorabji objects that God's failure to know tensed propositions would have serious consequences for us:

> If he cannot know that a sparrow is falling to the ground *now*, he cannot know that it needs his concern *now*. Nor again could he know when to intervene in human affairs, when, for example, to send his son, or to answer a prayer.[39]

Sorabji claims that there is action and emotion-guiding force to a proposition containing the token-reflexive *now*, which is missing from the tenseless proposition. A being that knows only tenseless propositions can be neither omniscient nor omnipotent.

Notice, however, that this objection can be sidestepped if God's knowledge is nonpropositional, as Aquinas maintains. This point is well put by William Alston.

> If God's knowledge simply consists in an intuition of one or more concrete realities, and does not involve a segregation of these realities into abstract propositions, this issue does not arise. I see the sun shining and register this fact by assenting to the indexical proposition that the sun is shining here and now. If the knowledge of a timeless or immutable deity is propositionally structured, we have to ask whether that deity knows just the proposition that I expressed by the words "The sun is shining now." And that will lead us into the question of whether some non-indexical proposition which that deity can know is the same proposition as the one I just expressed. But on the non-propositional account of divine knowledge the question is as to whether an immutable or timeless deity can have an intuition of the same concrete reality that I registered one abstract aspect of by assenting to the proposition "The sun is shining now." And there would seem to be no problem about that. What is there in that concrete hunk of space-time that would be unavailable to an immutable or timeless deity? If God is not confronted with the task of analysing reality into distinguishable propositions He will have no traffic with either indexical or non-indexical propositions concerning the current state of affairs. That being the case, we cannot specify some bit of knowledge that is unavailable to Him by focusing on indexical propositions. A deity that enjoys a direct intuition of the concrete reality has slipped through this net.[40]

So if God's knowledge is not propositional, the upholder of God's timelessness and omniscience need not defend tenet (d).

There is another way the upholder of timelessness need not be committed to (d). If both the temporal and atemporal modes of being are ontologically real, it may turn out that propositions true from one perspective are nontrue from the other. The truth of a proposition would be relative to a perspective on this view. So even if tenet (d) is false and tenses are not eliminable from propositions expressing truths from the temporal perspective, such propositions are not true from the atemporal perspective and, hence, it is no problem that God does not know them. This solution would mean that an omniscient being cannot simply be defined as one who knows the truth value of all propositions, since propositions would not be true *simpliciter*, but would be true from a certain perspective. To be omniscient God would know all propositions true from the atemporal perspective. His knowledge would include cognitive awareness of everything going on in the temporal realm, although the propositions he knows when he has such awareness would not be the same as the propositions known by a being in the temporal realm.[41]

We may question, however, whether God loses anything by knowing in this way. Some of those who defend the Boethian solution against the attack we are considering seem to think it important that God not only knows propositions, but that he knows all the same propositions any other being knows. In consequence, several philosophers have recently attempted to defend tenet (d).[42] One of the cleverest is Edward Wierenga's argument that God is aware of the haecceity of each moment of time and its coinstantiation with the events occurring at it.[43] I prefer, however, to suggest a simpler approach. I will argue that on the assumption that God knows propositions and that propositions are true or false *simpliciter*, not relative to perspectives, the main issue is whether the manner of knowing of a being is part of the object of knowledge. If it is not, then it is reasonable to accept (d). If it is, there is a problem with the concept of an omniscient being, but this problem arises whether or not God is in time.

As both Boethius and Aquinas have said in places quoted at the beginning of Section 2.1, it is reasonable to think that each kind of being knows in a manner appropriate to its kind. It would therefore not be surprising if a being that is essentially atemporal knows in a manner different from beings that are essentially temporal, and this difference would no doubt also be an essential difference. The mode of knowing of a temporal being would presumably include the temporal relation (if any) between the state of affairs known and the time at which the being knows. For atemporal beings, of course, there would be no such relation. This means, then, that a temporal being is essentially such that its mode of knowing an event can include that event's temporal relationship to itself and that such awareness is essentially lacking in the mode of knowing of an atemporal being.

Now what, exactly, is the relationship between the mode of knowing and the object of knowledge? It seems to me a good case can be made that relations between a knower and the state of affairs known, including spatial and temporal relations and such intentional relations as relief, regret, hope and anticipation, are not part of the object of knowledge. On this view, when I know that the Battle of Hastings is now over, my temporal relation to that event expressed by "now over" is like such intentional relations as relief or regret. The temporal relation is a relation between me and the object of my knowledge, just as relief or regret is a relation between me and the object of my knowledge, but it is not itself part of what I know. If so, the object of a temporal being's knowledge could be exactly the same as the object of an atemporal being's knowledge, even if the former would in some circumstances express the knowledge in tensed sentences and the latter would not and could not. If so, tenet (d) of the B-theory would be true and a commitment to it would be no objection to the Boethian solution.

But what if the manner of knowing *is* part of the object of knowledge? Prior has argued that what a student knows when he knows with relief that the examinations are over is different from what he knows when he knows with anxiety that they are still to come. And on his argument this is so even though his knowledge of the tenseless proposition *The examinations are over on May 24, 1988* is the same in both cases.[44] The difference between the two cases is a difference in the temporal and intentional relations between the knower and the date of the examinations. If Prior is right that the awareness of these relations is part of the object of knowledge, and assuming that temporal and atemporal beings are essentially different in their awareness of temporal relations, and that no being can be both temporal and atemporal, and assuming that there are both temporal and atemporal beings with knowing powers, it immediately follows that there can be no omniscient being.

The skeptic about eternity would probably conclude that this argument shows that there is no atemporal being with powers of knowledge, but this move would hardly help matters at all. This is because an infinite, omniscient, *temporal* being is as little able to know what we know on this view of the objects of knowledge as is an infinite, omniscient, *atemporal* being. The argument just given is not just a special problem within the doctrine of eternity. If God is in time, he can know that the Battle of Hastings is now over, and he cannot know that if he is not in time, but this is of little advantage, since his manner of knowing would still be radically different and, in fact, essentially different from the manner of knowing of any finite temporal being. An omnipotent and omniscient, infinitely perfect being simply would not know in the manner in which a finite being knows, whether or not such a being were temporal. Even if God were in time, he would not be related to the objects of knowledge in a way that would produce fear, hope, relief, regret, or many other intentional relations appropriate to finite temporal beings. This is because these intentional relations require either that there be a time at which the knower is ignorant or that power over the thing known is lacking. Nor would God know other beings and events as being far removed in space from himself. Thus, if the manner of knowing is part of the object known, an infinite being could not know everything a finite being knows. So the claim that spatial, temporal, and intentional relations appropriate to typical temporal beings are part of the object of knowledge is not a special problem for the view that God is eternal. It is instead a general problem for the view that an infinite divine being knows exactly what a finite and limited being knows.

There is, then, a general problem about God's omniscience that the third objection highlights. It is hard to see how an infinitely perfect being can know everything, including what it is like to be a finite, temporal being, with all the longings, fears, and limitations that human beings experience. But if what it is *like* to be finite is an essential part of *what* a finite being knows, no infinite being could know exactly what a finite being knows. The objection that an eternal being cannot know what it is like to hope for or look back on a temporal event is just a special case of that general problem in the doctrine of omniscience. But to put God in time is to gain very little, if anything, with respect to *that* problem. Even though an everlasting temporal being could know propositions expressible only by tensed sentences, such a being could hardly be said to know anything like what *we* know, since that being also knows the complete future and the complete past. So even if the third objection is correct in the claim that there are propositions not expressible tenselessly, this does not indicate that the theory of timeless omniscience has a problem that the theory of temporal omniscience does not have as well.

I conclude that the objection that an atemporal being is not omniscient because he does not know what is going on now *as* now is an instance of a deep problem in the concept of omniscience, a problem that is not solved by making God temporal. This problem must be solved whether or not God is in time and, even if it is true that God is temporal, this goes very little distance toward solving it. When a good solution is proposed, then, I do not see any reason why it could not apply to an atemporal God as well as to a temporal one.

I have argued in this section that either the mode of knowing of an atemporal being that is essentially different from that of a temporal being is not part of the object of knowledge, in which case a commitment to (d) is not a problem for the Boethian solution, or the mode of knowing is part of the object known, in which case there is a serious problem in explaining how God can know what we know. But, I argued, that problem is not significantly worse if God is atemporal than if he is temporal. This type of problem may show the philosophical importance of the doctrine of the Incarnation, but that is another topic. The problem does not threaten the use of the doctrine of eternity in solving the foreknowledge dilemma.

3.4. Fourth Objection

The fourth objection is that a common metaphorical way of understanding God's eternal knowledge of all temporal events is incompatible with divine providence. This objection comes from the later scholastic philosopher Luis de Molina.

On the standard interpretation of Aquinas endorsed by most Thomistic commentators before the late sixteenth century, Thomas holds that God knows future contingents with certainty solely because future entities, while not yet existing in time, nevertheless exist in eternity where they are present to the divine vision. God's knowledge of future contingents is therefore similar to perceptual knowledge, the main difference being that what is present to God's vision extends to all of space and time, whereas what is present to us is limited to the temporal present and to a small region of space. In the passage from the *Summa Theologiae* quoted on p. 40, Aquinas uses the vision model, and Boethius uses it both in the passage on p. 38, where he alludes to God's knowing as a "looking forth," and in the passage on p. 39, where he says you cannot escape the knowledge of God, just as "you cannot escape the sight of an eye that is present to watch."

One objection to this model, taken up in the second objection, is that it seems to require that the future is just as real as the past. One of Molina's objections is the same as the second objection, but he has another objection that I wish to address here.

In the introduction to his translation of Part IV of *The Concordia*, Alfred J. Freddoso discusses and endorses this objection. He says, "So stated, this solution apparently entails that God acquires His knowledge of vision from created things themselves and thus that true future contingents have their truth conceptually, if not temporally, prior to God's intending or permitting them to be true."[45] But, he says, this is incompatible with the doctrine of divine providence, since it seems to make God the passive recipient of knowledge about the world, whereas the knowledge of a providential God should be much more closely connected with the knowledge of his own will as creator and conserver of the world.

But although Freddoso says he thinks the vision model of divine knowledge *is* incompatible with the desired strong view of divine providence, he says it is not at all clear that Aquinas is guilty of taking such a view seriously, since he repeatedly makes it clear that God's knowledge is not passive: "To the contrary, in many places he states quite unambiguously that the created world is known by God as an artifact is known by the artisan who has fashioned it; and in equally many places he explicitly denies that created things are a cause of God's knowledge of them."[46]

But whether or not Aquinas believed God knows future contingents on the basis of a "vision" of the future, the vision model is an interesting theory about the way God knows and is in need of evaluation. Notice, however, that the vision model need not be used by a proponent of God's timelessness, whereas it can be used by someone who believes God exists *in* time.[47] This objection is therefore not an objection to the eternity solution *per se*, but to a positive explanation of the way God knows, which is commonly conjoined with the eternity view.

In Chapter 1 it was argued that the problem of a providential infallible foreknower is harder than the problem of a nonprovidential infallible foreknower, since the former not only knows, but wills or permits everything that goes on. And so, I argued, God cannot be seen as the passive finder and reader of "The Story of the World." If the vision model is committed to such a way of understanding God's foreknowledge, the model must be rejected.

It is quite possible, I think, that God is able to know things, including future contingents, in more than one way. Presumably on the vision model God's vision of my future act from the vantage point of eternity is *sufficient* for his knowledge of it, although it is quite compatible with this model that it is not necessary. And if it is not necessary God would not be undesirably passive. But even supposing that the vision model gives both necessary and sufficient conditions for God's knowledge of my future act, how does this make God weak, passive, or insufficiently providential? The doctrine of providence requires that nothing goes on without God's willing, or at least permitting, that it be so. But the vision model is not incompatible with this doctrine. Suppose that God timelessly wills to go along with whatever humans choose. I would not be able to choose without God's so willing, although God could still know what I will do in the future *because* he sees me do it from his eternal perspective. This way of understanding God's knowledge would not require that it be analogous to finding and reading "The Story of the World," since there would be no story at all without God's cooperation.

But on this view doesn't God's knowledge of my specific choice depend not only on his knowledge of his own will, but also on me? The answer is yes, but that hardly seems to be an unseemly kind of passivity. Giving human beings free will presumably involves giving us certain active powers with respect to which God is voluntarily passive. I do not see that this is inappropriate for a divine being or a sign of weakness. Furthermore, this model is compatible with most of the things we ordinarily say when referring to God's providential activity. Need an adherent of the vision model deny that God has the power to interfere with our free choices and to render them inefficacious? Need he deny that God can turn any human free act into the means to some providential good? Need he deny that God, by using his foreknowledge, can intervene before the choice is made in any manner he chooses? In each case the answer is no.

If God's knowledge is nonpropositional, as Aquinas maintains, the adherent of the vision model has an even stronger answer to this objection, since God would not know by "reading off" propositions outside of himself anyway. Instead, his knowledge is a vision, not of the outside, but of his own essence. God "sees" my future act by "seeing" himself. On this view, God knows by a single direct intuition of his own essence. The primary object of his knowledge is his own essence, but the secondary object is everything else. The primary object is therefore the same in all possible worlds in which God exists, since God's essence is the same in all worlds in which he exists. But since contingent facts differ from world to world, the secondary object of God's knowing state differs from world to world. I interpret this to mean that God has exactly one knowing state whose identity conditions are given by its primary object, and so it is the numerically same state in all worlds in which God exists. Such a state is secondarily a knowing of one contingent fact in one world and a different contingent fact in another world. God therefore knows that I do A in $w1$ by knowing his essence and knows that I do not A in $w2$ by the same knowing state. This theory will be discussed in more detail in Chapter 3. For the purposes of answering the present objection it is sufficient to point out that such a theory is well entrenched in Christian theology, and even though it is a kind of knowledge by vision, it is hardly passive.

At the beginning of this chapter I noted that some solutions to the foreknowledge dilemma have philosophical or religious implications that some people will find unacceptable. Those who find it religiously important to have a view of divine providence that is so strong as to be incompatible with the vision model will obviously wish to reject that model. I have no interest in attempting to defend a view of providence that is compatible with this model, since it seems to me that the model is not a necessary part of the Boethian solution and, in any case, I believe there are other solutions to the foreknowledge dilemma that are compatible with even the strongest notion of providence. Since my aim in this book is not to defend a unique solution, I do not believe it is necessary to defend all the philosophical and religious commitments of each one. Those who find this solution incompatible with their commitment to a very strong view of providence are probably right to reject it.

3.5. Fifth Objection

In this section I wish to propose what I think is the strongest objection to the Boethian solution. On this view the timelessness move is useless, since even though the eternality of God's knowledge solves the version of the foreknowledge dilemma based on the necessity of the past, it nevertheless generates a parallel dilemma based on the necessity of eternity. We might call it the Timeless Knowledge Dilemma. I think that the argument I will present shows that the view that God is timeless is not enough to solve the foreknowledge problem, but I no longer think that the solution is useless. This is because the intuition of the necessity of eternity is less well grounded in intuitions about eternity than the necessity of the past is grounded in intuitions about time. This means that the Boethian move still has some advantage over the solution I will support in Chapter 3.

Let us first review the ways in which the Boethian move solves the foreknowledge problem. First, if God's beliefs are outside of time, they are immutable. This means, of course, that they cannot change, but this is not to say they had to be what they are in the first place. After all, even though God's beliefs are immutable in all possible worlds, they are different in different possible worlds. So the immutability of God's eternal beliefs does not take away the logical contingency of those beliefs, and the Boethian solution is compatible with the logical contingency of human acts.

Furthermore, if God's beliefs are outside of time, there is no worry that they cause events in time in a way that takes away the causal contingency of human acts. As we will see in Chapter 4, if God's beliefs are in time they satisfy the conditions for being the cause of human acts according to a currently important theory of causation.[48] This problem is removed entirely if God's beliefs are not in time at all. The Boethian solution, then, is not incompatible with the causal contingency of human acts.

Again, since accidental necessity applies only to events in time, the Boethian solution is compatible with the accidental contingency of human acts. So even if every state of affairs in the past is fixed and inalterable, this has no effect on the Boethian solution. If God is eternal, then, his knowledge of all human choices is compatible with the logical, causal, and accidental contingency of those choices.

But what can be more fixed than eternity? Both ontologically and modally the realm of eternity seems to be much more like the realm of the past than of the future. It is ontologically real, like the past and unlike the future, and if p is some proposition about a timeless state of affairs, it is not very likely that there exists (timelessly) a potency for *not p*. As we saw in Chapter 1, Ockham connected his doctrine of the necessity of the past with the fact that the past has lost potency for being otherwise. So the reason used by Ockham for maintaining the necessity of the past seems to apply equally well to the eternal realm. Furthermore, the intuition that there is nothing I can do now about God's eternal immutable beliefs about my future acts is about as strong as the intuition that there is nothing I can do now about God's past immutable beliefs about my future acts. It seems as if there is nothing I can do about those beliefs that are now irrevocable, and eternal beliefs seem to be just as irrevocable as past ones. If the commonsense view of time discussed in Chapter 1 leads us to think that it is now impossible that actual past events did not occur, surely what little we know about the nature of the timeless realm leads us to think that it is now impossible that actual timeless events do not occur timelessly. So just as the inalterability of God's past infallible belief about the future seems to lead to necessity in the future, by the same reasoning the inalterability of God's timeless infallible belief also seems to lead to necessity in the future.

The objection, then, is that the timelessness solution solves one version of the dilemma only to fall into another one, for consider the following set of states of affairs.

Timeless Knowledge Dilemma

(1) God's being infallible (or essentially omniscient).

(9) God's timelessly believing that I do S at $t3$.

(3) My being free to refrain from doing S at $t3$.

If (1) obtains, then God's belief cannot be false. But when applied to the belief in (9), it seems to follow that no matter what I do at $t3$, I cannot make God's timeless belief about that act false. And this seems inconsistent with (3). This dilemma is exactly parallel to the one proposed in Chapter 1.

In discussing the medieval notion of accidental necessity, Adams makes a point that at least hints that she has a worry similar to mine. She says: "But if the necessity of the past stems from its ontological determinateness it would seem that timeless determinateness is just as problematic as past determinateness."[49] This suggests that the notion of accidental necessity relies on the intuition that the past has an ontological reality that the future lacks. But if there is a timeless realm as well as a temporal one, the timeless realm would no doubt have no deficiency in ontological reality. Presumably, then, it would be much more like the past than the future with respect to ontological reality and, hence, with respect to inalterability.

There is a further objection to the version of the eternity doctrine proposed by Stump and Kretzmann. On their view an eternal entity or event observed as eternally present, or just "as eternal" by some temporal observer, is ET-simultaneous with every temporal entity or event. I do not have a clear grasp of what it means for a temporal observer such as myself to observe some entity or event as eternal, but presumably some temporal being is in a position to predicate eternality to each of God's beliefs, even though none of us is in a position to know the propositional content of very many of them.[50] If some temporal being is in a position at any time to "observe" that God's belief about my act is eternal, it follows on the Stump-Kretzmann account that such a belief is ET-simultaneous with every temporal being or event, including myself before the act in question. Consider, for example, the fact that I am now sitting before my computer writing Chapter 2 of my book. I or some other temporal being seems to be in a position to observe that God's belief about this fact is eternal or eternally present. On the Stump-Kretzmann account this belief is consequently ET-simultaneous with every temporal entity and event. This means that God's eternal belief is ET-simultaneous with myself just prior to my deliberations about whether or not to sit down at the computer. From *my* temporal perspective before I decide what to do, God's belief about what I will do is ET-simultaneous with me. But if it is reasonable to worry that from my temporal perspective the past is beyond my control, it is reasonable to worry that from my temporal perspective what is ET-simultaneous with me in the past is beyond my control. This objection does not assume that the ET-simultaneity relation is transitive, as Stump and Kretzmann deny, but only that if A is ET-simultaneous with B and B is accidentally necessary, then A is accidentally necessary or necessary in a related sense.

So it seems that if a past state of affairs is beyond my control, so is a timeless one. If a principle of the Necessity of the Past is plausible, so is a principle of the Necessity of Eternity, and for parallel reasons. The Timeless Knowledge Dilemma should worry us, then, almost as much as the Accidental Necessity Version of the Foreknowledge Dilemma. I suspect that the only reason the Timeless Knowledge Dilemma is less vivid than the Foreknowledge Dilemma is that our grasp of eternity is weaker than our grasp of the past and certainly we have much less of a grasp on the notion of ET-simultaneity than on the before-than relation. But this reason is not very flattering to the theory.

The Foreknowledge Dilemma requires that there be some explanation of the relationship between God's past belief and my future act that makes it plausible that my future act is contingent in all senses required for freedom. As a first step some philosophers have suggested that the relationship is truly expressed by the following subjunctive conditional.

(10) If I were to choose *A* instead of *B* God would have known at all previous times that I would do so.

And as we will see in Chapter 3, many objections have been given to (10). But is it any better to say the following instead?

(11) If I were to choose *A* instead of *B* God would have timelessly known that I would do so.

Propositions (10) and (11) are, of course, in need of analysis, and that will be begun in Chapters 3 and 4. My point here is simply that whether or not God is timeless, the relationship between God's knowledge and my act needs to be explained, and prior to such an analysis it is not at all clear what advantage (11) has over (10).

Although my conclusion at this stage is that the Boethian move is not yet a solution to the Foreknowledge Dilemma because of the fifth objection, I think that the switch from the Accidental Necessity Version of the dilemma to the Timeless Knowledge Dilemma has some advantages. It may be less objectionable to say, for example, that my free act causes or brings about God's timeless belief than that it brings about a past belief. Also, if God's beliefs are not in time there is no dilemma analogous to the Causal Necessity Version of the dilemma that faces those who say God's beliefs are in time. For these reasons and others that I will discuss in Chapter 3, the Boethian move, while not yet a complete solution to the dilemma, may still be a worthwhile beginning.

4. Conclusion

In Section 3 I examined the strongest objections to the timeless knowledge solution I know of. I argued that none of them shows that the Boethian view must be rejected, although the Timeless Knowledge Dilemma shows that the move is not yet a solution to the foreknowledge problem. Since the Timeless Knowledge Dilemma uses the principle of the Necessity of Eternity, which is no doubt less well entrenched in our intuitions than the analogous Necessity of the Past Principle, this dilemma may be easier to solve, and so the Boethian move may still represent a conceptual advance.

In this concluding section I would like to outline briefly the reasons for thinking God is timeless that I find most compelling. These reasons are independent of considerations of knowledge and arise directly from a consideration of the nature of time.

A good many Judeo-Christian thinkers in antiquity and the Middle Ages, from Philo to Augustine to Aquinas, argued that there was a first moment of time. One reason for thinking so is the Aristotelian view that time cannot exist in the absence of motion. If we combine this view of time with the view that the physical universe had a beginning, it follows that time came into being with the rest of the physical universe. On this view it does not make sense to say time passed when nothing was in existence but God, who is immutable. But if there was a first moment of time, presumably it was created by God. It depends on God for its existence. Of course, if we take this position we must be careful not to refer to the atemporal existence of God "before" the creation of time. The term "before time" implies that there was a time before time and that is undoubtedly absurd. But this much we can say: God did not himself come into existence at the first moment of time. But then God must have been outside of time in order to create it.

But if God did create time, does that mean he is still outside of time? Couldn't he create it and then jump into it and ride along with the flow? I know of no conclusive arguments against this possibility but, since it is almost always thought that a timeless being is unchanging, this possibility could be eliminated if it implied a change. Does a being who creates time and then becomes temporal change? Intuitively the answer is yes, but the answer would be no on the following definition of an unchanging being proposed by Wierenga.

> x is unchanging $\longleftrightarrow$ there are no times $t1$ and $t2$ and change-relevant property P such that x has P at $t1$ and x lacks P at $t2$.[51]

A being who creates time and becomes temporal would be unchanging on this definition as long as he never loses a property while he is in time. My intuition is that if an atemporal being becomes temporal that being has certainly changed. If so, the possibility that an immutable God can create time and then become temporal should be eliminated.

Suppose, on the other hand, that the philosophers who argued that there was a first moment of time are wrong. Suppose that instead time is infinitely long in both directions. There was no first moment of time and there will be no last moment of time. This still does not settle the question of whether time is necessary or contingent. A similar point has been made by those upholders of the Cosmological Argument such as Copleston who allow for the possibility that the physical universe always was. Even if time is infinitely long, it does not follow either that it was self-caused or that it is impossible that it not exist. Are there any possible worlds with no time at all? If so, whether or not time is infinitely long, it is contingent, and if it is contingent, it must have the reason or source of its existence in a being outside itself. And such a being is presumably God. So if God is necessary and time is contingent, it seems that God must be timeless.

Finally, let us allow that time is necessary in the sense that there is no possible world without some temporal flow. But even if this is the case, does it follow that it is necessary that there be a single time—indeed, the particular time we experience? Could there not be many times—even, in fact, many times coexisting in the same possible world? Aren't there perhaps many times coexisting in the actual world? If so, which time does God exist in? Whatever is gained religiously in the idea that God is in time is lost unless God is in our time. The objections in the literature against timelessness are arguments that are supposed to lead us to conclude that God's now is our now, God's past is our past, and so on. But we know from the Theory of Relativity that there is no one answer to the question what distant events are going on simultaneously with events here. There are different answers, depending on the rates of relative velocity of the observers. If God has no state of motion or rest, what answer do we give for him? If he does have such a state, his now would not be identical with our now. But then even if he is in time, he would not know the temporally indexed propositions that give trouble to the timelessness view.

I suspect that the main reason people reject the timelessness doctrine is a distaste for the metaphysically abstruse. Presumably the best cure for metaphysical abstruseness is greater clarity, and I agree the doctrine could use more of that. But I see no cause to despair of such clarity. Furthermore, the doctrine of timelessness does have a certain advantage worth noting. It is simply more metaphysically exciting than the view that God is temporal. Whether this is a reliable indication of truth I am not able to judge.

3

The Ockhamist Solution

1. Introduction

Perhaps the most widely discussed solution to the foreknowledge dilemma in recent years is the Ockhamist solution. Many variations of it have been proposed, and some are probably not very close to Ockham's intention. I will consider a solution Ockhamist in spirit if it (a) takes accidental necessity seriously and at least initially identifies it with the necessity of the past, (b) assumes that God exists in time, and (c) denies that God's beliefs are accidentally necessary. The general idea behind this solution is that even though God had beliefs (more or less) in the past, and even though the past is (more or less) accidentally necessary, God's beliefs nonetheless escape accidental necessity. On the face of it, this solution is an attempt to have it both ways, but it can be seen as an attempt to push an insight I discussed in Chapter 1. There I argued that the problem of future truth is not as gripping as the problem of divine foreknowledge. The reason is that it is much less clear that the necessity of the past applies to the past state of affairs of some proposition's being true than to the past state of affairs of a person having a belief. But exactly how are we to distinguish the two cases? The Ockhamists claim either that some states of affairs that verbally are in the past are not really or strictly in the past, or that some past states of affairs are modally different from the rest of the past.

Interest in Ockham's way out of the dilemma in the contemporary literature began in the late 1960s with Marilyn Adams's paper, "Is the Existence of God a 'Hard' Fact?"[1] Since then a number of philosophers have defended some version of Ockhamism.[2] Most of this literature analyzes the concept of accidental necessity in an attempt to show that the necessity of the past may not apply to God's past beliefs. There have been two distinct approaches to doing this. The first, and generally earlier, approach was to distinguish between what is really or strictly past (i.e., the "hard" past) from what is only apparently or merely in part about the past (i.e., the "soft" past). The claim is that it is only the hard past, the past strictly speaking, that is fixed and hence accidentally necessary, yet God's past beliefs or God's past existence are in the soft past.

To be a successful negative solution this approach first needs to distinguish between hard and soft facts in a way that is not *ad hoc*. Ideally it should arise naturally from the analysis of time and the nature of facts and it should be carried out independently of the foreknowledge issue. It should then give a good case for the claim that it is at least possible that God's past beliefs are soft facts. If this can be accomplished, it leaves open the possibility that God's past beliefs do not limit our power to act; at least, our power is not limited by accidental necessity. I am sympathetic with the intuition behind this approach, but I know of no attempted solution of this type that has been successful.

The second and more recent approach is to bypass the distinction between the hard and soft pasts in favor of defining accidental necessity directly in terms of human power. This approach has been attempted by Plantinga and has been followed by others.[3] Briefly, the accidentally necessary at t is what I can do nothing about at t. To be successful this approach must suggest some means of picking out a class of facts I can do nothing about distinct from the logically and causally necessary. It should either be compatible with the intuitions about time that underly the concept of accidental necessity and the typical examples of necessity *per accidens*, or it should defend its superiority to those intuitions. This solution should then show that it is at least possible that God's past beliefs are not in this category. I do not know of a solution of this type that has accomplished this.

Both approaches concentrate on giving a precise definition of accidental necessity. It may be possible to show, however, that God's past beliefs may not be accidentally necessary by analyzing the concept of God's beliefs rather than the concept of the accidentally necessary. I think it is quite likely that God's beliefs are so different from other things in the past that even in the absence of a precise account of accidental necessity, a good case can be made that they are not in the category of the necessary *per accidens*. I believe this approach has not been investigated as much as it deserves.

In this chapter I will discuss the solution of William of Ockham as well as the two most common types of contemporary Ockhamism just mentioned. I will argue that neither of these is very promising. I will then use the Thomistic description of God's knowing to propose an Ockham-inspired solution of my own.

2. Ockham

Briefly, Ockham's solution to the problem of divine foreknowledge in his treatise *De Praedestinatione* is that propositions about God's knowledge of future contingents are themselves future contingent propositions. The objects of God's knowledge are true propositions. Each proposition is at all moments of time either determinately true or determinately false, and propositions cannot change truth value. Therefore, a true contingent proposition about the future was true at all times in the past. According to Marilyn Adams, Ockham rejects the following principle, which he attributes to Aristotle.

> (1) 'x is (was, will be) A at tm' is determinately true at tn, if and only if there is no potency in things at tn for x's not being (having been, being going to be) A at tm.

He replaces it with the following principle:

> (2) 'x is (was, will be) A at tm' is determinately true at tn if and only if at some time or other there is (was, will be) no potency in things for x's not being (having been, being going to be) A at tm.[4]

According to principle (1) the determinate truth of a proposition at a time is settled by something real or actual in the past or present relative to that time, and so by something past relative to any later time. But then, by the necessity of the past, if p is true now, p will be necessary at any later time. But by (2) it follows only that the determinate truth of a proposition at a time is settled by what is real or actual at some time or other. If it is settled at t_n, then at all times prior to t_n there is still a potency for the opposite. So even though the proposition *Peter denies Christ at t_m* is determinately true at all moments of time, there is potency in things for Peter's not denying Christ until t_m. Since the necessity of the past is connected with potency for the opposite, not with truth, this means that the past determinate truth of such propositions does not fall under the necessity of the past.

If there is potency in things for its being false that Peter denies Christ before t_m, since God is infallible, there is also potency in things for *God foreknows Peter denies Christ at t_m* to be false until t_m, even though it has always been true that God foreknew that Peter would deny Christ at t_m. Ockham says:

> And in that way [His knowledge] is not necessary, nor need it be granted that God has necessary knowledge regarding future contingents; instead,

[His knowledge regarding them] is contingent. For just as this or that future contingent contingently will be, so God knows that it contingently will be, for if He knows it He can not know that it will be.[5] (Translator's additions in brackets.)

So the past determinate truth of propositions expressing God's past knowledge about future contingent events does not fall under the necessity of the past either.

Ockham says very little about the basis for excluding these propositions from the category of the accidentally necessary. The passage generally thought to be the most suggestive, already quoted in part in Chapter 1, is the following:

Assumption 3. Some propositions are about the present as regards both their wording and their subject matter. Where such propositions are concerned, it is universally true that every proposition has [corresponding to it] a necessary one about the past—e.g., "Socrates is seated," "Socrates is walking," "Socrates is just," and the like.

Other propositions are about the present as regards their wording only and are equivalently about the future, since their truth depends on the truth of propositions about the future. Where such [propositions] are concerned, the rule that every true proposition about the present has [corresponding to it] a necessary one about the past is not true. . . .

Assumption 4. All propositions having to do with predestination and reprobation, whether they are verbally about the present or about the past, are nevertheless equivalently about the future, since their truth depends on the truth of propositions formally about the future. But Assumption 3 show that such true [propositions] about the present do not have a necessary one about the past [corresponding to them] but rather one that is merely contingent, just as the one about the present is contingent. From these [considerations] it follows that no proposition about the present having to do with predestination and reprobation has a necessary one about the past [corresponding to it].[6] (Translator's additions in brackets.)

Ockham admits that the way in which God is able to know future contingents is problematic. However, he attempts a rather unsatisfying explanation by analogy with human intuitive knowledge.

Despite [the impossibility of expressing it clearly], the following way [of knowing future contingents] can be ascribed [to God]. Just as the [human] intellect on the basis of one and the same [intuitive] cognition of certain non-complexes can have evident cognition of contradictory contingent propositions such as "A exists," "A does not exist," in the same way it can be granted that the divine essence is intuitive cognition that is so perfect, so clear, that it is evident cognition of all things past and future, so that it knows which part of a contradiction [involving such things] is true and which part false.[7] (Translator's additions in brackets.)

Ockham's contemporary supporters more than compensate for his lack of precision in distinguishing between what is only verbally about the past and what is really about the past. Surprisingly, very few such discussions connect the distinction to the Aristotelian act/potency distinction, as Ockham does, nor do they generally reflect much on the alleged ontological asymmetry between past and future. Instead, the method typically involves giving a definition of either "hard facts" or "accidentally necessary" which is consistent with a certain class of paradigm cases, and then arguing that God's past beliefs are not in this class of facts. The two most common approaches to doing this will be discussed in Section 3.

3. Contemporary Ockhamist Accounts

3.1. Hard Facts/Soft Facts

If the past is accidentally necessary because it is past, it might be thought important to get clear on what is *really* past, since every fact is logically equivalent to one about the past. For example, if it is a fact that I will go to Santa Barbara next week, that fact is equivalent to the fact that it was the case two weeks ago that I would go to Santa Barbara in three weeks, yet the latter seems to be about the past, whereas the former does not. For the same reason every fact is equivalent to one that seems to be about the past. But then which ones are accidentally necessary?

Much of the recent Ockhamist discussion is part of an ongoing attempt to answer the following well-known challenge by Pike in his first article on fatalism:

> If God existed at *T1* and if God believed at *T1* that Jones would do x at *t2*, then if it was within Jones' power at *T2* to refrain from doing x, then (1) it was within Jones' power at *T2* to do something that would have brought it about that God held a false belief at *T1*, or (2) it was within Jones' power at *T2* to do something which would have brought it about that God did not hold the belief He held at *T1*, or (3) it was within Jones' power at *T2* to do something that would have brought it about that any person who believed at *T1* that Jones would so S at *T2* (one of whom was, by hypothesis, God) held a false belief and thus was not God—that is, that God (who by hypothesis existed at *T1*) did not exist at *T1*.[8]

In this argument Pike makes use of a principle the generalization of which has been called by John Martin Fischer the Fixed Past Constraint (FPC), a principle that is said to articulate the basic intuition of the necessity of the past and is presumably intended to be a necessary truth.

FPC   A person never has it in her power at t so to act that the past (relative to t) would have been different from what it actually was.[9]

Ockhamists do not deny FPC; instead, they focus their attention on what it is to be genuinely in the past, since they claim that intuitively it is only the genuine past which is fixed by FPC.

Recall that in Chapter 1 it was argued that the common belief that the past is necessary is connected with the view that it is possible that the world end now, in which case there would be no future but, no matter what happens, it is not possible that there is no past. In fact, it is not now possible that anything other than the actual past be the past, although even if there is an actual future, it is possible now that something other than the actual future be the future. Past events cannot now not have happened; future events *can* now not happen. And this asymmetry between past and future means that whereas I have it in my power now to act so that the future will be different from what it actually will be, I do not have it in my power now to act so that the past would be different from it actually was. Something like this, I believe, is the intuitive defense of FPC.

So if the world ended now and there was no future, the past would still be. This means that at any moment of time t_n, relations between events/states of affairs at t_n and moments of time later than t_n are possibly such that they do not obtain and are therefore exempt from the necessity of the past relative to t_n. It is reasonable to say that such relations do not really obtain at t_n, since the future is not real, nor do any states of affairs that have such relations as components. The concept of being really or strictly in the past, then, is naturally explicated in terms of a lack of dependency on the future.

Adams used this intuition in a well-known response to Pike's article. She argued that Pike's three alternatives are unacceptable only if God's beliefs are really or strictly in the past. But both God's belief and God's existence itself are not in the strict or hard past, she argued.

To define "hard fact" Adams proposed the following:

D1   Proposition p expresses a hard fact about time $t =_{df} p$ is not at least in part about any time t' such that t' is later than t.

And the notion of being in part about a time was clarified as follows:

D2   Proposition p is at least in part about $t =$ $_{df}$ the happening or not happening, the actuality or nonactuality, of something at t is a necessary condition for p's being true.

There are numerous objections to Adams in the literature. The strongest attack may be that of Fischer, who argues that on Adams's criterion no fact is a hard fact.[10] This is because even a fact that intuitively ought to be hard at $t1$, such as that Jack is sitting at $t1$, entails that it is not the case that Jack sits for the first time at $t2$. But then, by D1 and D2, the fact that Jack sits at $t1$ is not a hard fact at $t1$.

It is not obvious, however, that Jack is sitting at $t1$ entails *It is not the case that Jack sits for the first time at $t2$*. If the latter proposition is committed to the existence of a moment of time $t2$, then what the former entails is rather *If there is a t2, Jack does not sit for the first time at t2*. An interesting recent modification of Adams's view is that of Widerker, who accepts Fischer's objection to Adams just given, but observes that the nonoccurrence of the event of Jack's sitting for the first time at $t2$ does not entail that $t2$ occur. The intuition behind the hard fact/soft fact distinction is that it is compatible with the hard facts at t that the world go out of existence immediately after t, whereas the soft facts at t entail that the world continues in existence after t. Widerker proposes a version of D2 that uses this intuition but that is not vulnerable to the Fischer objection. His definition, modified slightly by Fischer, is as follows.

D2$_w$ A fact F is about a time $t1$ if and only if F's obtaining entails both that $t1$ occurs and that something occurs at $t1$; a fact F about $t1$ is a soft fact about $t1$ if and only if F's obtaining entails that some later time $t2$ occurs.[11]

Fischer proposes an objection to this version of D2 as well. On D2$_w$ the fact that God believed at $t1$ that Jones would not do S at $t2$ is a soft fact about $t1$. Call it "*F1*". But suppose that exactly seven persons believe at $t1$ that Jones will not do S at $t2$. Call this fact "*F2*". Fischer argues that if *F1* is a soft fact about $t1$, *F2* should be also. But on D2$_w$ *F1* is a soft fact and *F2* is a hard fact. Furthermore, suppose that Jones can do S at $t2$. It follows that Jones can so act that *F1* would not have been a fact. That much is okay since *F1* is supposed to be a soft fact. But suppose that if Jones had done S at $t2$, the only person whose beliefs would have been different about that fact is God. In that case Jones would have acted in such a way that *F2* was not a fact either. But on D2$_w$ *F2* is a hard fact about $t1$ and the Ockhamist denies that anyone has the power at $t2$ to act so that a hard fact about *t1* is not a fact. Fischer concludes that $D2_w$ cannot be used by an Ockhamist.[12]

Most of the recent literature on Ockhamism includes a series of clarifications of D2, counterexamples to it, revisions of the definition, and more counterexamples. The intuition that remains constant throughout these discussions is probably something like D1, but D2 has been replaced by more and more elaborate and sophisticated definitions. For example, Freddoso worked out a complex definition of accidental necessity that is still fairly close to the spirit of Adams's original idea.

> D3   *p* is necessary *per accidens* at (w,t) iff (i) *p* is logically contingent and (ii) *p* is true at *t* and at every moment after *t* in every world *w** such that *w** shares the same history with *w* at *t*.[13]

> D3.1   Two worlds *w* and *w** share the same history at *t* iff *w* and *w** have identical series of $t_i < t$ and that for any submoment *k* and time $t_n < t$, *k* obtains *at* (w,t_n) iff *k* obtains at (w^*,t_n).

> D3.2   A submoment for any (w,t) is the set of immediate propositions true at (w,t).

> D3.3   An immediate proposition *p* is (i) an atomic, nonquantified, present-tense proposition and (ii) temporally indifferent, such that either (*a*) *p* is not logically contingent or (*b*) it is possible that *p*, as well as its negation, be true at a first, a last, or an intermediate moment of time.[14]

Even more elaborate definitions have subsequently been offered. Consider the definition proposed by Hoffman and Rosenkrantz. They first distinguish between eternal states of affairs (e.g., Socrates is walking at t_n) and unrestrictedly repeatable, present-tense, or tenseless states of affairs (e.g., Socrates is walking), and then suggest the following:

> D4   *r* is a hard fact iff
>
> (i)   *r* is the state of affairs: *s* at *t*;
> (ii)   *s* is an unrestrictedly repeatable, present-tense state of affairs;
> (iii)   *s* obtains throughout *t*;
> (iv)   either S is a simple state of affairs, or, if it is complex, all its parts are unrestrictedly repeatable, present-tense states of affairs;
> (v)   neither *r* nor *s* nor any of *s*'s parts entails either a simple unrestrictedly repeatable, present-tense state of affairs indexed to a time which does not overlap with *t*, or a complex unrestrictedly repeatable, present-tense state of affairs all of whose parts are unrestrictedly repeatable, present-tense states of affairs and which is indexed to a time which does not overlap with *t*;
> (vi)   *t* is a past time.[15]

More elaborate still is the definition proposed by Jonathan Kvanvig in his book, *The Possibility of an All-Knowing God.*[16] If the definition were written out together with all its subdefinitions, the result would be well over a page in length.

The methodology used in this series of definitions of hard facts is not uncommon, but I think ultimately misguided. In each case a definition is sought that has the following features: (i) it is consistent with the clear cases of hard facts and the clear cases of soft facts, and so has no counterexamples, and (ii) it has the consequence that God's past beliefs are soft facts. If so, we are not prevented from having power over them by their pastness. Some say, of course, that there is still some other reason why they are fixed but, if not, we have a solution to the foreknowledge problem on the grounds that we have counterfactual power over God's past beliefs.[17] It is interesting that even anti-Ockhamists in these discussions seem to accept the sufficiency of the preceding criteria and focus their attack on counterexamples. But I will not discuss here whether any of these definitions is vulnerable to counterexample, since I have no doubt that even if all of them are, it is possible to devise one that is not. Given some set of clear examples of hard facts and clear examples of soft facts, it is surely possible with enough ingenuity to devise a definition of hard facts that is consistent with the set and that has as a consequence that God's past beliefs are soft facts. But it is not at all clear what such a definition would accomplish. Even if some definition satisfies both criteria (i) and (ii), how would that give us any reason to think that it captures a real rather than a merely nominal distinction between the two types of fact? It is a tribute to the patience and the talent of philosophers that such elaborate recursive definitions of hard facts have been devised. But to present a definition is not to show that it bears any connection to a distinction in the nature of things.

An analogue from another area of philosophy might be helpful here. Suppose that the issue involved not the distinction between hard and soft facts, but the distinction between just and unjust acts. Imagine that some group of theorists are strongly inclined to deny that paying back a debt to Plantinga is a just act, whereas paying back a debt to anybody else *is* a just act. Suppose also that they are inclined to think so because it makes it easier to handle some other philosophical problem. They then propose a definition of "just act" that is compatible with every clear case of just acts they can think of, except that it has the consequence that paying debts to Plantinga is unjust. In the manner of good dialectical method they propose the definition as acceptable and invite counterexamples. The definition is then amended with additional clauses as counterexamples are given, and eventually it becomes very complex, although it still has the consequence that paying debts to Plantinga is unjust. Much simpler definitions of "just act" are available, but they do not have the Plantinga consequence.

I suspect that we would think that something had gone wrong with such a definition. We would think this partly because of its complex form, especially since such a form could be avoided if it were not insisted that a particular case be classified as unjust. Similarly, the elaborate form of the definitions of "hard fact" we have considered is largely due to the insistence that God's beliefs turn out to be soft. If the status of God's beliefs were not a consideration, it is pretty clear the definitions would be much shorter and simpler in structure.

The point I am making here is an instance of a general observation about concept definition. Suppose that both sides to a dispute agree that some set of examples $H1, H2, H3 \ldots Hn$ are genuine cases of H, and that some set of examples $S1, S2, S3, \ldots Sn$ are genuine cases of S, and the disputed case is Bg. It is surely possible for those who believe that Bg is in S to find some property that $H1, H2, H3 \ldots Hn$ have in common and that is lacked by Bg and $S1, S2, S3 \ldots Sn$, and some property that Bg has in common with $S1, S2, S3 \ldots Sn$ and that is lacked by $H1, H2, H3 \ldots Hn$. They can then use these respective properties to define H and S. The resulting definition has no counterexamples and has the consequence that Bg is in S. Both criteria (i) and (ii) are satisfied. But such an exercise should not by itself lead us to think that it has captured a helpful distinction between two classes of facts. The reason is that both sides can play the same game. Those who believe that Bg is in H can simply find some property that Bg has in common with the H's and not the S's and use that to define H instead. It will always be possible to find such a property as long as there is no limit on complexity.

Most people have strong intuitions about the necessity of the past in a large variety of cases, the past spilling of milk being the most common folk example. Past beliefs of persons would automatically be put in this category if it were not for the foreknowledge dilemma. If this intuition is strong enough, it may be reasonable to maintain it independently of an account of accidental necessity and, in fact, this might be seen as a constraint on any such account. That is, the intuition that past beliefs are really in the past may simply override any proposed criterion on which some of them are not. The intuitions are just stronger than the criterion. A soft fact is supposed to be something that can be seen to be not really in the past at all. It may be in the past verbally, or there may be an aspect of it that is later attributed to it retroactively (such as in typical cases of human foreknowledge) but, on reflection, we can see that it is an illusion to say that it is past. In the case of God's past beliefs, however, even on reflection, they still seem to be as past as past gets.

A good definition of the hard fact/soft fact distinction should do much more than satisfy criteria (i) and (ii). Since the underlying intuition is a fairly ordinary one, although admittedly vague, we should find that the definition illuminates the underlying notion. Simplicity is also a virtue. The less simple the definition, the more nervous it should make us. Furthermore, it should be explanatory. It should be helpful, not only to the foreknowledge issue, but to other issues arising from temporal asymmetry as well. If it does not do these things moderately well, it is *ad hoc*, and it seems to me that this is a much more serious problem for this approach than the question of whether we can find any counterexamples to the proposed definitions.

Incompatibilists about divine foreknowledge hold that the claim that God's past beliefs are either not really past or are such that our power is unaffected by them violates necessary truths about the structure of time. I have not defended the intuitions the incompatibilist relies on, but I argued in Chapter 1 that they are common enough and strong enough to be considered common sense. I think, then, that even a negative solution to the foreknowledge dilemma of the type we are considering must attack these intuitions directly. The supporters of this approach, unfortunately, do not do this. Until they do, we have no reason to think their distinctions are more than purely nominal.

3.2. The Counterfactual Power of Agents

In one of the earliest responses to Pike, Saunders argued that just as it is within my power so to act that my past decision would have been different, so it lies within my power so to act that God's foreknowledge would have been different.[18] Solutions that make use of the counterfactual dependency of God's belief on my act have been used repeatedly in the discussions following Pike's paper, notably in Plantinga's early reply in *God, Freedom, and Evil*.[19] In his paper, "On Ockham's Way Out," Plantinga suggests that the definition of accidental necessity be given directly in terms of counterfactual power over the past. In this paper Plantinga says that he endorses Ockhamism, but his reasoning about accidental necessity is quite different from Ockham's. Unlike Ockham, and perhaps in part because of a lack of patience with the hard fact/soft fact approach, he does not analyze necessity *per accidens* in terms of being strictly about the past. He argues that Newcomb's Paradox shows that there is a proposition strictly about the past that is not accidentally necessary.[20] His idea, then, is to eliminate reference to the past in the analysis of accidental necessity and simply to define it in terms of the counterfactual power of agents. A number of other philosophers have approved of this move, either calling it a successful negative solution to the dilemma or amending it in a friendly way.[21] In this section I will criticize this approach.

Plantinga's suggested definition is

> D5   *p* is accidentally necessary at *t* if and only if *p* is true at *t* and it is not possible both that *p* is true at *t* and there exists an agent *S* and an action *A* such that (1) *S* has the power at *t* or later to perform *A*, and (2) if *S* were to perform *A* at *t* or later, then *p* would have been false.[22]

It is interesting that the power referred to in this definition of accidental necessity is not the power of the past over the present and future, as might be expected, but rather the lack of power of the future over the past. The latter type of power raises grave difficulties about backward causation and related matters that could have been avoided if the definition had been constructed differently. Chapter 4 will address the question of whether D5 involves undesirable commitments of this kind. Here I would just like to point out that even if it is thought desirable to define accidental necessity in terms of human power rather than in terms of what is strictly in the past, it would seem to be closer to the intuitive concept to define it in terms of what limits my present power to choose rather than what I now have no power to affect.

In addition, Plantinga seems to have forgotten that on the previous page of his paper he had remarked that accidental necessity is supposed to be distinct from logical and causal necessity, yet his definition would cover both logically and causally necessary facts since we have no power over those facts, either.[23] And even if he amended the definition by adding a clause that excludes the logically and causally necessary, there is still the problem that good definitions should not be negative. Such a definition would not tell us anything about what the class of facts *is* that are neither logically nor causally necessary, yet are such that we can do nothing about them. But even though I believe this makes D5 inadequate as a definition of accidental necessity, it is probably true that Ockhamist compatibilists wish to claim that D5 is satisfied by accidentally necessary propositions. If so, it is still important to consider whether D5 is helpful at all in solving the foreknowledge issue, even if it is not satisfactory as a definition.

On the face of it, this approach seems *ad hoc*, but it can be seen as a natural extension of the hard fact/soft fact approach. Recall that that approach began with the intuition that a soft fact is one that depends on the future. Adams suggested that something is a soft fact as long as there is something in its future that is a necessary condition for its being a fact. Since it is possible that there is no future, it is possible now that some given soft fact about the past is not a fact. Hence, it is not accidentally necessary. The type of dependency in question is problematic, but it seems likely that it is counterfactual dependency that is intended.[24] But what, exactly, could a past fact counterfactually depend on in the future? Perhaps in some cases the answer is a human free choice. But if so, this means that there is something I have the power to do in the future that is such that if I did (did not) do it, then some particular past fact would have been different than it is. Something like D5, then, is naturally suggested by an extension of the hard fact approach.

There are counterexamples to D5 in the literature that I will not discuss.[25] Aside from such objections, I cannot see that the proposed definition of accidental necessity is helpful to the foreknowledge problem. Notice first that to say of some true proposition p that it is not accidentally necessary is just to say the following on D5.

> D5a   There exists an agent S and an action A such that (1) S has the power at t or later to perform A, and (2) if S were to perform A at t or later, then p would be false.

But, of course, the intuition of the necessity of the past is the intuition that D5a is not possibly satisfied for any S, A, t, and p if p is about some state of affairs earlier than t, for that contradicts FPC, a principle that is said to be a necessary truth. If p_1 is a proposition expressing God's state of knowledge before t_1, then to say it is possible that p_1, t_1, and some S and A satisfy D5a is to say it is possible FPC is false. But then Plantinga ought to offer reasons for thinking FPC is possibly false. Otherwise his claim that something might satisfy D5a does not give a solution to the foreknowledge dilemma. It merely gives directions for the formulation of a solution.

A person who finds strong intuitive support for FPC is not going to be much impressed with Plantinga's account of accidental necessity. Those who worry that necessary features of the structure of time preclude the counterfactual dependency of the past on the future will not have their worries laid to rest by being told without argument that there might be something A that S can do that is such that if S were to do it the past would have been different. As an example, Plantinga argues that the following situation is possible: Paul has the power to mow his lawn and if he were to mow his lawn it would have been false that a colony of carpenter ants moved into his yard last Saturday. It would have been false because God would have foreknown the mowing and prevented the ants from moving in. By the same reasoning, he says, virtually all of the past is excluded from the category of the accidentally necessary. In defense of the possibility of this situation, Plantinga says simply, "what I have called the 'facts of the matter' certainly seem to be possible." [26] I will say more about the analysis of this example in Chapter 4, but it seems to me unconvincing as a defense of the possibility of this situation simply to declare that it "seems possible." The contrary intuitions expressed by those who think it is intuitively obvious that FPC is a necessary truth should be confronted directly.

I have objected that D5 is unhelpful to the foreknowledge problem because there is no reason to think there is any p and t, where p is about a state of affairs prior to t, that satisfies D5a. Such a case seems on the face of it to violate the intuition of the necessity of the past. Plantinga recognizes that D5 does not illuminate "our deep intuitive beliefs about the asymmetry of past and future with respect to power," and he subsequently suggests that D5 be strengthened by adding "necessarily" to the outside of clause (2).

> D6 p is accidentally necessary at t if and only is p is true at t and it is not possible both that p is true at t and there exists an agent S and an Action A such that (1) S has the power at t or later to perform A, and (2) necessarily, if S were to perform A at t or later, then p would have been false. [27]

The result, he says, is that barring one or two exceptions, a logically contingent proposition about the past is accidentally necessary if and only if it is true and strictly about the past. [28]

If Plantinga is right that D6 succeeds in capturing the intuition that the accidentally necessary corresponds (almost) to the necessity of the past, the objection I have just given to D5 would not apply. I argued that worries about the necessity of the past cast doubt on the possibility that D5a is satisifed when p is about a state of affairs prior to t. Plantinga seems to be claiming, however, that D6 is compatible with those intuitions.

But what reason do we have to think that it is? The point of D6 is to exclude God's forebeliefs from the range of the accidentally necessary, but not to exclude other obvious examples of facts strictly about the past from the accidentally necessary. But if this is the point of D6, it does not succeed. Consider again the following proposition.

> (3) A colony of ants moved into Paul's yard last week.

Plantinga says that there might be something Paul can do now, namely, mow his lawn, which is such that if he were to do it, then (3) would have been false. But there is nothing Paul can do that *entails* that (3) is false, so (3) is accidentally necessary on D6. But what does it mean to say (3) is accidentally necessary on D6? Plantinga has not taken back his claim that there is something Paul now has the power to do, which is such that if he were to do it then (3) would be false. In fact, he reiterates this claim.[29] And he has admitted the same can be said for any proposition about the past, at least as far as we know, for how do *we* know what God would have arranged differently in the past had some choice of ours been different in the future? But then how has D6 captured the connection between accidental necessity and the necessity of the past? Even if all the right propositions about the past turn out to be accidentally necessary on D6, they *all* might be such that for each one there is something I can do that would be such that if I were to do it the proposition would be false. And what kind of accidental necessity is that? Again, Plantinga has simply denied FPC, and if he is going to do that, he should say so and justify it.

Sometimes discussions of the Ockhamist move are carried on as if there is a confusion that can be cleared up by making a three-way distinction.

(P1) Jones has the power at t to do something R that would make it the case that whereas God had a certain belief prior to t, God had a different (incompatible) belief prior to t.

(P2) Jones has the power at t to do something R that would bring it about that God had a different belief prior to t than one that he did, in fact, have.

(P3) Jones has the power at t to do something R such that if he were to do R, God would have had a different belief prior to t than one that he did, in fact, have.

Let us consider one at a time.

Proposition (P1) says that Jones can alter the past and almost everybody believes that is incoherent. Certainly that is the case if the structure of time is anything close to what people ordinarily take it to be. But even though the structure of time may make the denial of (P1) a matter of common sense, it is less obvious that that structure is necessary and that the negation of (P1) is logically necessary. For example, Lewis has suggested that the hypothesis that time is circular or has some other shape, even if false, is nonetheless possible.[30] If so, the negation of (P1) may not be logically necessary and, if so, (P1) is a logically contingent proposition and would permit a successful demonstration of the logical consistency of:

God is essentially omniscient.
God believes prior to t that Jones will do S at t.
Jones is free to refrain from S at t.

However, a negative solution of this kind would not be satisfactory, since it would make use of a known falsehood and therefore could not be used in the formulation of a successful positive solution.

Proposition (P2) says there is a case of backward agent causation of a strong sort. Jones has the power now to bring about something in the past. In fact, he has the power to bring about something that did not happen in the actual past. As noted in Chapter 1, Mavrodes has argued that it is possible to do just that. Note that (P2) does not entail (P1), since it is possible that even though events are fixed once they occur, fixedness is independent of the causal connections among events, and the cause of some event may still be something in its future. Furthermore, Mavrodes argues, it may still be possible (but not actual) that some event occur that would have caused something to be different in the past. But again, even if such backward causation is logically possible, it is still incompatible with the world as we know it to be, and it is *this* world in which we are interested. Even if causal relations could have had a structure different from the one they in fact have, this does not help the foreknowledge issue, since it is the actual structure of causation that counts, not a merely possible one. So (P2) should be rejected for the same reason as (P1). It makes use of a known falsehood and so is useless for a positive solution to the foreknowledge dilemma.

But what about proposition (P3)? Counterfactual dependency of the past on the future may not entail causal dependency of the past on the future or, to be more accurate, a type of dependency of the past on the future truly expressed by a subjunctive conditional may not entail causal dependency. Recent discussions of the Ockhamist move often concentrate on the question of whether (P3) entails (P2). Philip Quinn calls a principle that would allow the inference from (P3) to (P2) a Power Entailment Principle (PEP), and he says he doubts there is a true PEP.[31]

This discussion puzzles me. Ockhamists are right to reject backward causation, but why do they worry about PEPs? Either God's past belief is not *really* past, in which case my causing it is not really backward causation, or it *is* really past, in which case backward counterfactual dependency seems to be ruled out just as well as backward causation, for how can the hard past counterfactually depend on the future any more than it can be caused by it?[32] Doesn't the rejection of (P3) come immediately out of a certain very common view of time? If so, it does not matter whether (P3) entails (P2) or not, since (P1), (P2), and (P3) are all ruled out by the necessity of the past. The reason is that there *is* no future. The future is not real. But then it seems to follow that the past can no more counterfactually depend on the nonexistent future than it can be caused by it.

So even if (P3) does not entail (P2), the Ockhamist is hardly any better off. It is difficult to see how we can accept the claim that it is possible that we have counterfactual power over the past without a clarification of what is strictly in the past.[33] And so this approach will only succeed if the first one does. If the notion of being strictly about the past were successfully elucidated independently of the foreknowledge dilemma and the concept of accidental necessity defined in terms of it, Plantinga's D5 and D6 would be explanatory. But since this has not yet been accomplished as far as I know, Plantinga's solution does not explain at all how it can be possible that we have counterfactual efficacy over God's past beliefs.

3.3. Can Essential Omniscience Make Beliefs Soft?

Several current analyses of the hard fact/soft fact distinction have the consequence that God's past beliefs are soft only because of God's essential omniscience. This is true of the positions of Adams, Plantinga, and Kvanvig. Plantinga, for example, claims in "On Ockham's Way Out" that both soft facthood and hard facthood are closed under strict equivalence. So any proposition strictly equivalent to one that is a soft fact about the past is itself a soft fact about the past. Similarly, he says, "any proposition equivalent (in the broadly logical sense) to a proposition strictly about the past is itself strictly about the past."[34] That is, a proposition strictly equivalent to a hard fact about the past is itself a hard fact about the past. Now if God is essentially omniscient, the proposition *Eighty years ago God believed that Paul will mow his lawn in 1999* is strictly equivalent to the proposition *Paul will mow his lawn in 1999*. Using the principle that soft facthood is closed under strict equivalence, Plantinga argues that since the latter is not strictly about the past, neither is the former. For this reason, he concludes, the Edwardsian argument fails.[35]

But this argument can go either way, since hard facthood is also closed under strict equivalence. A skeptic about the Ockhamist solution need only point out that since *Eighty years ago God believed that Paul will mow his lawn in 1999* is strictly about the past, so is *Paul will mow his lawn in 1999*. So even though Plantinga may be right that if one of these propositions is a soft fact, so is the other, the skeptic is likewise right that if one is a hard fact, so is the other. We are not told why we should take Plantinga's preferred line of reasoning rather than the alternative.

Furthermore, notice that the arguments that God's past beliefs are soft because of his essential omniscience can be easily modified to show that God's past beliefs are soft because of their infallibility at a time. If q is soft and q strictly implies p, then p is soft. But infallibly believing p at t strictly implies p just as much as believing p and being essentially omniscient strictly implies p. So if p is soft, infallibly believing p is soft also. So it is not only essential omniscience that gets the result that God's beliefs are soft on the Ockhamist criteria; infallibility does so as well. But it seems to me that the claim that an infallible belief is any less past than any other belief leads to some strongly counterintuitive results.

To see this, suppose some being George is not infallible. All the past beliefs of George are really or strictly past, according to the Ockhamist. And suppose that one of George's beliefs in the past is that he will attend a conference next month. Now consider what happens if George acquires the property of infallibility. Remember that on the definition of infallibility given in Chapter 1, if George is infallible at t, George cannot make a mistake at t. And unlike essential omniscience, it is possible for infallibility to be acquired.[36] But now that George is infallible, all his beliefs about the future become soft on the Ockhamist criterion. This is because George's infallibly believing C at t strictly implies C. This means that whereas before infallibility George's belief that he would attend a conference next month was hard (i.e., strictly in the past), now that he is infallible, his belief in that same proposition, his belief that he will attend the conference next month, becomes soft. That belief is now no longer in the strict past. And it is not in the strict past simply because George has acquired another property—a property independent of his belief—the property of infallibility. This seems to me to be a totally unacceptable consequence of the Ockhamist position that whereas most beliefs in the past are hard, the beliefs of an infallible being are soft.

If God really has beliefs, then the fact that he has a certain belief seems to be a fact that is independent of the fact that he is essentially omniscient or infallible. At least, the way in which the two properties are dependent on each other does not have anything to do with pastness. So it is very difficult to see how having the property of either essential omniscience or infallibility can affect the intrinsic pastness of a certain belief. An Ockhamist of the Plantinga sort rather than the Adams sort might simply respond that essential omniscience does not affect the pastness of the belief, although it affects our power over it, but then the Ockhamist solution has been given up, since now it is clear that FPC is simply being denied outright. In that case, as I said in Section 3.1, the intuition of the necessity of the past must be addressed directly and either rejected or shown not to have the consequence that FPC is true. I have no idea if and how this could be accomplished.

In my opinion no Ockhamist solution can succeed if it either (a) relegates God's past belief to the same category as the quasi-past facts standardly given as examples of soft facts, or (b) depends on God's essential omniscience to save its softness. Believing something at t_1 just seems to be in the same logical category as jumping off a bridge at t_1. It is very difficult to see it in the same logical category as being-such-that-the-SCP-would-be-founded-in-30-years. And if one past belief is hard, they all are. If both God and Paul's wife believe that Paul will mow the lawn next Saturday, how can God's belief be any less past than hers? God's past belief that p is surely a different fact than his essential omniscience, and although the latter assures the truth of the former, it is hard to see how the property of essential omniscience could make the belief weak on pastness.

We do not need a formal account of accidental necessity to know we cannot do anything about spilled milk, and God's past beliefs seem just like spilled milk. Ockhamists, of course, do not deny that *generally* past beliefs are like spilled milk. It is just in the special case of *God's* past beliefs that they are unlike spilled milk. So a successful Ockhamist solution must identify something distinctive about God's past beliefs that removes them from the category of the necessity of the past. As far as I can see, however, the current Ockhamist solutions have not done so.

A more promising approach, I think, is to explore the possibility that God's past knowledge is so different from human knowledge that it cannot be considered a state of affairs in the past, not because it is like the paradigm cases of soft facts, but because it is so unlike all cases of *either* hard *or* soft facts. I suggested at the beginning of this chapter that instead of defending the accidental contingency of God's past belief through an analysis of accidental necessity, it might be more fruitful to do it through an analysis of God's beliefs. I will discuss this approach in the next section.

In Chapter 1 I explained the intuitions in common sense and in Aristotelian metaphysics that I think ground the concept of the necessity of the past. I did not defend these intuitions, but simply pointed out their existence and widespread acceptance. Incompatibilists about divine foreknowledge, I believe, almost always justify their position by appeal to these intuitions, whether explicitly or implicitly. One principle that has been said to come out of these intuitions is the Fixed Past Constraint

(FPC). Ockhamist compatibilists have an interesting position. They claim to accept the intuition of the necessity of the past (and presumably the set of related intuitions that are commonly connected with it), but they exempt God's foreknowledge from the necessity of the past. So far I have argued in this chapter that this project cannot succeed unless either it is clear that the Ockhamist solution really is compatible with these intuitions, or it attacks the intuitions directly and shows how they are misguided. If it cannot be made intuitively plausible to assert that God's past beliefs are not strictly past, then we have good reason to think that any claim that we have counterfactual control over them conflicts with FPC. I know of no successful demonstration that God's past beliefs are not really past. Therefore, I conclude that this solution conflicts with FPC.

4. A Defense of Thomistic Ockhamism

4.1. *The Status of God's Mental States*

Discussions of the Ockhamist solution, both pro and con, have typically been carried on as if it is assumed that God's beliefs, although infallible, are much like our beliefs in other respects. They occur at moments of time and are individuated in a way very like ours. That is, God's past beliefs are distinct from his future beliefs, so God's past belief that A is distinct from God's future belief that A. And God's belief that A is distinct from his belief that B. It is also generally assumed that the object of God's belief is a proposition or something accurately expressed by a "that" clause. All Ockhamists, of course, also assume that God exists in time and, for the purposes of this chapter, I will not question that assumption. Instead, I wish to question some of the other assumptions just mentioned, since I believe that doing so may lead to a viable solution to the foreknowledge problem. This approach is not *ad hoc*, since these assumptions would be problematic anyway, given the differences between infinite and finite nature. I will suggest a way in which a successful solution might be devised that is very different from any of the Ockhamist approaches I know, although Ockhamist in the sense in which I introduced the term at the beginning of this chapter. That is, it assumes that God exists in time and takes seriously the necessity of the past.

First, we can question the assumption that God has beliefs at all. At the beginning of Chapter 1 I proposed the foreknowledge dilemma in a way that assumes that God has beliefs only in a very loose, pretheoretical sense of "belief." I left open the possibility that on analysis it may turn out that God does not have beliefs, properly speaking. There is, of course, a tradition in Christian philosophy according to which God does not have beliefs, since knowledge precludes belief. Recently Alston has denied that God's knowledge has belief as a component, and he says this is the case whether or not knowledge is propositional.[37]

Consider first Alston's argument from the position that God's knowledge is nonpropositional. Alston uses Aquinas's exposition of this view, an account that is striking for its consequences for the arguments of this chapter. According to Thomas, since God is simple, there is no real distinction between his knowledge and its object. Since its object is the divine essence, God's knowledge is itself simple and not split up into propositional bits. "God does not understand by composing and dividing," says Aquinas.[38] Alston does not attempt to defend Aquinas' view, but he says:

> It seems plausible to suppose that the propositional character of human knowledge stems from our limitations. Why is our knowledge parcelled out in separate facts? For two reasons. First, we cannot grasp any concrete whole in its full concreteness; at most we cognize certain abstract features thereof, which we proceed to formulate in distinct propositions. Second, we need to isolate separate propositions in order to relate them logically, so as to be able to extend our knowledge inferentially. Both these reasons are lacking in the divine case. God can surely grasp any concrete whole fully, not just partial aspects thereof. And God has no need to extend His knowledge, inferentially or otherwise, since it is necessarily complete anyway.[39]

Since belief is a propositional attitude, says Alston, it follows that a being whose knowledge involves no propositional structure has no beliefs as components of his knowledge.

But, Alston argues, even if God's knowledge *is* propositional, it is still the case that it does not have belief as a component. This is because the "intuitive" conception of knowledge is superior as an understanding of divine knowledge to any belief + . . . construal. On this view, God's knowledge of a proposition is simply an immediate awareness of it. In such a case, the mental attitude of judging or accepting, which characterizes belief, is superfluous. Alston says:

> In its present guise the point is that if God is immediately aware of all facts, there is no point to His assenting to propositions. Such activity has a point only when one does not already have effective access to the facts. If one's best shot at reality is to pick out those propositions that, so far as one can

tell, have the best chance of being true and assenting to them, well and good. But if one already has the facts themselves, what is the point of assenting to propositions? It would be a meaningless charade.[40]

Alston concludes, then, that whether or not God's knowledge has propositional objects, it does not have belief as a component.

This position gives a simple answer to the Accidental Necessity Version of the Foreknowledge Dilemma according to Alston since, he says, a case of knowledge is clearly a soft fact, whereas a belief is not. Knowledge has its object as a component, so if its object is something in the future, such knowledge is not completely in the past or present.

> If we are right in denying that divine knowledge involves belief at all, and in denying that God has beliefs, the way is blocked to Pike's strengthening of the argument [for incompatibilism]. We are forced back to the version in terms of divine foreknowledge, a version that is decisively refuted by the point that foreknowledge is only a soft fact.[41] (Bracketed addition mine.)

I find these arguments very interesting, and I am satisfied that there is at least some doubt that God's state of knowing can also be accurately described as a state of believing. But even if Alston is right that God has no beliefs, it seems to me that this does not by itself help matters for the foreknowledge problem. The only reason a person's past knowledge of the future is generally taken to be soft is that the mental state of that person can be described either as knowledge or belief, depending on what happens in the future. But the mental state itself is hard. In the special case of divine knowledge, however, the combination of the presumed hardness of God's past mental state, together with his infallibility, generates a strong foreknowledge dilemma whether that mental state is described as one of knowing or one of believing. The only way to retain the intuition of the necessity of the past, maintain God's infallibility, and still claim that his past knowledge is soft is to either deny that his mental state itself is hard, a claim that seems highly implausible, or to say that one and the same mental state would have been a case of knowing A or of knowing not A, depending on what happens in the future, and that seems equally implausible.[42] I conclude that questioning the view that God has beliefs is not a promising line to take in devising an Ockhamist solution. However, Alston's arguments have led me to think of another approach.

Ockhamist solutions are implausible because of their tendency to assume that God's mental states are like ours in every respect except the one picked out for discussion. It is usually taken for granted that the object of any belief is essentially related to the belief, and that the object of a belief is either a proposition or something accurately expressed by a "that" clause. A particular belief would not be that very belief if its object were a different proposition. So if God believes Mary will eat a box of candy on Valentine's Day 1998, this belief is distinct from his belief that $2 + 2 = 4$, from his belief that there are more ants than roses, and so on. Since it is also assumed that knowledge has belief as a component, the same assumption is made about cases of knowledge. If God knows M, that is a bit of knowledge distinct from his knowing that G.

In the case of human beliefs it is reasonable to say that they are individuated in part by their objects, that their objects are picked out by a "that" clause, and that a state of knowing is like a state of believing both in its object and in the way it is individuated. Since it is often assumed that God's beliefs are like ours except for their infallibility, it is assumed that their objects and individuation are like ours. I believe this view is false, whether or not belief is a component of God's knowledge.

Recall the description of God's knowledge given by Aquinas. Primarily and essentially God knows only himself.[43] To know anything else primarily would be to focus the divine gaze on the imperfect. But in his simple and direct intuition of his own essence, God knows secondarily everything else. This is because God's essence contains exemplars of the infinitely many ways his essence can be represented in finite reality: "God knows Himself as primarily and essentially known, whereas He knows other things as seen in His essence."[44]

Since the primary object of God's knowledge is his own essence, and since his essence could not have been different, it follows that God's mental state of knowing is the same in all possible worlds. His knowing state would have been the same state even if contingent truths had been different—even, in fact, if he had decided not to create a world at all. So God's state of knowing everything there is to know in the actual world is the very same state as his state of knowing everything there is to know in a different world, even a world containing no created beings. This may seem peculiar, since it is natural to think that since one world is incompatible with another, the objects of knowledge in one world are incompatible with the objects of knowledge in another, and if difference of object of knowledge makes a difference in the state of knowing those objects, God's state of knowing in one world could not be identical with his state of knowing in another.

This line of reasoning makes good sense when we are examining the knowing states of beings like ourselves. If I know a proposition A it is reasonable to think that the fact that my knowing state is directed affirmatively toward A is an *essential* property of that state. Our knowing states in typical cases are directed outward toward propositions or some other objects outside ourselves, and those objects are at least partially constitutive of the knowing state in question. So if I had known *not-A* instead that would have been a numerically and qualitatively different state from my state of knowing *A*.

But as Aquinas describes God's epistemic state, the primary object of God's knowledge is neither *A* nor *not-A*. The primary object is not a proposition or anything divisible into discrete bits, or even anything outside himself. We might conclude from this that God's knowing state is *essentially* a state of knowing his own essence and only *accidentally* a state of knowing, say, *A* rather than *not-A*. So the single state of knowing his own essence that constitutes God's epistemic state in all possible worlds has the accidental property of secondarily knowing one set of contingent truths in one world and another set of contingent truths in another world.

This means that there is no distinction in God's knowledge between his knowledge of one fact and his knowledge of another, since both are contained in the same simple vision of his own essence. On this view it is not correct to say that God's knowledge (or belief) that Mary eats a box of candy on Valentine's Day 1998 is distinct from his knowledge that $2 + 2 = 4$ and from his knowledge that some particular event will occur in the year 2000. In fact, it is not even distinct from his knowledge in another possible world that such an event will *not* occur in the year 2000. God's knowledge is not divided up into bits, each of which has a distinct object. There is numerically one belief or state of knowledge that God has and which he has essentially. Of course, we may have no choice but to use the way *we* express knowledge when we speak of God's knowledge, that is, by using the form of words, "*S* knows that *A*." So we say that God knows *M* and God knows *G* and God knows *C*. But it is still the case that God's mental state of knowing that *M* is identical to his knowing that *G* and his knowing that *C* and his knowing of everything else knowable.

On this view God's knowing state is so different from our own that we are forced to resort to the language of analogy in an attempt to understand it. I will present an analogy from the area of human visual acts. The key idea for what follows is the distinction between an essential object of an act of seeing or believing and an accidental object of such an act.

Suppose you see a young man's face. Even though it is difficult to individuate acts of seeing, it is reasonable to say that a certain pattern of his features can be the object of a single visual act. That object is essential to that particular visual act; it would not be *that* act of seeing if it were not directed toward *that* particular pattern of features. Furthermore, we can imagine that the pattern of his features is the *only* object of the visual act essential to it. Even if this is not true of every case of seeing a person's face, surely there are some visual acts with this character. Let us call the visual act in question V. If we were using Aquinas' terminology, we would call the pattern of the young man's features the *primary* object of V.

A visual act can have a secondary object as well, and a secondary object is not essential to it or, at least, need not be. Let us suppose that the secondary object of V is the features of the young man's mother. You see the mother's features *through* the features of the son. The seeing of the secondary object is not a distinct act of seeing, given the way it is related to the primary object, yet in this case it is plausible that the secondary object is only accidentally related to V. That is, if you had not seen the mother in the son it would still have been the same visual act. V could have occurred without the secondary object; it would have been a complete visual act, in fact, *that* complete visual act, without it.

So now we have a case in which an act of seeing is essentially directed toward one object and accidentally directed toward another object. It is an essential property of V that it is of the son's features, but only an accidental property of V that it is of the mother's features. But if a visual act can have one object as an accidental property, why not another? You might have seen something else in seeing those facial features instead. Perhaps you might have seen the father's features or something entirely different. Maybe it is even possible to see many things in the features of a face. If so, in some possible worlds when V occurs it has secondary object $O1$, in other worlds V has secondary object $O2$, in still other worlds V has secondary object $O3$, and so on. There are also worlds with no secondary object at all.

Now suppose that God's knowing state is like V. The primary object of God's knowing is the divine essence. That object is essential to the act of knowing itself, and no other object is essential to it. In particular, no contingent truths, objects, events, and the like, are essentially related to *that* act of knowing. That particular act of knowing would be complete even if there were no contingent objects to be objects of knowledge. This means that there is numerically one divine epistemic state, and that epistemic state exists in every world in which God exists. We can then suppose that the difference in contingent truths in different worlds is the difference in what is "reflected" in God's essence in different worlds. God's knowing all contingent truths is like seeing them through the "features" of his own essence. He "sees" that Q and R and S through his essence in a way analogous to your seeing the mother through the son. God might not have seen that Q; in other worlds he sees *not-Q* instead. This is to say that in other worlds the divine nature reflects different truths. But since these objects are accidental properties of the divine epistemic state, the divine epistemic state is still the same in different worlds, even though in one world it involves secondarily knowing Q and in another world it involves secondarily knowing *not-Q*. There are also certain truths that the divine nature reflects in all worlds. These are the necessary truths.

An important conclusion for the argument against the compatibility of foreknowledge and free will follows immediately if God knows in the way I have just described. This account of God's knowing makes premises (3) and (3') of the argument from Accidental Necessity false. Those premises, as they were stated at the beginning of Chapter 2, are as follows.

(3) God's belief at *t1* strictly implies my act at *t3*.
(3') God's belief at *t1* is strictly equivalent to my act at *t3*.

Premise (3) was used in the argument based on the infallibility of God's past beliefs, while premise (3') was used in the argument based on God's essential omniscience. But the account of God's epistemic state proposed in this section makes both premises false. God's belief at *t1* does not strictly imply my act, since the numerically same belief occurs in worlds in which I do not perform the act in question. What is essential to God's belief at *t1* is its primary object, namely, God's own essence. It is only an accidental property of that belief that it is a belief that I do *S* rather than that I do not do *S*. The numerically same belief occurs in worlds in which I do not do *S*. It follows that the Thomistic account of God's knowing allows us to reject the argument that divine foreknowledge is incompatible with free will quite apart from any question of the accidental necessity of God's past belief. We turn next to the argument that the Thomistic account allows us to reject that premise as well.

4.2. Two Reasons Why God's Past Beliefs Are Not Accidentally Necessary

4.2.1. GOD'S BELIEFS ARE ONE

If the Thomistic description of God's knowing is right, there is trouble for the Ockhamist compatibilist. As we saw in Section 2, Ockham wished to claim that God's belief yesterday about something prior to yesterday is now accidentally necessary, whereas his belief yesterday about a (still) future contingent is now accidentally contingent. But if Aquinas is right in the explanation of God's knowledge in the preceding paragraph, what God believed yesterday about something last year and what he believed yesterday about something next year is the numerically *same* belief. How could the one be accidentally necessary and the other accidentally contingent if the beliefs are identical? Ockhamist compatibilists have focused most of their attention on giving an account of accidental necessity on which it is at least possible that God's past belief about the future is not accidentally necessary. But in not addressing the issue of how God's beliefs are individuated, they may be missing a significant objection to their project. For if it is not reasonable to say that certain beliefs God has at t are distinct from certain other beliefs God has at t, it is not reasonable to propose principles for distinguishing the accidentally necessary ones from the nonaccidentally necessary ones. If God has uniquely one epistemic state, then either it is accidentally necessary, it is accidentally contingent, or accidental necessity and contingency do not apply to it. Since everything God knows, past, present, and future is contained in this state, by far the most plausible position is that accidental necessity and contingency simply do not apply.

4.2.2. GOD'S BELIEFS ARE ESSENTIALLY INDEPENDENT OF TIME

According to the Christian philosophical tradition, it follows from God's essential aseity that God is essentially independent of everything outside himself. God not only creates, but conserves in existence everything but himself, and he does so at every time in every world. To say that God is essentially independent of some x outside of him is to say much more than that there is *some* possible world in which God is not related to x. That would amount merely to the claim that it *might have been* the case that God bears no relation to x and would be satisfied as long as x is contingent. But for God to conserve every x in existence at every moment in every world, it must also be true that he maintains his independence of x *at every moment of time in every world*. God does not lose the possibility of being unrelated to x at any time in any world. Furthermore, God's independence of entities outside himself is not limited to contingent things. If there are any necessary entities outside of God, God is independent of them as well.

In order to understand God's independence of everything outside of him, let us first define a type of possibility that is relativized to moments of time at particular worlds.

> It is possible-at-t-in-w- that p = There is a world w^* possible relative to w at t in which t exists, and p is true at t in w^*.

Unlike logical possibility, this sense of possibility is relativized to times and worlds. It can happen that it is possible-at-$t1$-in-$w1$ that p, but not possible-at-*t2*-in-*w1* that *p*, and not possible-at-*t1*-in-*w2* that *p*. Logical possibility is not relativized in this way. If *w1* and *w2* are accessible to each other, then if it is logically possible at *t1* in *w1* that *p*, then it is logically possible at *t2* in *w1* that *p*, and it is logically possible at *t1* in *w2* that *p*, and so on. A proposition *p* is logically possible at any time in any world as long as there is some time in some (accessible) world in which *p* is true.

God's essential aseity requires that his independence of any *x* outside himself is stronger than that expressed by the claim that it is logically possible that God exist and have no relation to *x*. Since God's independence of everything outside himself can never be lost at any time in any world, his aseity requires the truth of at least the following.

> For every *x* outside of God, God is essentially independent of *x* → For every time *t* and world *w*, it is possible-at-*t*-in-*w* that God has no relation to *x*.

On the doctrine of divine aseity it cannot turn out that there is any *x* outside of God, time *t*, and world *w* at which it is not possible-at-*t*-in-*w* that God has no relation to *x*. That would be to make God dependent on *x at that time*.

Now let us consider the case in which the entity *x* in question is time itself. On the assumption that time is something outside of God, it follows from God's aseity that for every time *t* and world *w* it is possible-at-*t*-in-*w* that God has no relation to time. God is essentially independent of time *at every moment of time in every world*. Furthermore, if God is independent of time and if, as we have said, the primary object of God's knowing is his own essence, then his state of knowing must also be independent of time. Let us call God's knowing state *K**. It follows that even if *K** is temporal, it could not be essentially temporal. It must be, in fact, essentially independent of time in that for every moment of time *t* in every world, it is possible-at-*t* that *K** exists without existing *at* or *in t*.

How are we to understand God's independence of time if he is, in fact, a temporal being? This is difficult for us to comprehend since in all our experience every temporal being is essentially temporal and essentially dependent on time. We, of course, are temporal beings, and the same goes for our knowing states. Whenever we conceive of a temporal knowing state we think of it as tied to time in the same way our own knowing states are tied to time. That is, we tend to think of them as essentially dependent on time. I claim that it is more faithful to the religious tradition of the West to say that even if God is temporal, he is only accidentally temporal and, furthermore, that his essential aseity requires that throughout time he is as independent of time as he is independent of anything outside himself.

The point I am making here is no less valid if time is necessary rather than contingent. Nothing I will say in proposing the solution of this section is committed to the contingency of time. If time is necessary, God's independence of time is like his independence of numbers, whereas if time is contingent, God's independence of time is like his independence of matter. At every time t it is possible-at-t that God is independent of time, of matter, of numbers, of everything else outside himself. For any x outside of God, if God had no relation to x, x would go out of existence, but God would not. If x is a (logically) necessary entity and God has a (logically) necessary relation to x, it is still the case that if *per impossibile* God had no relation to x, x would go out of existence. I have given an account of such propositions, which I call "counterpossibles," elsewhere.[45]

We are now ready to use the notion of aseity to show that God's existence is not accidentally necessary at any time. And if God's existence is never accidentally necessary, neither is his epistemic state, K^*. To avoid complexity, I will assume that each of the statements in the following argument is relativized to the actual world.

Argument that God's existence is never accidentally necessary

(1) God is essentially independent of everything outside himself (essential aseity).

(2) For any x outside of God and every time t it is possible-at-t that God has no relation to x.

(3) Time is outside of God.

(4) For every time t it is possible-at-t that God has no relation to time. (2,3)

(5) It is possible-at-$t3$ that God has no relation to time. (4, universal instantiation)

(6) If God's existence at $t2$ is accidentally necessary at $t3$, then it is not possible-at-$t3$ that God does not exist at $t2$ (definition of "accidental necessity").

(7) If it is not possible-at-$t3$ that God does not exist at $t2$, then it is not possible-at-$t3$ that God has no relation to time.

(8) If God's existence at $t2$ is accidentally necessary at $t3$, then it is not possible-at-$t3$ that God has no relation to time. (6,7 HS)

(9) But the consequent of (8) conflicts with (5).

(10) Therefore, it is not the case that God's existence at $t2$ is accidentally necessary at $t3$. (5,8 MT)

We know that God's epistemic state K^* is not accidentally necessary at any time by replacing every occurrence of "God" in the preceding argument by "K^*." The conclusion is that accidental necessity never applies to K^*. It does not follow, however, that K^* is accidentally contingent, either. It is much more likely that accidental necessity and contingency do not apply to K^* at all, but apply only to states of affairs that are essentially temporal.

I have called this an Ockhamist solution to the foreknowledge dilemma because it (1) assumes that God is in time, (2) takes seriously the claim that past events/states of affairs are accidentally necessary, and (3) denies that accidental necessity applies to God's beliefs. It should be obvious, however, that it is very different from any solution usually considered Ockhamist. It does not try to minimize the pastness of God's beliefs, a move that I have argued in this chapter is very implausible, nor does it attempt to claim we have counterfactual power over a certain class of past events, a class that includes more than God's beliefs. This also I have argued is implausible. The relation between God's beliefs and time is wholly different, I think, than the relation between creaturely states/acts and time. Even if God's beliefs are really in time, and as much in the past as anything is, it does not follow that they ever have to be in the past or in time at all. If they do not have to be in the past or in time, there is no worry that they acquire the special property of fixity or accidental necessity that essentially temporal events acquire automatically. Since my solution in this chapter blends Aquinas' understanding of God's knowing with the Ockhamist position on God's temporality and the necessity of the past, we might call it Thomistic Ockhamism.

Although the solution I have proposed in this section is serious about the necessity of the past, it requires a modification of that notion that is intuitively plausible and has as a consequence that only nondivine states of affairs have the necessity of the past. By this modification, the necessity of the past and FPC apply to those states of affairs in the past that are essentially temporal and not to any nonessentially temporal states of affairs.

In Section 4.1 I described the Thomistic account of God's knowing and argued that apart from Aquinas' view that God is timeless, such an account has the consequence that God's state of knowing my future act does not strictly imply my future act, and so premise (3) of the strong argument for theological fatalism we have been considering in this book is false. In Section 4.2 I offered two reasons for thinking that the Thomistic account also makes premise (1) of that argument false. That is, the simplicity of God's knowing leads to the conclusion that his state of knowing or believing is not accidentally necessary *even if* he exists in time. I have called this view Thomistic Ockhamism. It is my opinion that Thomistic Ockhamism makes more sense than Ockhamist Ockhamism.

5. A Solution to the Timeless Knowledge Dilemma

In Chapter 2 I rejected the Boethian/Thomistic solution on the grounds that it generates a new dilemma—what I called the Timeless Knowledge Dilemma. Now that we have examined the other features of the Thomistic conception of God's knowing, we can see that even though timelessness alone is not sufficient to make divine foreknowledge and human free choice compatible, these other features are sufficient to make it reasonable to claim that God's knowing state does not have the necessity of the past even if temporal. But since I have not taken a stand on God's temporality, let us return to the possibility that he is timeless. Can the view of God's knowing defended by Aquinas solve the Timeless Knowledge Dilemma as well?

In this chapter I have given two reasons for rejecting the view that God's epistemic state is accidentally necessary: (1) God has numerically one epistemic state and so it cannot be that at any given time some of his beliefs are accidentally contingent and some accidentally necessary; and (2) accidental necessity and contingency apply only to essentially temporal states of affairs, but God's beliefs are not essentially temporal even if temporal. The second of these reasons has a parallel if God's beliefs are timeless. Clearly, if the accidental necessity/contingency distinction applies only to essentially temporal state of affairs, but God's belief state is atemporal, then it does not apply to God's belief state.

The argument in Section 4.1 also holds if God is timeless. There it was argued that the Thomistic conception of God's knowing makes premises (3) and (3') of the arguments for theological fatalism false. They are false because God's unique epistemic state does not strictly imply my contingent act, and this is true whether or not God is in time.

This means that for those readers who prefer straight Thomism to what I have called Thomistic Ockhamism, a solution to the foreknowledge/timeless knowledge dilemma is available. So if other objections to the timelessness view can be met, I see no problem with taking the position that God is outside of time. I have argued, however, that what makes Aquinas's position work in solving the foreknowledge dilemma is not the timelessness part of it, but his view on how God knows, and that this view works whether or not God is in time. Should we accept this solution? I think there is no doubt that when taken in isolation, Aquinas's view on God's knowing will seem to many readers to be so metaphysically abstruse as to be much too high a price to pay to solve the dilemma. But much of the persuasiveness of the Thomistic view on how God knows comes from its place in a much broader metaphysical theory of great subtlety and explanatory power. The more a reader is persuaded by other aspects of the general Thomistic theory, the more she will be convinced of the usefulness of the position I have described in this chapter. This is quite rationally proper. It also means that this solution is not apt to persuade in the absence of the other attractions of Aquinas's philosophy. But with greater clarity and refinement I think this theory can be developed into an acceptable positive solution to the dilemma of freedom and foreknowledge.

4

Foreknowledge, Causal Relations, and Subjunctive Conditionals

1. Introduction

Contemporary Ockhamists generally say very little about the relationship between God's past belief and my future act other than to make the modest claim that it can be truly expressed by subjunctive conditionals going in both directions. That is, both of the following propositions are true.

(1) If I had done S at t, then God would have believed prior to t that I would do S at t.

(2) If God had believed prior to t that I would do S at t, then I would have done S at t.[1]

In fact, not only Ockhamists, but almost any compatibilist will assert propositions of the form of (1) and (2). A compatibilist is not, of course, forced to make these two claims. She may simply eschew the use of subjunctive conditionals, either because of their logical peculiarities or for some other reason. But if a compatibilist is not willing to accept (1) and (2), she is not left with much to say about the relation between my act and God's prior knowledge of it. The relationship between divine beliefs and human acts seems to be reduced to utter mystery, and this makes compatibilism an uncomfortable position. If anything at all can be said about the way God's foreknowledge relates to human acts, it should at least include what is expressed by (1) and (2). I will therefore assume that (1) and (2) are a practical commitment of any compatibilist position that has a hope of being developed into a positive solution to the foreknowledge problem. For this reason I am treating these propositions separately from my discussion of Ockhamism. If they have unacceptable consequences, that is much worse than a problem for Ockhamism; it is a problem for compatibilism.

Subjunctive conditionals are remarkably uninformative. They are uninformative partly because so many different relationships are expressed through subjunctive conditionals and, in this case, they are uninformative partly because the relationship expressed by (1) and (2) is much weaker than what we know to obtain from other sources. That is, (1) and (2) tell us less about how God's knowing relates to my act than we already know from other elements of the Christian tradition. We will return to this point later in this chapter. Nevertheless, (1) and (2) are a good place to start an analysis of this relationship since, in spite of their apparent innocence, they have been strongly attacked.

Foreknowledge compatibilists maintain that I am able to perform free acts in a sense of freedom that is incompatible both with causal necessity and with accidental necessity*. This is generally taken to imply that when I do *S* freely I have both the power to do *S* and the power not to do *S*. And when I freely refrain from *S*, I also have the power to do *S* and the power not to do *S*. So, on the compatibilist position, there are instances of *S* and *t*, where *S* is an act I freely refrain from doing, for which (1) and (2) are true as well as:

(3) I have the power at *t* to do *S*.

The conjunction of (1) and (3) yields:

(4) I have the power at *t* to do *S*, and *S* is such that if I had done it at *t*, God would have believed prior to *t* that I would do *S* at *t*.

Notice that (4) is almost exactly like one of Plantinga's proposed definitions of a nonaccidentally necessary proposition.[2]

But it is generally acknowledged that it would be ruinous to the compatibilist position if either (1) or (2) implied a causal relation, and the same thing applies to (4). To say that God's prior belief causes my act is to say that my act is not causally contingent and hence not free. On the other hand, to say that my act causes God's prior belief is to say there is backward agent causation and, as I said in Chapter 1, I assume that is impossible. In this chapter I will first attempt to demonstrate that neither (1), (2), nor the even more bothersome (4) implies a causal relation and will give what I think is a satisfactory solution to the Causal Necessity version of the Foreknowledge Dilemma proposed in Chapter 1. I will also argue that the defense of (1) is only helpful if it can be shown that (1) is not like a class of cases that are consistent with the incompatibilist position, and I will argue that the conjunction of (1) and (3) to yield (4) is not as straightforward as it may seem. Notice that if I am right about this, it makes a problem noted earlier even worse. That is, the subjunctive conditionals (1) and (2) now look *very* uninformative. We will then be left with the unenviable task of explaining what relation *is* expressed by (1) and (2). This problem will lead to a discussion of metaphysical laws as a prologue to a theory on the relationship between God's belief and human acts.

2. Backward-Looking Subjunctives and Causal Relations

2.1. Back-Tracking Counterfactuals

The first thing to be noticed about backward-looking subjunctives such as (1) is that they are deviant. Relationships of subjunctive dependency are usually forward-looking; that is, a later event subjunctively depends on an earlier one, not the other way around. So even though there may be true backward-looking subjunctive conditionals and we will examine several examples of them, it must be admitted that temporal order is of some importance.

Lewis has argued that the asymmetry between backward- and forward-looking counterfactual conditionals is connected with time's arrow—a point familiar from our discussions in Chapters 1 and 3.[3] Lewis says that we assume that facts about earlier times are counterfactually independent of facts about later times, but facts about later times are counterfactually dependent on facts about earlier times. He considers and rejects other ways of formulating temporal asymmetry, concluding that the asymmetry between past and future amounts to nothing but this asymmetry of counterfactual dependence.[4] The past is counterfactually closed, whereas the future is counterfactually open. Backward-looking counterfactuals are therefore false because they are inconsistent with the asymmetry of time. However, Lewis argues, since counterfactuals have a certain degree of vagueness, it is possible to interpret some "back-tracking" counterfactuals as true under a special resolution of their vagueness. Still, all backward-looking counterfactuals are false under the standard resolution.

Lewis considers an example he borrows from Downing. Jim and Jack quarreled yesterday and Jack is still mad today. It is true that if Jim asked Jack for help today, Jack would not help him. But since Jim is such a prideful fellow, he wouldn't ask for help unless he knew Jack would not refuse. So it is reasonable within this context to say that if Jim were to ask Jack for help today, there would have to have been no quarrel yesterday. And that means if Jim asked Jack for help today, Jack would help him after all.

On the standard account of the truth conditions of a counterfactual conditional $A > B$, the conditional is (nonvacuously) true just in case in the world closest to the actual world in which the antecedent is true, the consequent is true. More precisely, some world in which A and B are true is more similar overall to the actual world than any world in which A is true and B is false. The inherent vagueness of counterfactuals consists in the vagueness in specifying which worlds count as the closest A-worlds. In some contexts it may be natural to say that the closest A-worlds are worlds in which the past is different from the actual world in various ways. This is because the assumption that the world is now different in some way is to assume that past causally relevant conditions did not lead to actual present events. A world that preserves sensible causal connections between the present and the past but that has a different past may be more like the actual world for the purposes of a certain discussion than one that has the same past but an unexpectedly different present. So we may say that to imagine a world just like this one except that A is true is to also imagine a causal history for A that is different from the actual past. This is what we are asked to do when we say

(5) If Jim were to ask Jack for help today, there would have been no quarrel yesterday.

The lack of a quarrel yesterday is causally connected to Jim's asking for help today.[5]

Another example of a back-tracking counterfactual of this type is the following.

(6) If I were flying to Chicago in a half hour, I would have packed by now.

This seems true because in worlds close to this one there is a certain sequence of events causally connected with taking a trip. Packing a certain amount of time before leaving is not a necessary condition for leaving and is not a cause of going, but both packing and leaving for a trip are probably joint effects of the decision to go, and packing prior to leaving on trips does occur in worlds fairly close to this one. For this reason the resolution of the vagueness involved in specifying the close worlds in which I go to Chicago in a half hour may favor those in which the past is somewhat different.

But, Lewis argues, (5) is still false on the standard resolution, and presumably the same reasoning would apply to (6):

> Under this standard resolution, back-tracking arguments are mistaken: if the present were different the past would be the same, but the same past causes would fail somehow to cause the same present effects. If Jim asked Jack for help today, somehow Jim would have overcome his pride and asked despite yesterday's quarrel. . . . Some special contexts favor a different resolution of vagueness, one under which the past depends counterfactually on the present and some back-tracking arguments are correct. . . . But when the need for a special resolution of vagueness comes to an end, the standard resolution returns. . . . Although we tend to favor the standard resolution, we also charitably tend to favor a resolution which gives the sentence under consideration a chance of truth.[6]

As we have seen, one reason the standard interpretation that disallows back-tracking is standard on Lewis's account is that it is required by the asymmetry of past and future. But there is another reason. If back-tracking is allowed in some contexts, it is difficult to draw the line. This is because the desire to maintain a smooth causal flow from the present counterfactual assumption back into the past and then again into the present and future may lead to an endless succession of amendments of the facts. If we are going to allow back-tracking in the case in which the earlier event is in the direct causal line leading up to the later event, why not also in those cases in which an earlier counterfactual event is part of the broad causal nexus most closely associated with the assumption of the truth of the antecedent? For example, suppose that if I were to go to Chicago this afternoon, I would have packed earlier, and since I would have packed earlier, I would have opened a suitcase that contains my friend's valuable book which he has been searching for for weeks, and this would have led me to call him immediately. This might make it reasonable to assert the truth of the following:

(7) If I were going to Chicago in a half hour, I would have called Tom about the book before now.

But perhaps calling Tom about the book would have started an elaborate causal sequence, leading us to say that indefinitely many events would have been different than the ones that actually occurred. Considerations of this sort show how we can extend these cases indefinitely to what Lewis calls "back-tracking unlimited."[7] The more back-tracking, the less similarity to the past events of the actual world, and the closest A-world to the actual world in such contexts may not be recognizably close at all. But this may lead us to lose our hold on the point of counterfactuals, which is to say what would have happened if the actual world had been different in some respect. It threatens to make counterfactuals useless. So we have another reason to reject a resolution of vagueness that validates very much back-tracking.

John Pollock disagrees with Lewis's view that standardly interpreted, backward-looking counterfactuals are always false. But his disagreement is no comfort to the foreknowledge compatibilist.

> Lewis is certainly correct that it is hard to find true backwards-directed conditionals, but one case in which such conditionals seem clearly true is when they result directly from instantiation in physical laws. Consider, for example, a match that was struck and then lit. We cannot conclude that if it had not lit it would not have been struck. If it had not lit, something else might have gone wrong besides its being struck. By suppose *C* comprises a complete list of conditions under which, according to true physical laws, a struck match lights. There is no obstacle at all to our concluding that if the match had not lit, then either it would not have been struck or else conditions *C* would not have obtained. This conditional is as clearly true as counterfactuals ever get. It is precisely because it results directly from instantiation in a law that it is so clearly true.[8]

This argument is of no help to the compatibilist use of (1) since Pollock justifies these conditionals only because of a causal relation in the forward direction. Pollock gives no other example of true backward-looking counterfactuals that I can find. So neither Pollock's discussion nor Lewis's standard resolution of backward-looking counterfactuals interprets (1) in a way useful to the foreknowledge compatibilist.

Still, as long as Lewis allows that there *is* an interpretation of some backward-looking counterfactuals that makes them true, perhaps we can return to those cases for help, even if they are nonstandard. What use do these examples have for the compatibilist defense of (1)?

John Turk Saunders has offered examples structurally similar to (5) and (6) in defense of (1) and indirectly for (4). He argues that (1) is no different than the following proposition:

> (8) If I ran instead of skipped at *t2*, my decision at *t1* would have been different.

Saunders claims that since it is plainly true that I have the power to run even if I am skipping, and since (8) is true, I have the power to do something that is such that were I to do it, the past would have been different.[9] So this case is apparently intended to be a true instance of (4).

But I think our discussion of Lewis shows that the context in which (8) is true is quite different from the context in which the issue is my power to do something (i.e., run), which is such that if I did it the past would have been different. Either my power to run at this instant requires that I *already* decided to run or it does not. It it does, then I simply do not have the power to run at this instant (although, of course, I retain the power to run at the next instant). If my power to run at this instant does not require a previous decision, then my present power to run is compatible with the truth of (8) only if (8) permits the exceptional case in which I run without a previous decision. In no case do I have the power to do something that is such that were I *now* to do *it*, the past would have been different. A proposition like (8) expresses something quite different than what is needed to show counterfactual power over the past. What it says is that the closest world(s) to the actual world in which I run instead of skip at *t2* is also a world that differs from the actual world prior to *t2*. That is, the resolution of the vagueness in specifying the relevant close worlds in which I run favors those in which I also decided to run previously. But then (8) is unhelpful to the foreknowledge compatibilist.

Saunders's response to this argument may simply be that he is using a conditional notion of power, one that is compatible with determinism, according to which I have the power to run even if I never run without a previous decision to run and I have not made a previous decision to run. Alston has argued, in fact, that this is the notion of power that must be used by those who favor the truth of propositions of the form of (4).[10] But this is to give up the view that the analysis of these propositions aids the type of foreknowledge/freedom compatibilism we have been considering in this book.

My argument against Saunders applies as well to (5) and (6). Even if I have not packed a suitcase because I do not intend to go anywhere, we can suppose that I have the power to fly to Chicago in a half hour (assuming optimal conditions at the airport). But even though there is a context of discussion in which (6) is true, this in no way implies that I now have the power to do something—namely, hop on a plane—that is such that were I to do it I would have packed before now. If the truth of (6) means that past packing really is a requirement for future leaving, then I do not have the power to leave. If it is not, then we can maintain the truth of (6) only if (6) allows me to do the exceptional thing of leaving without packing. I do not have the power to do something that is such that were I to do that thing, I would have already packed. Similarly, if Jim were now to ask Jack for help, given that they did quarrel yesterday, the fact that there are contexts in which (5) is a reasonable thing to say in no way implies that Jim now has the power to do something such that were he to do it the quarrel would not have happened after all. Either he has the power to do the unusual thing of asking for help after a quarrel, or he does not have the power at all. Otherwise, (5) is just false. This suggests that the contextual differences in interpreting propositions of the form of (1) and (3) make it questionable whether they can be conjoined in the form of (4). And it also shows that examples such as propositions (5), (6), and (8) are of no help to the compatibilist.

The point of the ordinary cases of back-tracking arguments is not to indicate a way the world might still turn out should something occur in the future. Instead, they are intended to show an alternative way the world could have gone, a way that is now forever lost. This is probably the reason these back-tracking counterfactuals sound more natural if the antecedent is in the past tense rather than the future tense. It sounds perfectly okay to say:

(9) If I had run instead of walked into my office this morning, I would have decided to run previously.

But it is a little strange to say:

(10) If I were to run instead of walk into my office at the next moment, I would have decided to run before now.

What is strange about (10) is that the use of the future tense in the antecedent seems to leave it open whether I run or walk, whereas the past tense of the consequent implies that the matter is already closed. In the case of (9), however, there is no implication that it is still open to me to run, and the proposition says just that among some class of worlds similiar to this one there are worlds in which there is a deviation in the manner of my entrance into my office this morning, and these are also worlds that deviate from the actual world at a previous point as well.

It is interesting that even backward-looking counterfactuals with future-tense antecedents may seem true as long as there is a detachment from any question of deliberating about the future. It is in contexts of this kind that (5), (6), and (7) are true. If I were genuinely deliberating about whether or not to go to Chicago, I would never assert (6) or (7). Similarly, if Jim were seriously considering asking Jack for help, we would not assert (5) in that context. It is only because the option for the future event in the antecedent is lost that we can use back-tracking counterfactuals. But we can do so because we are treating the antecedent as if it is already past. As far as we are concerned, our perspective on it is no different than the uninvolved perspective we have on the past. For this reason it is possible to see (10) as no different than (9). But the perspective that supports (10) prevents it being the case that I now have the power to do anything about the antecedent.

We have seen that Lewis makes a distinction between a special resolution and a standard resolution of the vagueness of back-tracking counterfactuals. I wish to suggest that the difference between these two perspectives is the difference between the detached, nondeliberative perspective used in comparing alternative courses of events from a purely objective, timeless standpoint, and the involved, potentially deliberative perspective used from an agent-centered standpoint. The former is typically used in judging the past, while the latter is typically used in judging the future. It is possible to take the former standpoint about the future, but it is not possible to take the latter standpoint about the past. Perhaps this is yet another way to look at the asymmetry between past and future.[11]

Incompatibilists can agree that there is a sense in which back-tracking counterfactuals can be true, but it is not a sense that supports the compatibilist's claim that there is something I can do now that is such that were I to do it, God would have had a different belief in the past. This is, of course, no argument for incompatibilism. It merely means that examples such as propositions (5), (6), and (8) give no support for compatibilism. If the compatibilist wishes to support her position by identifying a class of true backward-looking counterfactuals that entail that there is something I can do now that is such that were I to do it, the past would have been different than it is, she must look elsewhere.

2.2. Power Over the Past

It was argued in Section 2.1 that even if there are true propositions of the form of (1) and (3), this does not necessarily support the argument compatibilists often want to make with it. That is, even if it is true that

(3) I have the power to do S

and

(1') If I did S, K would have been different in the past,

this does not necessarily mean that I now have the power to do something that is such that were I to do it the past would have been different. This is because the usual instances of (3) and (1') are cases in which (1') is true only in a context in which it is no longer open that I do S. So (1') and (3) are not true in the same context. This makes the conjunction of (1) and (3) to get (4) very problematic.

The problem of conjoining (1) and (3) to get (4) can be brought out by comparing the scope of the power expressed in (3) with that of (4). (3) says that I have the following power: to do *S*. (1) tells us that if I had done *S*, God's past belief would have been different. But how does it follow from that that I have the following power: to do something such that had I done it God's past belief would have been different? The conjunction of (1) and (3) to get (4) requires that the scope of my power to do *S* includes all the counterfactual implications of doing *S*. But we do not know that, at least not without further clarification. Lacking such clarification, (1) and (3) do not seem to entail enough to be of interest to the compatibilist's argument.

There are those who claim that, on the contrary, (1) and (3) entail too much. Some philosophers have argued that if compatibilists are committed to (1) and (3), they are committed to (4), and (4) entails that I have an unjustified power over the past. It is unjustified because it is a form of backward agent causation, and even if a few recherché cases of backward causation are permitted, backward *agent* causation is simply impossible. Furthermore, the objection can be made in a way that does not rely on any special analysis of the causal relation. The point is just that it is impossible to *bring about* the past, whether or not bringing about is, strictly speaking, a causal relation.

Quinn has suggested in a paper defending Plantinga against Pike that this dispute could be settled if the incompatibilist could defend the truth of a logical principle that would justify the inference from (4) to a proposition that says I can bring about the past. Since (4) is structurally identical to (P3) of Chapter 3, the issue is whether the proposition

(P3) Jones has the power at *t* to do something *R* such that if he were to do *R*, God would have had a different belief prior to *t* than one which he did in fact have

entails the unacceptable

(P2) Jones has the power at *t* to do something *R* which would bring it about that God held a different belief prior to *t* than one which he did in fact have.[12]

Hasker calls such a principle a Power Entailment Principle (PEP), and there has been much discussion recently about whether there is a true PEP and what this signifies for the foreknowledge problem.

In Chapter 3, Section 3.2, I remarked that PEPs have been discussed in the literature within the context of an Ockhamist solution. I expressed puzzlement over this since, on Ockham's account, God's past beliefs are not wholly or strictly in the past. But if so, there should be no worry about either backward-looking counterfactuals or backward causation since on that view (4) is not *strictly* a backward-looking counterfactual. On the other hand, if (4) *is* a backward-looking counterfactual in the strict sense, it should be rejected outright, whether or not it is also committed to an impossible power over the past. That is, it would not matter whether there is a true PEP permitting the inference from P3 to P2, since P3 would be unacceptable by itself. This would be the case if David Lewis is right that the necessity of the past just *is* the fact that the past is counterfactually closed.

I do not have much hope for (4), then, although my argument in Section 2.1 shows that (4) can be rejected without rejecting (1) and (3). (1) and (3) are not individually incompatible with the necessity of the past. Unfortunately, however, the account so far leaves the compatibilist position verging on the mysterious. (1) and (3) are turning out to be quite unhelpful.

But the situation for the compatibilist is even worse than mysterious. Even apart from subjunctive conditionals and their peculiarities, compatibilists do assert propositions such as (3). But, as we will see from (3) and certain other common compatibilist claims, the PEPs seem to show a commitment to backward agent causation after all. In answering Quinn's request for a principle that would justify the inference from (4) to a proposition asserting the existence of power over the past, Talbott and Hasker have given something much more important than that, for even if compatibilists ignore (4) and any subjunctive conditional relating God's knowledge and my act, in fact, even if they have the position that (4) is incoherent, as I am inclined to do, the PEPs still seem to show that they are committed to an impossible power over the past. The PEPs are important because they relate only the power necessary for free will with the relationship that holds between God's knowing and my act. None of them are in the subjunctive mood. This means that we need not sort out the nature of subjunctive reasoning to appreciate the threat of the PEPs. I will argue in this section that none of the PEPs I know of are justified.

In his book *God, Time, and Knowledge* Hasker proposes a series of PEPs that he claims are true. The first two come from Talbott.

(PEP 1) If (a) it is within S's power to bring it about that p is true and (b) it is within S's power to bring it about that p is false and (c) p entails q and *not-p* entails *not-q*, then it is within S's power to bring it about that q is true.

(PEP 2) If (a) it is within S's power to bring it about that p is true, (b) p entails q, and (c) q is not a necessary condition of S's having the power to bring it about that p is true, then it is within S's power to bring it about that q is true.[13]

Talbott says that PEP 1 "seems not only true but obviously true," and Hasker quotes this approvingly, adding "It seems to me that this is absolutely correct."[14] Talbott attempts a proof of PEP 2, which Hasker calls "both elegant and conclusive."[15]

But Hasker looks for even more such principles. The following principle, he says, is somewhat simpler than PEP 2, although PEP 2 can be easily derived from it.

(PEP 3) If it is in S's power to bring it about that p, and p entails q, and q is false, then it is in S's power to bring it about that q.[16]

Hasker claims self-evidence for PEP 3 and says Quinn has said in correspondence that he now accepts PEP 3.[17] Hasker then proposes two more principles that are obtained by logical transformations on PEP 3. Since these latter principles stand or fall together, it is not necessary to consider them separately. Taking on PEP 1 to PEP 3 will be quite enough to do.

The threat of the PEPs to the compatibilist position on foreknowledge is based on the fact that the conjunction of the proposition that God's belief and my act are strictly equivalent and one of these PEPs has the consequence that I can bring about God's past belief. But that seems to be at least a very unwelcome consequence, if not a logically impossible one. Notice, however, that the PEPs are no threat to compatibilism if we accept the Thomistic account of God's knowing outlined in Chapter 3 since, on that view, God's belief and my act are not strictly equivalent. They are not strictly equivalent nor does my act entail God's belief because God's belief that I do S is the numerically same belief as the belief he has in another possible world that I do not do S. Furthermore, it is the numerically same belief as his belief that Caesar crossed the Rubicon. This is because God has numerically one epistemic state. But it would be very peculiar to say that my act entails God's belief that Caesar crossed the Rubicon. Even if there is some attenuated sense of entailment in which this is true, it surely is not the sense in which the concept of entailment is used in the PEPs. So the PEPs are no threat to the view I called Thomistic Ockhamism. Nonetheless, I will argue that they are probably false anyway.

Notice that PEPs are versions of TNP 2 discussed in Chapter 1. On that principle, if ϕ is W-necessary and ϕ is strictly equivalent to ψ, ψ is W-

necessary. Since the relevant types of necessity are those that involve our powerlessness, this means that

> I am powerless over ϕ.
> ϕ is strictly equivalent to ψ.
> $\vdash$ I am powerless over ψ.

Such a principle has strong intuitive support, and the logical relationship between it and the PEPs is part of the ground of the intuitive support for the latter. I will present arguments against the PEPs here and arguments against the TNPs in Chapter 6. However, reasons for rejecting the one are no doubt connected to reasons for rejecting the other.

I will give three sets of counterexamples to the PEPs. Although I will argue that these principles are false, the acceptance of some of my examples requires the rejection of some common views on the conceptual connections among the notions of power, possibility, and counterfactuals. To give a really convincing case, it would be necessary to give a much more extensive discussion of the metaphysics of modality than I will give. But since the burden of proof is on the defender of these principles, I do not need to do that here. It should be enough to show that there are alternatives to the conventional way of looking at the connection between free choice and modality and that the nonconventional way has intuitive support. It also has the consequence that the PEPs are false.

2.2.1. FIRST ARGUMENT AGAINST THE PEPS

First, if any necessary truths and their negations can be brought about by anybody while others can be brought about by nobody, all of these PEPs are false. Descartes is said to have taken the position that God created modal structure and had the power to do it differently. This has been interpreted as the position that for every necessary truth, God made it the case that it is true and necessary and could have made it the case that different propositions were necessary instead, for example, that $2 + 2 = 5$. This view, known as universal possibilism, has well-known problems, and I will not assume its truth in my arguments. But although I believe universal possibilism is implausible, this is not to say that universal nonpossibilism is plausible. Even though God may not be able to bring about the truth of *every* necessary truth, he may still be able to bring about the truth of *some* necessary truth. A limited possibilism, then, may be true and, in fact, it has been argued by Curley that this was Descartes' position.[18] Although not standard, this view does not seem to me to be unreasonable. If so, it is too hasty to declare that any of the PEPs are obviously true.

In this section I wish to focus on a special category of truths that may be necessary and that yet are definitely in the category of those brought about by God. These are truths involving God's plan of salvation. For example, consider the proposition

(11) If there is a Fall, God sends his Son to redeem the world.

God brings about the truth of (11) and it seems to me to be compatible with the goodness of God that he not bring about (11) if he so choose. That is, God has the power to bring about (11) and the power to bring about the negation of (11). But couldn't God decide to send a redeemer in *any* circumstance in which there was a fall? Doesn't God have the power to decide that no matter what happened, if there was a fall, there would be a redemption? If so, it would be the case that (11) is a necessary truth, true in all possible worlds. And it would be a necessary truth precisely because God decided in a certain way, a way in which he could have decided differently. But, if so, we can construct a counterexample to PEP 1.

Let S = God. For *q* substitute the proposition *God exists*. For *p* substitute the proposition (11). Now, even if it is within God's power to bring it about that (11) is true and within God's power to bring it about that (11) is false, and even though (11) entails *God exists* and the negation of (11) entails *It is not the case that God exists*, it is not within God's power to bring about the truth of *God exists*.

We can apply the same example to PEP 2. For a counterexample to this principle we need a case of a necessary truth God can bring about and another necessary truth God cannot bring about that has nothing to do with the one he can bring about. This principle is not as easy to discuss as the first one, since the intended sense of a necessary condition for having a power is not clear.[19] It could, of course, be simply declared that every necessary truth is a necessary condition for everything else, but I have been appealing to the intuition that necessary truths are not all on a par, especially when it comes to a question of God's power. If there are necessary truths that are not "conditions" of God's power and that are also such that God cannot bring them about, then there are counterexamples to PEP 2. I suggest that if we let *p* = (11), and *q* = The Law of Identity, we get an instance of such a counterexample.

Finally, let us turn to PEP 3. If it is within God's power to bring it about that (11) is false, we can also formulate a counterexample to PEP 3. Let *p* = not (11) and *q* = *God does not exist*. Then it is within God's power to bring about the negation of (11) and the negation of (11) entails *God does not exist*, but it is not within God's power to bring it about that God does not exist.

I do not expect this brief argument to establish that God has power over any necessary truths. It is enough, however, to call attention to the fact that the PEPs make certain assumptions about the status of the necessary that are not yet established. The relationship between the necessary and God's will is by no means fully understood. It is instructive to note, then, that if it is even *possible* that there is a being who can bring about some necessary truth and its negation but not some other necessary truth, all of the proposed PEPs are false. And even if it is not possible that there is such a being, surely that is not self-evident, as Hasker maintains. It depends on much more argument on the nature of modality than anyone has yet given.[20]

We are used to thinking of modal structure as fixed in a sort of Platonic heaven that is ontologically prior to everything else. As such, it constrains the choice of all free beings, including God. We generally do not ask where modal structure came from. It is probably thought that that structure could not have been otherwise and that the fact that it could not have been otherwise is sufficient to answer the question "Why is it the way that it is?" This question is supposed to be answered by the claim that what is possible is necessarily possible, what is impossible is necessarily impossible, and what is necessary is necessarily necessary. But it seems to me that this claim goes no distance at all toward answering the question of what grounds modality. *Why* is the necessary necessary, the possible possible, and the impossible impossible? I am not able to propose an answer to this question, but I think that any good answer will be forced to distinguish within the class of necessary truths those that are necessarily necessary and those that are not necessarily necessary.

I have argued that we should think that it is at least possible that God chooses to make some of what is necessary necessary. It also seems clear that God's choice probably does not extend to everything necessary, for example, his own existence. So a limited possibilism is true. This way of looking at modality requires a modal system weaker than $S4$. This is because the characteristic axiom of $S4$, $\Box P \rightarrow \Box \Box P$, requires that if P is true in all worlds possible relative to some world w, P is true in all worlds possible relative to any world. But that is just what I have been denying in my counterexample to the PEPs. It is true in all worlds possible relative to the actual world that (11), but if God has the power to make (11) false, then there is some world w^* such that (11) is false in some world possible relative to w^*. It is interested to note that Hugh Chandler and Nathan Salmon have both argued that $S4$ must be rejected anyway.[21]

The modal metaphysics associated with this view deserves extensive analysis that I cannot provide here. But for the purpose of casting doubt on the PEPs, it is sufficient to show that those principles make common but unargued assumptions about the relation between modality and the power to choose. In the case of divine power, I seriously doubt these assumptions are correct.

2.2.2. SECOND ARGUMENT AGAINST THE PEPS

What about the case of human power? It is, after all, human power that is at issue in the foreknowledge dilemma. I believe that as long as God can determine that certain contingent states of affairs are strictly equivalent, we also can construct counterexamples to the PEPs based on human power.

Let A be some ordinary human act that I have the power to bring about and the power not to bring about. Suppose also that from all eternity God decided that whenever I would do A he would do B subsequently, and that he would do B only when I do A, and that this decision would obtain no matter what else was the case. We need not concern ourselves with the question of whether such a decision is determined by the divine nature or whether it is free in some stronger sense. It matters only that I played no part in the decision myself. In addition, suppose that God is essentially omniscient, so it is true in every possible world that whenever I do A God knows that I do A, and whenever God believes that I do A, I do A. It would then be the case that

$$\Box \ (\text{I do } A \ \longleftrightarrow \ \text{God does } B).$$

The propositions *I do A* and *God does B* would be strictly equivalent, and their strict equivalence would be something brought about by God, not me. Finally, suppose that I know nothing about B, am incapable of even understanding B, and therefore cannot form the intention of acting in such a way as to bring about B.

In this case we have a counterexample to each of the PEPs. I have the power to bring it about that *I do A* is true, and I have the power to bring it about that *I do A* is false. *I do A* entails *God does B* and *It is not the case that I do A* entails *It is not the case that God does B*. Yet I do not have the power to bring it about that *God does B is true*. The truth of that proposition is brought about by God. So PEP 1 is false.

Next consider PEP 2. I have the power to bring it about that *I do A* is true, *I do A* entails *God does B*, *God does B* is not a necessary condition for my having the power to bring it about that *I do A* is true, and yet I do not have the power to bring it about that *God does B* is true.

To get this counterexample to PEP 2 we must make the reasonable assumption that not every proposition strictly equivalent to some proposition p is a necessary condition for someone having the power to bring about the truth of p. Of course, the intent of "necessary condition" in this version of PEP is unclear, but notice that it cannot just be declared that every proposition strictly equivalent to some proposition p is a necessary condition for my bringing about the truth of p without making PEP 2 empty.

Next consider PEP 3. Suppose that I do not do A at t. I have the power at t to bring it about that $I\ do\ A$ is true, $I\ do\ A$ entails $God\ does\ B$, $God\ does\ B$ is false, yet I do not have the power to bring it about that $God\ does\ B$ is true since, again, it is God who determines that he does B if and only if I do A and that that is the case necessarily.

It seems to me that much of the plausibility of the PEPs comes from the fact that we usually think that *nobody* brings about strict equivalences. So if you have the power to bring about p and p is strictly equivalent to q, then you have the power to bring about q only because you have no competitors. If not you, who else? But if there is somebody who brings about the strict equivalence, then it no longer looks like you are the one who brings about q, at least in some cases.

2.2.3. THIRD ARGUMENT AGAINST THE PEPS

My final argument against the PEPs requires that there be some true counterfactuals of freedom. Consider one such proposition, *If my son asked me for an apple I would not give him poison*. Let us symbolize this proposition as $A > \sim P$. In Lewis's account of counterfactuals, this proposition is (nonvacuously) true as long as there is some world in which A is true and P is false that is closer to the actual world than any world in which A is true and P is true. All possible worlds can be ranked according to their degree of similarity to the actual world. Take the set of worlds closer to the actual world than the closest A/P world. All of these worlds are $A/\sim P$ worlds. Since this set of worlds is similar to at least a certain fixed degree to the actual world, they all have a certain property in common that is lacking in all the A/P worlds. Call this property ϕ. Now form the counterfactual conditional $(A\ \&\ \phi) > \sim P$. This conditional is necessarily true. In every world in which it is true that A and ϕ, it is false that P. This means, of course, that it is necessarily false that $\sim [(A\ \&\ \phi) > \sim P]$. So as long as counterfactuals can be reduced to strict implications based on comparative similarity of worlds in a Lewis manner, and as long as there are true counterfactuals of freedom, there are also true strict implications of freedom.[22]

Now who brings about the truth of a counterfactual of freedom? As we will see in Chapter 5, Banez thought that God does, whereas Molina thought that nobody does; its truth is an ultimate fact. But isn't it more likely that the agent is the one who makes them true?[23] In fact, if there are any true counterfactuals of freedom and if they are analyzed as in the previous paragraph, to say that the agent brings about or is responsible for their truth may be the only way to maintain the agent's freedom. That is, a counterfactual such as $A > \sim P$ and the corresponding strict conditional are true because I would freely choose to make $\sim P$ true in the requisite circumstances. So I have the power to make it the case that $(A \mathbin{\&} \phi) > \sim P$ and I have the power to make it the case that $\sim [(A \mathbin{\&} \phi > \sim P]$ instead. But the proposition $\sim [(A \mathbin{\&} \phi) > \sim P]$ is strictly equivalent to $2 + 2 = 5$. However, I do not have the power to make $2 + 2 = 5$ true. We have, then, another counterexample to PEP 1 to PEP 3.

3. Forward-looking Subjunctives and Causal Relations

3.1. *John Pollock on the Causal Conditional*

Contemporary philosophers interested in the technical analysis of causal statements are highly motivated to give such an analysis in terms of subjunctive conditionals. However, they have been unable to do so in any straightforward sense. Pollock, for example, distinguishes four kinds of standard subjunctive conditionals, none of which is equivalent to the causal conditional. So if the worry that (1) and (2) express a causal relation is based solely on the fact that the conditional is in the subjunctive mood, that is surely mistaken. Not only is it not the case that every subjunctive conditional is equivalent to a causal conditional, *no* standard subjunctive conditional is equivalent to the causal one. As Pollock points out, one reason for this is that the causal conditional is transitive, yet no known subjunctive conditional has the property of transitivity.[24] Pollock subsequently defines a strong subjunctive conditional in which transitivity and adjunctivity are built in, but even then he finds that the resulting conditional is not sufficient for defining the causal relation, and he has to add the provision that the antecedent expresses a condition prior in time to the consequent. Pollock concludes that since no counterfactual condition can distinguish between nomically equivalent states of affairs (defined shortly), no purely counterfactual analysis of causation can succeed.[25] This suggests that any claim that (1) or (2) express a causal relation must await a satisfactory account of causation, and such an account will not show a straightforward connection between subjunctive conditionals such as (1) and (2) and causation.

In Section 2.2 I argued that the recent arguments that (1) is committed to backward agent causation are unsuccessful. These arguments use so-called PEPs, that we have not been given sufficient reason to accept. So neither on the basis of the form of (1) alone nor on the basis of PEPs can it be shown that (1) is committed to backwards causation. (2), however, is another matter. In (2), at least the counterfactual order is the right one for a causal relation. And even though the form of (2) alone should not lead us to conclude that it is committed to a causal connection between God's foreknowledge and my act, it turns out that (2) satisfies the conditions for the causal conditional given by Pollock.

On Pollock's account, we can define the notion of nomic implication between states of affairs as follows.

$X \underset{w}{\Rightarrow} Q$ (X nomically implies Q at w) $=_{df}$ necessarily, if the union of the state of affairs X and the basic subjunctive generalizations true in w (L_w) is such that it obtains, then Q obtains.

Note that the L_w are assumed by Pollock to be physical laws, but he does not say anything that prevents us from extending the definition to include any other laws expressible by subjunctive conditionals.[26]

Two of the subjunctive generalizations true in any world w will be the following.

$L_w 1$. If a person had performed a certain act at any time t, God would have believed that she would prior to t.

$L_w 2$. If God had believed prior to t that a person would perform an act at t, then she would have performed that act at t.

Since, necessarily, the union of $L_w 1$ and the state of affairs of my act at t_n is such that if it obtains then God's belief at t_{n-1} that I would perform the act obtains, my act nomically implies God's belief. And since, necessarily, the union of $L_w 2$ and the state of affairs of God's belief at t_{n-1} is such that if it obtains, then my act at t_n obtains, God's belief nomically implies my act. My act at t_n and God's forebelief at t_{n-1} are therefore nomically equivalent states of affairs.

My act and God's belief are actually even more closely related than nomic equivalence; they are strictly equivalent, true in exactly the same possible worlds. Pollock does not consider cases of events that are not merely nomically equivalent, but also strictly equivalent, since he says that strictly equivalent events are the *same event*.[27] The possibility that two distinct events can be strictly equivalent and causally unrelated does not arise in his treatment of the causal relation.

Pollock's definition of the causal conditional, $P \rightarrow\!\!\!\rightarrow Q$, can be paraphrased informally as follows.

> $P \rightarrow\!\!\!\rightarrow Q$ obtains at w if and only if for each world that is P-accessible from w, a minimal change which removes P removes Q, and a minimal change which does not remove P does not remove Q.[28]

Pollock says that this conditional is transitive and adjunctive.

The analysis of the causal relation between states of affairs P and Q is as follows.

> P causes $Q = [P \& Q$ obtain & $(P \rightarrow\!\!\!\rightarrow Q)$ & P is earlier than $Q]$.[29]

An interesting feature of this analysis if that if two states of affairs are nomically equivalent, the earlier is *designated* the cause. Proposition (2) therefore satifies Pollock's strong conditions for expressing the causal conditional. God's forebelief comes out as the cause of my act.

Pollock's analysis of the causal relation in terms of a specially defined strong subjunctive conditional is interesting for its consequences for the issue of this book. As far as I can see, however, we have been given no reason to accept his account of the causal conditional as it relates to (2). Pollock declares without argument that the laws grounding subjunctive conditionals are physical or causal laws, and this makes sense, given his interests. But, of course, it begs the question to designate the "broad subjunctive generalizations" true in a given world (i.e., L_w1 and L_w2, as causal laws). Furthermore, Pollock admits that his efforts to reduce the causal conditional to some ordinary subjunctive conditional are a failure. There is no argument at all that nomically equivalent events are such that the earlier is the cause of the later. Pollock is no doubt right that it violates basic intuitions about causation to designate the later event as the cause, but why must either one be a cause of the other in every case?

The causal relation is little understood, and it is forgivable that philosophers concerned with the nature of causation would be motivated to reduce it to some better-understood relation. But it is unfortunate when this attempt involves the ignoring of laws other than causal laws. The fact that subjunctive conditionals are related to law statements may be important, but the fact that subjunctive conditionals are not directly related to *causal* law statements seems to me to be good evidence that there are laws other than causal laws that should be taken into account. Of course, many philosophers will reply that they knew that anyway. What is significant for our present problem is the fact that those who claim that subjunctively expressed relations such as the ones given by (1) and (2) necessarily involve causal relations or the power to bring about something have a very weak defense. It is interesting that God's forebelief satisfies Pollock's conditions for being the cause of my future act, but it is even more interesting to see how little philosophical argument supports this result.

3.2. The Causal Necessity Version of the Foreknowledge Dilemma

In Chapter 1 two versions of the dilemma of divine foreknowledge were proposed: the Accidental Necessity Version and the Causal Necessity Version. Most of the discussion in this book so far has centered on the Accidental Necessity Version, and it is that version that has usually captured the philosophical imagination. In this section I would like to look at the Causal Necessity Version and propose a solution to it.

The argument that if God has foreknowledge then my future acts are all causally necessitated can be formulated as follows:

1) God's belief at $t1$ that I will do S at $t3$ is causally sufficient for my choice to do S at $t3$.
2) If A has occurred and A is causally sufficient for a human act B, then B is causally necessary.
3) So if God believes at $t1$ that I will do S at $t3$, my act at $t3$ is causally necessary.
4) If an act is causally necessary, it is not free.
5) So if God believes at $t1$ that I will do S at $t3$, my act at $t3$ is not free.

As we have seen, on Pollock's account of causation, it follows that God's belief at $t1$ is causally sufficient for my future act, so (1) follows. The defense of (1) comes from the idea that for an act to be causally contingent there must be a possible world with a past history exactly like this one up to the time of the event in which the event does not occur. The criterion might be formulated as follows.

(12) S's doing x at t is causally contingent at t only if there is a possible world w that has a history up to t indistinguishable from the actual world and in which S does not do x at t.

Now it seems to me that (12) does not express a necessary condition for causal contingency. It is much too strong. To say that S's doing x at t is causally contingent, we need not consider the entire past history of the world up to t, but only those events $C1$, $C2$...Cn that are part of the causal history of x at t. We ask if these events could have occurred though x itself does not. Not every event in the past history of the world is part of the causal chain leading up to x. In fact, it is doubtful whether there is *any* event that is such that the entire past history of the world is part of its causal history, and it is doubtful whether very much of the past history of the world is part of the causal history of typical events. If the entire past history of the world were part of the causal history of some event, we would not expect such an event to occur if anything in the past had been different. And this is true even when the event in question is much broader in its significance than typical human acts. For instance, when someone asks, "If the money supply increased, would the interest rates go down?", the question is not whether the rates would go down if *everything* that has happened in the past happened and the money supply increased. We assume that if there is a causal connection between lower interest rates and previous events, it is not to every previous event that the connection holds. Many, in fact most, events in the past are no doubt causally unrelated to it, for example, the invasion of Poland by the Tatars in 1287. But, likewise, to show that the fall of interest rates is causally contingent it would not be necessary that there be a world exactly like ours up to just before the interest rates fall in which the rates do not fall. It would be sufficient if there is a world like this one in the causally relevant respects. Perhaps there is no such world, but that is not the point. If there is such a world, it would suffice to show the causal contingency of this event.

Similarly, if we want to know if my act at $t2$ is causally contingent, we do not mean to ask if there is a world exactly like this one up to $t2$ in which my act does not occur at $t2$. We mean to ask if there is a world that at some time has the same causal history as my act, but in which my act does not occur. Of course, there are problems in specifying what belongs in the causal history of an event and what does not. But such problems do not change the point of what causal contingency means. (12) takes the safest approach of excluding nothing in the past from the causal history of a given event and, of course, the satisfaction of this criterion is sufficient to show an event contingent. But the fact that this approach bypasses the difficulty of having to sort out which events are causally related to a given event and which are not is not a reason for us to accept its truth.

In my early foreknowledge paper, I suggested the following criterion of causal contingency:

A proposition p true in a world w is causally contingent in w if and only if there is a possible world maximally similar to w relative to p in which p is false.

Possible worlds w and w' are maximally similar relative to p if and only if they share the same causal history relative to p.

The causal history of an event S = those events in its past that are causally necessary for S—those events without which S would not occur.[30] The question then becomes whether the causally necessary events for S are also causally sufficient.

I now prefer to apply the concept of causal contingency to events/ states of affairs rather than to propositions, so the definition must be revised. The one I suggest is as follows:

Let S be an act which A does at t in w. Let $CS1$, $CS2$, $CS3$, . . . CSn be the causal history of A's act S, performed at t in w.

Definition of causal contingency

An act S is causally contingent at t in w if and only if there is a possible world w' in which $CS1$, $CS2$, $CS3$, . . . CSn occurs at t and in which A does not do S at t.

The incompatibilist of the causal necessity variety can offer only one reason for thinking that God's previous knowledge that A would do S at t in w is one of $CS1$, $CS2$, $CS3$, . . . CSn. That reason is simply that God's act of knowing is prior to S. But to think so is to use a notion of causal history that is much stronger than is normal. Not only is it unusual to think of every event that occurs prior to some given event as causally relevant to it, to do so is incompatible with many of the causal statements we actually make. We think that a given causally determined event would have occurred even if many things had been different in the past, and we do not think this because these differences are just alternative causal routes. We think of them as causally irrelevant.

Suppose that I strike a dry match in the right conditions and it lights. It is reasonable to say that striking the match in those conditions caused it to light. What needs to be put into those conditions is, of course, problematic, but it is clear that they do not include everything that has happened in the entire previous history of the world. Many events before the striking of the match could have been different without affecting the causal sequence. For example, it is highly probable that the match would have lit even if J.L. had not moved to Paris from Lyons in 1968. This means that ordinary causal statements such as

Striking the match in conditions C at $t1$ caused it to light at $t2$

entail a host of subjunctive states such as

Even if J.L. had not moved to Paris from Lyons in 1968, and the match was struck in conditions C at $t1$, it still would have lit at $t2$.

If someone wanted to uphold the causal contingency of the lighting of the match, she need only claim that there is a world that shares the causal history of the lighting of this match and in which the match is struck but does not light. It is not necessary to claim that there is a world that includes the fact of J.L. moving to Paris from Lyons in 1968 and in which the match is struck and does not light. Such a fact is no doubt irrelevant to the question of whether the lighting of the match is causally contingent.

Suppose, however, that there is no world relevantly similar to the actual world in which J.L. moves and the match does not light. Some philosophers might be inclined to take that as a demonstration of the causal connection between the move and the lighting. They would probably be so inclined because the causal relation is so little understood that the temptation to reduce it to subjunctive relations is difficult to overcome. I agree that if this were the case it would show that there is some sort of modal connection between J.L's move and the lighting of the match. I have tried in this section, however, to motivate the view that such a relation need not be causal.

Similarly, although there is no world in which God believes that I will do S and I do not subsequently do S, there is no reason to see that as having the consequence that God's foreknowledge is in the causal history of my act, even though that indicates that there is some sort of necessary or other modal connection, most likely of a metaphysical variety, expressible by subjunctive conditionals.

There is another response that we could make to the Causal Necessity Version of the foreknowledge dilemma if my alternative way of looking at the relation between choice and modality in Section 2.2 is right. In that section I suggested that we do not know that the possible and the impossible constrain us rather than the other way around. It has not been established that modal structure is ontologically prior to free choice, whether divine or human. But if it is the other way around, my act could be free even if it is not causally contingent on the definition I have given.

So even if there is not a possible world in which $CS1$, $CS2$, . . . occurs and in which my act S does not occur, I may still have the power not to do S. This line of reasoning will be pursued more fully in Chapter 6.

4. Subjunctive Conditionals and Metaphysical Laws

I have argued in this chapter that the attacks on (1) and (2) by incompatibilists on the grounds that they are committed to unacceptable causal claims are not well founded. Nonetheless, (1) and (2) are not holding up very well. In the first place, I have argued that it is highly doubtful that (1) can be conjoined with (3) to get the more interesting (4). I have also argued that we have seen no examples of backward-looking conditionals like (1) which help the compatibilist's case. In the absence of such an account, (1) does not look very informative. Furthermore, even (2) does not look very informative if it does not imply a causal relation. My efforts to defend (1) and (2) against attack have left us with a very flimsy account of the relation between God's beliefs and our acts. If we are ever going to get a positive solution to the divine foreknowledge dilemma, we must either look in an entirely different direction or make (1) and (2) both informative and plausible. I will try to do a little of both in this section.

A model of the relation between a human act and God's foreknowledge would be nomically equivalent events in which there is no causal relation in either direction. This means that the two events are unrelated by physical laws, even though they occur in time. Since nomically equivalent events are connected by some sort of law, if it is not physical, it must be metaphysical. A good place to look for a foreknowledge model, then, would be a metaphysical law that has a temporal instance.

Suppose that God is essentially provident and suppose that that means he watches over every creature he creates and that he would have watched over every creature he would have created. Consider the following pair of subjunctive conditionals.

(13) If God had not created Adam, he would not have watched over him.

(14) If God did not watch over Adam, he would not have created him.

(13) is forward-looking, whereas (14) is backward-looking. They are true because of God's essential providence. The only case in which God would not watch over some possible being is the case in which that being does not exist. Adam's creation and God's providential care are therefore

nomically equivalent. Furthermore, they are strictly equivalent. That is, they occur in the same possible worlds.

Now compare (13) to

(15) If God had not believed at $t1$ that I would do S at $t2$, I would not have done S at $t2$.

(15) is structurally identical to (2). Compare (14) to:

(16) If I had not done S at $t2$, God would not have believed that I would at $t1$.

(16) is structurally identical to (1).

(16), like (14), is backward looking. (15) and (16) are true because of the essential omniscience of God, just as (13) and (14) are true because of the essential providence of God. In each case the pair of subjunctive conditionals is grounded in a metaphysical law.

(13) and (15) are true for parallel reasons. (13) is true because God watches over only created things. (15) is true because I do only things God believes I do. (14) and (16) are true for parallel reasons. (14) is true because God creates only things he watches over. (16) is true because God believes only things I do.

We have for consideration now two pairs of nomically equivalent events. It is probable that in each case one of the pair is ontologically or explanatorily more basic. I cannot say whether God's providential care of Adam or his creation of Adam is more basic. That depends on whether we think God watches over whomever he happens to create for whatever reason, or that God creates Adam in order to watch over him. Either way, this example illustrates the point that nomically equivalent events need not be on a par ontologically. A positive account of the relation between God's foreknowledge and human free choice should explain the ontological basicality of one of these classes of events over the other.

Perhaps (13) and (14) do not seem problematic because God is the agent for both equivalent events. God's nature and decisions ground both. But (15) and (16) are different because God is not the agent for one of the events. Intuitively, the object of a belief is ontologically, or at least explanatorily, more basic than the belief itself, so my act would be more basic than God's belief that it would occur. Of course, this deserves an account of the mechanism by which God believes contingent things. If such an account supports the intuition that my act is ontologically or explanatorily more basic than God's belief that the act occurs, it is reasonable to assert that God believes what he does *because* of my future act, although, of course, not in a causal sense of "because."

It is often thought that physical laws just *are* generalized subjunctive conditionals expressing relations between physical events. Metaphysical laws, on the other hand, seem to be more than the subjunctive conditionals grounded in them. This makes it much more difficult to give a positive account of the relations between nomically equivalent events that are related by metaphysical laws. An account of the subjunctive conditional relating the two sorts of events is just not sufficient to explain them. In short, no positive solution to the foreknowledge problem can be given, I believe, until a very comprehensive explanation of the relationship between God and contingent events has been accomplished.

5

The Molinist Solution

1. Introduction

1.1. What Middle Knowledge Is

Perhaps the most ingenious solution to the dilemma of foreknowledge and freedom was devised by the sixteenth-century Jesuit philosopher, Luis de Molina, in his theory of *scientia media*, or middle knowledge. This theory has lately attracted some attention and now has a number of adherents.[1] As we will see, if the theory is true, it has the advantage of solving at least two and perhaps three important theological problems simultaneously. In this chapter I will examine the theory as a solution to the foreknowledge dilemma and only incidentally will consider its other virtues.

Middle knowledge is said to be the knowledge of what any possible free creature would freely choose in any possible circumstance. Molina called it "middle" knowledge because it stands midway between God's natural knowledge, or his knowledge of what is necessary and possible, and God's free knowledge, or his knowledge of what is actual. Middle knowledge is like free knowledge and unlike natural knowledge in that its objects are metaphysically contingent propositions. All of God's natural knowledge, in contrast, is of metaphysically necessary propositions. So if God knows that A is necessary, the proposition A *is necessary* is itself necessary; if God knows that B is possible, the proposition B *is possible* is itself necessary, and so on. But if by middle knowledge God knows the proposition *In circumstance C Peter would do S*, that proposition is contingent and, hence, in a distinct category from the objects of natural knowledge. On the other hand, middle knowledge is like natural knowledge and unlike free knowledge in that it is prevolitional. It is logically or explanatorily prior to God's will to bring about what he does in the creation. All other contingent propositions except those expressing God's will itself are postvolitional. That is, they depend for their truth on the

125

fact that God has willed what he has willed. So the objects of God's middle knowledge are both contingent and prevolitional.

This means that God's foreknowledge of contingent states of affairs is logically or explanatorily subsequent to his middle knowledge. Freddoso explains how middle knowledge gives rise to foreknowledge as follows:

> On Molina's view, then, the source of God's foreknowledge of absolute future contingents is threefold: (i) His prevolitional natural knowledge of metaphysically necessary states of affairs, (ii) His prevolitional middle knowledge of conditional future contingents, and (iii) His free knowledge of the total causal contribution He Himself wills to make to the created world. By (i) He knows which spatio-temporal arrangements of secondary causes are possible and which contingent effects *might* emanate from any such arrangement. By (ii) He knows which contingent effects *would in fact* emanate from any possible spatiotemporal arrangements of secondary causes. By (iii) He knows which secondary causes He wills to create and conserve and how He wills to cooperate with them via His intrinsically neutral general concurrence. So given His natural knowledge, His middle knowledge and His free knowledge of His own causal contribution to the created world, He has free knowledge of all absolute future contingents.[2]

So on Molina's theory, God's free knowledge, or his knowledge of the actual, can be fully explained by his natural knowledge, His middle knowledge, and his knowledge of his own will. Since all foreknowledge is contained in free knowledge, this theory explains foreknowledge.

For the theory of middle knowledge to be a successful solution to the foreknowledge dilemma it is not actually required that God know what every *possible* free creature would freely choose in each possible circumstance, but only what every *actual* free creature would so choose. So the well-known difficulties with individuating possible but nonactual beings, while a problem for the full theory, are not a problem for that part of it relevant to foreknowledge.

The objects of middle knowledge are supposed to include propositions such as the following:

(1) If Peter were asked if he knows Christ (at a certain place and time), he would (freely) deny it.

(2) If Elizabeth were offered a (certain) grant, she would (freely) accept it.[3]

In modern parlance, conditionals such as (1) and (2) are called *counterfactuals of freedom*. So this theory explains God's foreknowledge of the consequents of (1) and (2) by the combination of his knowledge of (1) and (2) and his knowledge of the antecedents of (1) and (2).

Middle knowledge would solve the foreknowledge dilemma provided that for every actual contingent event expressed by a proposition ϕ, including every human choice, there is some true subjunctive conditional $\psi > \phi$ that has the following features: (a) $\psi > \phi$ is knowable by God logically prior to his knowledge of his own creative will, and (b) ψ is knowable by God independently of anything but his prevolitional knowledge and his knowledge of his own will.

How can God know the antecedents of (1) and (2) by using only his natural knowledge, his knowledge of counterfactuals of freedom, and his knowledge of his own will? Call the proposition expressing what God originally wills to create $\psi1$. Suppose that $\psi1$ includes the creation of Adam and Eve. If God also knows counterfactuals of freedom about Adam and Eve, his knowledge of other contingent states of affairs $\psi2$ can be explained. By knowing other counterfactuals of freedom about the actions of creatures in circumstances expressed by $\psi2$, as well as anything God chooses to directly bring about in $\psi2$, he would know further contingent states of affairs, $\psi3$, and so on. God's knowledge that Peter exists and finds himself in certain circumstances can then be explained simply by his knowledge of $\psi1$, his knowledge of counterfactuals of freedom, and his knowledge of his own will.[4]

Molina was embroiled in a vicious controversy with Banez over the status of the objects of middle knowledge. As Freddoso describes this dispute, both Molinists and Banezians accepted the fact of middle knowledge, but the Banezians denied that any metaphysically contingent state of affairs could be logically prior to God's decreeing that it obtain.[5] They therefore denied clause (a) (two paragraphs preceding) and claimed instead that counterfactuals of freedom are true because God has willed them to be true. In my opinion, this position is highly unappealing. If God brings about the truth of a counterfactual of freedom by willing it to be so, God is responsible for the fact that if I were in a certain circumstance I would freely bring about evil. But even if this is possible, it is surely distasteful. I therefore take the Molinist view of middle knowledge to be the most compelling version of the theory, and it is this version that I will investigate in this chapter. For those readers who prefer the Banezian version, the discussion of whether the theory satisfies clause (a) is, of course, irrelevant.

The theory of middle knowledge is remarkably powerful. If it succeeded, it would go a long way toward producing a positive solution to the foreknowledge dilemma. This is because it aims at much more than a simple demonstration of the logical consistency of foreknowledge and freedom that, as we have seen, is only the weakest form of compatibilism.

By giving a theory of *how* God knows the future, it aims at showing that divine foreknowledge and human free will are coplausible, not just copossible. Furthermore, middle knowledge can easily be combined with the Thomistic theory of divine knowing, either with or without the doctrine of timelessness, and it attempts to answer the mystery of how God can know what *I* freely do by knowing his *own* essence. As Molina himself expresses it:

> Finally, the third type is *middle* knowledge, by which, in virtue of the most profound and inscrutable comprehension of each free will, He saw in His own essence what each such will would do with its innate freedom were it to be placed in this or that or, indeed, in infinitely many orders of things— even though it would really be able, if it so willed, to do the opposite. . . .[6] (Emphasis mine.)

Middle knowledge has other advantages. Recall that in Chapter 1 I argued that the dilemma of a divine and infallible foreknower has special problems not encountered by the dilemma of a nondivine but infallible foreknower, a point stressed by Freddoso.[7] Any acceptable solution to the dilemma must at least be compatible with the doctrine of divine providence. The theory of middle knowledge is not only compatible with that doctrine, it helps to explain it in a way that seems to preserve both God's sovereignty and human free will. This advantage of the theory is enthusiastically expressed by Craig.

> Since God knows what any free creature would do in any situation, he can, by creating the appropriate situations, bring it about that creatures will achieve his ends and purposes and that they will do so *freely*. When one considers that these situations are themselves the results of earlier free decisions by creatures, free decisions which God had to bring about, one begins to see that providence over a world of free creatures could only be the work of omniscience. Only an infinite Mind could calculate the unimaginably complex and numerous factors that would need to be combined in order to bring about through the free decisions of creatures a single human event such as, say, the enactment of the lend-lease policy prior to America's entry into the Second World War. Think then of God's planning the entire course of world history so as to achieve his purposes! Given middle knowledge, the apparent contradiction between God's sovereignty, which seems to crush human freedom, and human freedom, which seems to break God's sovereignty, is resolved. In his infinite intelligence, God is able to plan a world in which his designs are achieved by creatures acting freely. Praise be to God![8]

In addition, the theory of middle knowledge was reinvented by Plantinga as a solution to the problem of evil. In much of his discussion, Plantinga uses the possible worlds interpretation of counterfactuals discussed in Chapter 4.[9] On that interpretation, a counterfactual conditional $A > B$ is (nonvacuously) true just in case there is a world in which A and B are both true that is closer to the actual world than any world in which A is true and B is false. Of course, some of the propositions that are the objects of middle knowledge are not *counter*factuals, since the antecedent is true, and it is these that allow middle knowledge to give rise to foreknowledge on Molina's theory. But it is usually thought that the analysis of counterfactuals applies to these conditionals, also. So if both A and B are true in the actual world, there is obviously a world in which both are true that is more similar to the actual world than any world in which A is true and B false, namely, the actual world itself.

Plantinga argues that God's middle knowledge can be used to show that it is possible that a certain set of counterfactuals of freedom are true that are such that if they are true, God cannot actualize certain possible worlds. Such worlds are *unrealizable*, to use Robert Adams's terminology. So even if there are worlds that contain a better balance of good over evil than ours, and even if some of those worlds contain free creatures, it might be that God cannot bring them into existence. The theory deserves a more lengthy discussion than I can give for the purposes of this chapter but, since it is well known, I will simply present my own simplified version of it in what follows.

There are good reasons for holding that God does not create a complete possible world, but only the foundations of a world. We might say he creates a world-germ. A world-germ probably contains certain substances and laws and the results of any direct action by God on these substances. We need not settle just how far God's direct action goes in the creation, since the point is that whatever God does, he does not bring about a complete world. His creative activity is compatible with a great number of possible worlds, probably an infinite number of them. What makes the actual world this particular world rather than some other one compatible with what God has created is determined by both God's direct action in the world subsequent to the creation and by the free action of the creatures God has made.

So for each world-germ God might have created, there is a set of possible worlds compatible with that world-germ. Let us call each such set of worlds a galaxy. So galaxy 1 is the set of worlds compatible with world-germ 1, galaxy 2 is the set of worlds compatible with world-germ 2, and so forth. This can be represented diagrammatically as follows.[10]

world-germ 1	world-germ 2 . . .	world-germ n
↓	↓	↓
world w1.1	w2.1	wn.1
w1.2	w2.2	wn.2
w1.3	w2.3	wn.3
w1. . . .	w2. . . .	wn. . . .
GALAXY 1	GALAXY 2 . . .	GALAXY N

Now suppose that there are possible worlds that contain free creatures who always choose good. Why doesn't God just create those worlds? The short answer is that it is *possible* that there are true propositions such as the following:

(i) If God created world-germ 1, world w1.2 would be actual,
(ii) If God created world-germ 2, world w2.4 would be actual,
(iii) If God created world-germ 3, world w3.1 would be actual,

where *in each case* the world that would have resulted given God's creative activity would have been one containing evil—perhaps very great evil.

So even if, say, worlds w1.1, w2.3, and w3.2 have no evil in them, they would not result even if God did *his part* in bringing them about. It is not God's fault, then, that there is evil, even if there are possible worlds with free creatures and no evil. Such worlds are unrealizable.

This way out of the problem of evil requires that God have middle knowledge, for God could not know which world would result given any one of his own creative options unless he knew in particular each event that would actually occur given any creative choice of his own. And it assumes that God himself does not choose to make counterfactuals such as (i) to (iii) true. Even if God wills them in the sense of permits them to be true, their truth is logically or explanatorily prior to God's willing them to be so. Plantinga's theory, then, requires a Molinist rather than a Banezian version of middle knowledge.

The theory of middle knowledge therefore has many advantages. If successful, not only can it account for the compatibility of divine foreknowledge and human freedom, it can also account for the compatibility of divine providence and human freedom, and it can be used in the formulation of an interesting solution to the problem of evil. Furthermore, it blends well with traditional theories about the nature of God and his knowing, particularly the views of Aquinas. The theory's conceptual importance, then, makes it deserving of a sympathetic hearing.

1.2. The Middle Knowledge Solution

In this book we have looked at a number of responses to two arguments that divine foreknowledge would make our future acts unfree. How does the Molinist theory of middle knowledge respond to these arguments? Freddoso discusses Molina's answer to a version of the argument from accidental necessity in more detail than Molina gives it himself.[11] According to Freddoso, Molina explicitly rejects three common responses to this argument: the Aristotelian move of denying that future contingents have a truth value, the Thomistic move of denying that God knows anything *as future*, and the Ockhamist move of denying that God's past beliefs are really or strictly past. Freddoso says:

> At this point it might seem that Molina has closed off every viable avenue of escape. And, indeed, I can attest from personal experience that at first glance his response to the argument is apt to strike one as rather astonishing. In a word, he rejects . . . the thesis that accidental necessity is closed under entailment.[12]

Freddoso's rendition of the argument from accidental necessity is similar to the version of my argument that uses the weaker TNP.

Transfer of Accidental Necessity Principle 1

If *A* is accidentally necessary and *A* entails *B*, then *B* is accidentally necessary*.

In my second version of the argument, I use an even more plausible principle on line 2.

Transfer of Accidental Necessity Principle 2

If *A* is accidentally necessary and *A* is strictly equivalent to *B*, then *B* is accidentally necessary*.

Molina's move is to accept the position that God's past beliefs are necessary in whatever sense other states of affairs in the past are necessary but to deny TNP 1.

> . . . even if (i) the conditional is necessary (because . . . these two things cannot both obtain, viz., that God foreknows something to be future and that the thing does not turn out that way), and even if (ii) the antecedent is

necessary in the sense in question (because it is past-tense and because no
shadow of alteration can befall God), nonetheless the consequent can be
purely contingent.[13]

There is no indication that Molina considered my second version of the
argument from accidental necessity, but it looks as if his only way out of
that argument would be to deny TNP 2 as well as TNP 1. Even though
this may seem like a hopelessly implausible move, I will present an
argument in Chapter 6, Section 2.2, that shows, I think, that even the
denial of TNP 2 is reasonable. I will do this in the context of one of my
own solutions to the foreknowledge dilemma rather than the middle
knowledge solution. In both Molina's solution and my own, the way out
of the dilemma is to present a model for understanding the relation
between God's knowledge and human acts that makes it plausible to deny
the TNPs. How does the middle knowledge solution accomplish this?

As Freddoso explains it, Molina allows no power of any sort over the
past, so Peter cannot cause it to have been true that God never foreknew
that he would sin at t. Nor, presumably, can Peter cause it to have been
true that God did not know the counterfactual of freedom that explains
God's knowledge that Peter sins at t. But since Peter's sin at t will be free,
it is true at some time prior to t that Peter has the power to contribute
causally to its being false that he sins at t.

> So even though Peter cannot now cause it to be true that God never
> believed that he would sin at T, he nonetheless can now cause something,
> viz., his not sinning at T, such that had it been true from eternity that he
> would cause it if placed in the relevant circumstances, God would never
> have believed that he would sin at T. And, significantly, the theory of
> middle knowledge provides an intuitively accessible model on which both
> parts of this claim come out true.[14]

It is not perfectly clear to me from Freddoso's account just how middle
knowledge is connected with the denial of the TNPs, but I can think of
ways the former might make the latter more plausible. Molina's position
seems to be that before t Peter cannot cause it to be true that God never
believed he would sin at t, yet he has the power to cause it to be true that
he does not sin at t, and this clearly involves denying TNP. The theory of
middle knowledge makes the claim plausible provided that Peter's power
before t not to sin at t does not entail the power to make it false that in
circumstances C Peter sins at t. Presumably, Peter has no power over the
truth of the counterfactual of freedom or God's knowledge of it. That is,
Peter cannot cause it to be true that in circumstances C he does not sin at

t, nor can he cause it to be true that God never believed that in circumstances *C* he would sin at *t*. But as long as power not to sin does not involve power over a counterfactual of freedom, the fact that God knows the truth of the counterfactual of freedom and Peter has no power over its truth explains God's knowledge of Peter's future sin *and* is compatible with Peter's power not to sin at *t*.

So Molina's theory of middle knowledge can give a way out of both the accidental necessity and causal necessity versions of the foreknowledge dilemma, but it does so at the cost of denying the intuitively plausible TNP, and the plausibility of this in turn requires denying that power over the truth of *S* involves power over the truth of *C* > *S*. The price may be worth paying but, as far as I know, little attention has been paid to it in discussions of middle knowledge.

2. Conditional Excluded Middle and the Asymmetry of Time

In Chapter 4 we examined the logical peculiarity of backward-looking subjunctive conditions. We related the fact that such conditionals are not true as standardly interpreted to the asymmetry of time. We noted, in fact, that Lewis claims that the best, if not the only, way to express temporal asymmetry is to say that there is an asymmetry of counterfactual dependency. Later times counterfactually depend on earlier times, but earlier times do not counterfactually depend on later times.

In my view, the connection between temporal asymmetry and the problems with backward-looking counterfactuals can help us to understand ordinary forward-looking counterfactuals. The reason backward counterfactuals are so strange is that the relation between the antecedent and consequent states of affairs in a counterfactual conditional is like the relation between the present and the future. In some cases, states of affairs in the present are sufficient to determine that something obtain in the future, and in those cases it is true that $A_{\text{present}} > B_{\text{future}}$, but the openness of the future means that the totality of states of affairs in the past and present is not sufficient to determine that the future be what it is going to be. So *The totality of present and past > actual future* is false. That is, it is false that if the past and present were just as it is, the actual future *would* follow. Alternative futures *might* follow instead.

To take a particular example, consider the following subjunctive conditional, where the antecedent is about the actual present and past and the consequent is about the future:

(4) If I lived my life the way I have up to now (May 1988), I would be living in Chicago in 1999.

It seems to me that (4) is false. Defining the might-counterfactual in terms of the would-counterfactual, as Lewis and Pollock do, (4) is equivalent to the following.

(5) ~ (If I lived my life the way I have up to now (May 1988), I might *not* be living in Chicago in 1999).

But (5) is surely false, and it seems false because it seems true instead that the following:

(6) If I lived my life the way I have up to now (May 1988), I might be living in Chicago in 1999.

(7) If I lived my life the way I have up to now (May 1988), I might *not* be living in Chicago in 1999).

I have not proposed an account of counterfactuals in this book, but it is clear to me that there is a large class of paradigm cases of the might-counterfactual in which the antecedent is about the actual past or present and the consequent about the future. In these cases we think that both $A > might\ B$ and $A > might\ not\ B$ are true. This means that the principle of Conditional Excluded Middle (CEM), $(A > B)$ or $(A > \sim B)$, is false when A is about the actual past and present and B is about either the actual or possible future. CEM fails in these cases because one mark of the difference between the future and the past is just that the future is such that there is more than one alternative that might be the future, whereas there is only one alternative that (now) might be the past. The ordinary notion of time explained in Chapter 1, then, supports the rejection of CEM for propositions in this category.

In a similar fashion, it seems to me that we use counterfactual conditionals when we want to treat the past as if it were still future. Suppose I say the following:

(8) If I had taught a course on Aristotle last semester I might have assigned the Categories.

or

(9) If I had taught a course on Aristotle last semester I might *not* have assigned the Categories.

I suggest that to understand these propositions we consider the time immediately prior to the time at which the antecedent would have obtained. The future, relative to that time, was still open. There were many ways things could have turned out in the course I would have been planning. Each possible future can be represented by branching paths on some of which I assign the Categories and on some of which I do not assign the Categories. So I might have assigned the Categories but, then again, I might not have. Of course, some of those branching paths represent futures farther removed from the way the actual world turned out than others. But it still seems likely that some world in which I assign the Categories is just as similar to the actual world as one in which I do not.[15] And even if the interpretation of (8) and (9) in terms of similarity of worlds is not accurate, I am more sure of the truth of (8) and (9) than I am of the semantics for counterfactuals currently in use.[16]

The truth of (8) and (9) is contained, then, in the intuition of the openness of the future, the idea that there are many possible futures, but only one possible past. And if (8) and (9) are true, given the interdefinability of might- and would-counterfactuals, the following propositions are both false:

> (10) If I had taught a course on Aristotle last semester I would have assigned the Categories.
> (11) If I had taught a course on Aristotle last semester I would *not* have assigned the Categories.

As pointed out by Robert Adams, it is compatible with the falsity of both (10) and (11) that the following is true:

> (12) If I had taught a course on Aristotle last semester I would *probably* have assigned the Categories.

And it is compatible with the falsity of (10) and (11) that the following is true:

> (13) If I had taught a course on Aristotle last semester I *probably* would *not* have assigned the Categories.

So even though (12) is incompatible with (13), each is compatible with the negations of (10) and (11).[17]

So both (10) and (11) are false, and this means that principle CEM is false for counterfactuals as well as for subjunctive conditionals with true antecedents about the present. I have not argued, however, that there are *no* true would-counterfactuals with an antecedent such as (10) and (11). In fact, I am reasonably confident that there *are* some, and some no doubt express propositions about my free choices. So there are true counterfactuals of freedom. For example, I would claim the truth of the following:

(14) If I had taught a course on Aristotle last semester, I would not have primarily assigned readings from Hegel.

The truth of (14), means, I think, that certain well-known objections to middle knowledge are misplaced. We will look at some of these in the next section. My point here is simply that even though there are pairs of states of affairs, one earlier, one later, in which the obtaining of the earlier one is sufficient to determine that the later one *would* obtain, and even if some of the latter are freely brought about by human beings, we should not expect that given any state of affairs, it is either true that it would obtain, given its past, or it is true that it would not obtain, given its past.

We have considered subjunctive conditionals with true antecedents about the present and consequents about the future and subjunctive conditionals with false antecedents about the past and have seen that CEM fails in both cases. Subjunctive conditionals with true antecedents and where both antecedent and consequent are about the past form a special category. These propositions are peculiar, and I think there is more than one way to understand them. Suppose that I did, in fact, teach Aristotle last semester and that I did, in fact, assign the Categories. To assert (10) would certainly be misleading, since the form of (10) suggests that the antecedent is false. However, I might assert a structurally similar proposition about someone else if I did not know whether or not the antecedent is true.

(15) If David Blake had taught a course on Aristotle last semester, he would have assigned the Categories.

One way to understand propositions such as (15) is to see them as no different than the first category we have considered. We imagine a time prior to the time Blake teaches the Aristotle course and, since the future was open and Blake might or might not have assigned the Categories at that time, (15) is false, even though both antecedent and consequent are true. So on this way of interpreting (15), CEM fails for this group of subjunctive conditionals as well. We might call this the forward-looking interpretation of counterfactuals about the actual past. They are forward looking because we imagine a time in the past when the consequent of the conditional was still future. My preferred way to handle propositions in this class is to interpret them all as forward looking, but my argument in this section does not depend on it.

There is, however, another way to interpret (15). We can examine it from the viewpoint of the present. When doing so, we are looking backward on the states of affairs expressed in (15). In this case (15) seems true, unlike (6), which seems to me to be false even if both antecedent and consequent are true. Why is there this difference between (15) and (6)?

Our inclination to treat the two cases differently, I submit, can again be explained by the asymmetry of time. We treat the *counter*factual past as like the present or future, with an open future laying ahead of it, but we treat the factual past as fixed. That is, it seems fixed when we look backward on it from the vantage point of the present. If the antecedent is not about the actual past, it does not come under the necessity of the past, and so its counterfactual implications are open, just as they are for the future. If antecedent and consequent *are* about states of affairs in the actual past, the negation of the consequent is now precluded, although it is instructive that we usually do not use subjunctive conditionals at all in such cases. So at best, CEM holds for propositions about the actual past, but only because of the necessity of the past. I suggest that this is the reason there is a tendency to put *counter*factual conditionals in a separate category from the rare *factual* subjunctive conditionals in the past tense, and why *deliberative* future subjunctives are put in the same category with the counterfactuals, whether or not they are contrary to fact.

If I am right that counterfactual conditionals are a way of speaking about the past as if it were future, we can see what is wrong with a certain common argument in favor of the principle of CEM. There must be *something* I would assign if I taught Aristotle, the objector says, and of any option I would have, either I would choose it or I would not. A good way to *tell* what I would choose, although not a foolproof method, is actually to teach the course. For each pair of choices, whichever one I *do* choose is the one I *would* choose.

But if I am right about the connection between counterfactuals and the asymmetry of time, this objection misses the point. If CEM holds, there are no true might-counterfactuals except those entailed by would-counterfactuals. There are no pairs of true propositions of the form $A >$ *might B* and $A >$ *might not B*. But surely the *point* of might-counterfactuals is to indicate more than one branching path of possibilities compatible with the antecedent. And in the case of either the future, or any moment of time considered *as if* it were either present or future, there are branching paths ahead. To bring about the antecedent in order to find out if the consequent obtains is irrelevant, since then the imagined future becomes past.

CEM might get some of its plausibility from a confusion between the counterfactual "would" and the use of "would" to express the simple future relative to some past time. If ϕ is a nonconditional (absolute) future contingent,

It was true that it would be the case that ϕ

just means

The proposition *It will be the case that ϕ was* true.

So

(18) It was true in 1900 that Reagan would be elected president in 1984

is interpreted as

(19) The proposition *Reagan will be elected president in 1984* was true in 1900.

But this use of "would" is not the same as the use of "would" in the consequent of a counterfactual. So the truth of (18) and (19) should not lead us to think it is also true that

(20) If ϕ occurred in 1900, Reagan would be elected president in 1984.

The use of "would" in the consequent of a subjunctive conditional indicates a certain relation with the antecedent, a relation I have argued indicates the lack of branching paths from the state of affairs described in the antecedent to any state of affairs precluded by the consequent. So as long as it was the case in 1900 that Reagan might not be elected in 1984, (20) is false, even if (18) is true. At best, (20) is true only in those cases in which ϕ is something that *did* happen in 1900. And even then, it is true only when interpreted in the backward-looking rather than in the forward-looking manner.

Counterexamples to CEM have already appeared in the literature.[18] Some of the more well-known ones are unfortunate choices, however, and the defenders of middle knowledge are right to point out that these examples prove nothing.[19] For instance, Lewis offers the following as a counterexample:

(21) If Verdi and Bizet were compatriots, Bizet would be Italian.
(22) If Verdi and Bizet were compatriots, Bizet would not be Italian.

On Lewis's reasoning, there are worlds in which Verdi and Bizet are both French that are equally close to the actual world as worlds in which they are both Italian. Hence (21) and (22) are false and CEM fails.

Kvanvig and Wierenga have pointed out that propositions such as (21) and (22) both seem false largely because of our substantial ignorance about the intentions, inclinations, and opportunities of Verdi's and Bizet's respective parents. Furthermore, they claim, even if neither (21) nor (22) is true, this does not necessarily threaten middle knowledge, since the version of CEM required for middle knowledge does not require the truth of either (21) or (22).[20]

To see this point, consider the fact that on counterfactual logic, even if neither $A > B$ nor $A > \sim B$ is true, one of them may be true if the antecedent is strengthened. In other words, the fact that CEM fails for certain propositions A and B does not demonstrate that CEM fails if A is conjoined with some suitable proposition. The criteria for a successful theory given at the beginning of this chapter require only that for each set of possible circumstances A and possible choice B, there is some proposition ϕ that, when added to A, is such that either $(A \text{ and } \phi) > B$ or $(A \text{ and } \phi) > \sim B$ is true and that is knowable by God independently of anything but his prevolitional knowledge.

However, the argument I have given against CEM holds against this version as well. Assuming we have eliminated the possibility that $(A \text{ and } \phi) > B$ is backward looking, ϕ can include only states of affairs present or prior to the imagined states of affairs expressed by A. But, if so, no matter how much A is strengthened, no ϕ will be strong enough to eliminate the openness of the future relative to that time. Except for certain cases of true counterfactuals of freedom already noted, there will always be branching paths indicating the ways the future might turn out, and these branches are not eliminated even if we pack *all* of the past into the antecedent. So even though Kvanvig and Wierenga are quite right that middle knowledge does not require the truth of certain forms of CEM, my objection based on the asymmetry of time would hold against any version, including that required for middle knowledge.

Sometimes upholders of middle knowledge say that they are more sure that there are true counterfactuals of freedom than they are of the possible worlds interpretation of counterfactuals. So when they are confronted with an objection based on that semantics, they can always reject the semantics rather than the truth of their favorite examples of counterfactuals of freedom. Since I do not deny that there are true counterfactuals of freedom, this move is not directed against my position. But I think it fair to point out that the same argument can be made against the principle of CEM. I find that I am more sure of the truth of both (8) and (9) and the falsehood of both (10) and (11) than I am of the principle of CEM.

Defenders of middle knowledge often concentrate on arguing for the truth of particular counterfactuals of freedom. I have not denied that there are some and, for all I know, (1) and (2) might be examples, although I doubt it. In Chapter 4 I argued that there may even be strict implications of freedom, a claim I have not heard even from defenders of middle knowledge. However, I see no reason to believe that the principle of CEM holds for counterfactuals. In fact, I think there are strong intuitive reasons against it, at least as strong as the intuitions supporting the truth of anyone's favorite example of a counterfactual of freedom. Furthermore, these intuitions hold equally against the version of CEM required for middle knowledge.

In this section I have argued that the relation between the antecedent and the consequent of a counterfactual conditional is like the relation between the present and the future. Given that the present is what it is, there are many ways the future might be. It might include the election of one president or it might include the election of another; it might include my moving to one city or to another, or I might stay where I am. Each way the future might be can be represented by a branching path extending from the single path representing the actual past up to the present. There are also some ways the future *would* be, given that the past is what it is, so every branching path may include the same event. Some of these events are logical or causal consequences of the past, but not all are. As we saw in Chapter 4, the failure to reduce the causal relation to any common counterfactual shows that the counterfactual relation includes more than the relation of causal or logical necessity. So some ways the future would be, given the past, are not logical or causal consequences of the past, and some of these may even be determined to be so by human free choice.

So there are counterfactuals of freedom, but CEM is false. If it were true, this would in effect be to say that given the present as it is, there is only one future that would follow and no other future that might follow. But this is to think of the future as no different than the past. If I am right that the antecedent of a counterfactual conditional is considered like the present and the consequent like the future, CEM must be false for counterfactuals. This means it is not the case that for each contingent state of affairs, including each human choice, ϕ, there is a true proposition $\psi > \phi$, where ψ is knowable by God without knowing any contingent proposition except his own will, and where $\psi > \phi$ is knowable by God independently of everything except his prevolitional knowledge. This theory therefore cannot explain how God knows ϕ.

3. Objections to Middle Knowledge

A number of intriguing objections to middle knowledge have appeared in the literature, particularly those of Robert Adams and, more recently, William Hasker. In my opinion, some of these objections are overstated, and this weakens the position of those opposed to the theory. It seems to me to be fairly clear that the proponents of middle knowledge are right that certain counterfactuals of freedom are true. I suggested (12) as an example. Plantinga has claimed the truth of the following:

(23) If Adams were to ask me to go climbing at Tahquiz Rock the next time I come to California, I would gladly (and freely) accept.[21]

Weirenga has suggested that:

(24) If my daughter asked me for bread, I would not give her a stone.

I have no objections to the truth of (23) or (24), and it seems to me to obfuscate the problems with middle knowledge to insist that these propositions are false.[22] But the defense of the truth of certain carefully selected examples of counterfactuals of freedom is nowhere near sufficient to show the truth of the theory of middle knowledge, or even its plausibility. In Section 2 I argued that many free choices are not counterfactually implied by even the totality of the past up to the time of the choice, so God cannot know these choices by knowing counterfactuals and his own will. In this section I will consider some of the more important objections to middle knowledge already in the literature. I am sympathetic with some of these objections, but not others.

3.1. The No-grounds Objections

Adams has said that he does not know "what it would be" for counterfactuals of freedom to be true. Hasker has expressed his agreement with this objection and has, in addition, proposed a variation of it. There is no one, he says, who could coherently be said to "bring about" the truth of a counterfactual of freedom. Both Adams and Hasker say they are looking for the grounds of truth for such counterfactuals, and both argue that there aren't any. Both of them conclude that all such counterfactuals are false, although Adams had earlier taken the more cautious position that none are true.

Consider first Hasker's query about who or what could bring about a counterfactual of freedom. Hasker argues that a counterfactual of freedom must be contingent if it is to be applicable to middle knowledge, and apparently he thinks that all contingent propositions need somebody or something to bring about their truth.[23] We must be careful, however, of talk about *bringing about* the truth of any proposition. Such terminology suggests a causal relation that is, at best, misleading. I have no objections, though, to saying that the ground of truth of some proposition is my concrete act. So the truth of the proposition *Linda Zagzebski is looking at her computer screen* is grounded in my actual act of looking at the screen. The same relationship holds between modalized propositions and my acts in other possible worlds. For example, the proposition *It is possible that Linda Zagzebski visit Antarctica* is true in that there is some possible world, no doubt not the actual one, in which I visit Antarctica. We might take this to mean that my act in some *other* world grounds the truth of a proposition in *this* world. But there is nothing mysterious about this unless possible worlds semantics is itself mysterious, and it certainly does not suggest that my act in one world causes the truth of a proposition in another.

Now consider the proposition *If Linda Zagzebski hadn't read so many novels this year, she would have finished her book sooner.* On the possible worlds interpretation of this proposition, it is to be understood as saying that in some other world I read fewer novels and finish my book sooner than I do in the actual world, and that such a world is closer to the actual world than any world in which I read fewer novels and do not finish my book sooner. But what is so mysterious about that? To say I bring about the truth of this proposition in one world by my act in another world is only unacceptable if that relation is thought to be causal. But since the relation between acts and truth is probably not causal anyway, there is no worry that this interpretation of counterfactuals of freedom implies that my act in one world causes something in another. The possible worlds interpretation of counterfactuals gives us a way of understanding what those propositions say, and what they say is that certain things go on in some other possible worlds. But any modalized proposition does that much. If it is not bothersome in the case of *It is possible that Linda Zagzebski visit Antarctica*, it should not be bothersome in the case of counterfactuals of freedom either.

Adams's version of the objection is not primarily ontological. He says he cannot "see how" a counterfactual of freedom can be true. First, he considers and rejects the possibility that the antecedent of such a conditional necessitates the consequent, either logically or causally. I believe he is right to reject that possibility. Next he considers the possibility that the antecedent provides nonnecessitating grounds for the consequent in the agent's intentions, desires, and character. He argues that these character-istics would ground the truth of a "would probably" counterfactual, but not a "would" counterfactual. Apparently, he thinks that whatever the connection is between antecedent and consequent in a true "would" counterfactual, it prevents the consequent from being contingent in the senses needed for free will.

Adams's argument here is more convincing than it should be because he is probably right about his example. Although I have said there are true counterfactuals of freedom, I am very doubtful about the truth of

(25) If David remained in Keilah, Saul would besiege the city,

which is Adams's main example. However, I deny that we should reject the truth of (25) because the connection between antecedent and conse-quent in a true counterfactual precludes the consequent from having the contingency needed for free will. The best way to see this, I think, is to consider the failure of the current attempt to define the causal relation in terms of any commonly used subjunctive conditional. As we saw in Chapter 4, this failure demonstrates that the relation between the antece-dent and consequent in a counterfactual is weaker than that between a propostion and its logical or causal consequence. An act can therefore be both logically and causally contingent and related to some circumstance as the consequent is related to the antecedent in a "would" counterfac-tual. I have not, of course, said here *what the relation is* that holds between antecedent and consequent in a counterfactual, but only that whatever it is, it is weaker than the relation of logical or causal necessity. Adams need not worry, then, that the freedom of an act expressed as the consequent of a true counterfactual is precluded by lack of logical or causal contingency.

As a third possibility for the ground of truth of a counterfactual of freedom, Adams considers Suarez's view that the property of being an agent who would in circumstance S freely do a is a primitive property that some being c has, "although there is nothing either internal or external to c, except the property itself, which would make or determine c to have one of these properties rather than the other." But in response to this Adams says:

I do not think I have any conception, primitive or otherwise, of the sort of *habitudo* or property that Suarez ascribes to possible agents with respect to their acts under possible conditions. Nor do I think that I have any other primitive understanding of what it would be for the relevant subjunctive conditionals to be true.[24]

I am sympathetic with Adams's worry here, but I find it difficult to express the worry very clearly. Part of the problem may be an intuition that the property of being such that he would freely do *a* in circumstance *S* cannot be a primitive property because of the grammatical form in which the property is expressed. A similar form is used to express dispositional or supervenient properties—properties that are parasitic on more primitive properties, so it is natural to think this one also must be parasitic on more primitive properties of the agent. Whatever the underlying properties are, they must be dependent on the agent's will. Otherwise, it is hard to see how the agent can be responsible for the property of being such that he would freely do *a* in *S*. If I understand Adams correctly, he cannot bring himself to understand a counterfactual-of-freedom property as primitive and, at the same time, he is not hopeful that an account of such a property in terms of more primitive properties can be given. I also cannot bring myself to take Suarez's view that such a property is primitive. I know of no argument to that effect. On the other hand, I am more hopeful than Adams is that it can be understood as supervenient or in some other way derivative from other properties. As I have argued in Section 2, however, I find it impossible to believe that for *every* act-option and possible circumstance, I possess the property of what I would do in that circumstance. I have already defended this claim by examples and by the intuition of the asymmetry of time.

3.2. The Circularity Objection

There is another interesting objection to middle knowledge in the literature, and this one, I think, successfully refutes the Molinist version of the theory. This is an objection proposed by Adams and by Kenny. The objection is formulated in a way that assumes the similarity-of-worlds interpretation of counterfactuals, but I do not think the heart of the objection relies on the standard semantics. The objection does not deny that there are true counterfactuals of freedom or that God knows them. What it denies is that God can know them independently of his knowledge of anything but his natural knowledge. So clause (a) of the criteria for a successful theory given in Section 1.1 is violated. This means that even if there is such knowledge, it is not useful to God either in the creation or as a basis for foreknowledge. Wierenga has called this the "Not true soon enough" objection.

Adams expresses the objection as follows:

Consider a deliberative conditional,

[(26)] If I did x, y would happen.

Is [(26)] true? According to the possible worlds explanation, that depends on whether the actual world is more similar to some world in which I do x and y happens than to any world in which I do x and y does not happen. That in turn seems to depend on which world is the actual world. And which world is the actual world? That depends in part on whether I do x. Thus the truth of [(26)] seems to depend on the truth or falsity of its antecedent.[25]

Kenny expresses what I take to be the same objection this way:

Prior to God's decision to actualize a particular world those counterfactuals cannot yet be known: for their truth-value depends . . . on which world is the actual world. It is not simply that God's knowledge of these counterfactuals cannot be based on a decision which has to be taken subsequent to knowledge of them. . . . The problem is that what makes the counterfactuals true is not yet there at any stage at which it is undecided which world is the actual world. . . . The difficulty is simply that if it is to be possible for God to know which world he is actualizing, then his middle knowledge must be logically prior to his decision to actualize; whereas, if middle knowledge is to have an object, the actualization must already have taken place. As long as it is undetermined which action an individual human being will take it is undetermined which possible world is the actual world—undetermined not just epistemologically, but metaphysically.[26]

Plantinga dismisses the objection of Adams by pointing out that the "depends on" relation is not transitive. He says:

This argument, I fear, does not warrant the trust Adams apparently reposes in it. It is true that

[(27)] the truth of [(26)] depends upon which world is actual

in the sense that [(26)] is true in some worlds and false in others; it is also true that

[(28)] which world is actual depends on whether the antecedent of [(26)] is true

again, in the sense that the antecedent of [(26)] is true in some worlds and false in others. It doesn't follow, however, that the truth of [(26)] depends on the truth of its antecedent. Consider the following analogue:

[(27*)] the truth of The Allies won the Second World War depends on which world is actual;

[(28*)] which world is actual depends on whether I mow my lawn this afternoon;

therefore,

[(29*)] the truth of The Allies won the Second World War depends on whether I mow my lawn this afternoon.

Clearly, the relation expressed by the relevant sense of "depends on" isn't transitive.[27]

Plantinga's rejoinder is quoted approvingly by Wierenga in his discussion of middle knowledge.[28]

I cannot see, though, that Adams's and Kenny's point depends on the transitivity of the "depends on" relation. Their argument calls attention to a certain feature of the Molinist version of middle knowledge, the position that the truth of counterfactuals of freedom and God's knowledge of them is logically or explanatorily prior to God's volitional and postvolitional knowledge, or his knowledge of the actual. We might call this the Molinist constraint to distinguish this version of the theory of middle knowledge from the Banezian version. According to Banez counterfactuals of freedom are true *because* God wills them to be true; they are part of God's volitional knowledge. But given the Molinist constraint, the truths about the actual world are graded in a logical or explanatory order. Metaphysically necessary truths come first and are the objects of God's natural knowledge. Counterfactuals of freedom come next. They are contingent, yet prevolitional. Next come the truths about God's own will. God decides to bring about certain states of affairs directly and knows what these are. Finally, there are all other contingent truths, and these constitute the objects of God's postvolitional knowledge. The point of the theory of middle knowledge, of course, is that the truths in the final category can be fully explained by the truths in the other categories. That is, all God needs to know in order to have postvolitional knowledge is his natural knowledge, his knowledge of counterfactuals of freedom, and his knowledge of his own will.

If I understand Adams's and Kenny's argument, the possible worlds understanding of counterfactuals of freedom violates the Molinist constraint. The point is not that there are no true counterfactuals of freedom or that God knows them. The point is that their truth cannot be logically or explanatorily prior to the truth of all the contingent truths that are in the category of God's volitional and postvolitional knowledge. The argument does not require the transitivity of "depends on." It requires only that it be asymmetrical, as it surely is in this context. So the argument does not proceed from (27) and (28) to the conclusion of Adams and Kenny. Instead, the argument goes as follows.

(27) The truth of (26) depends on which world is actual.

That is, by the possible worlds interpretation of (26) the fact that a particular world is actual is logically prior to the fact that (26) is true. However,

(28**) Which world is actual depends on the truth of (26).

That is, by the Molinist constraint, the fact that (26) is true is logically prior to the fact that a particular world is actual. But (27) and (28**) are inconsistent.

Plantinga's response to this objection, I believe, would be to deny (27) in the sense of "depends on" intended in (27). Let us use the expression "the actual world" to refer attributively to whichever world is the actual world. So in *w1* "the actual world" refers to *w1*, in *w2* "the actual world" refers to *w2*, and so on. Plantinga points out that the truth of a counterfactual in the actual world is determined by the truth values of antecedent and consequent in worlds similar to the actual world, and that, of course, depends on which world is the actual world. But he seems to deny this in the sense of "depends on" that indicates logical or explanatory order. This is because one thing that helps determine similarity between worlds is the degree to which they share their counterfactuals. Plantinga says:

> Of course this means we can't look to similarity, among possible worlds, as explaining counterfactuality, or as founding or grounding it. (Indeed, any founding or grounding in the neighborhood goes in the opposite direction.) We can't say that the truth of $A \rightarrow C$ is explained by the relevant statement about possible worlds, or that the relevant similarity relation is what makes it true. But it doesn't follow that the possible worlds account of counterfactuals is viciously circular or of no use. In the same way we can't sensibly explain necessity as truth in all possible worlds; nor can we say that p's being true in all possible worlds is what makes p necessary. It may still be extremely useful to note the equivalence of *p is necessary* and *p is true in all possible* worlds: it is useful in the way diagrams and definitions are in mathematics; it enables us to see connections, entertain propositions and resolve questions that could otherwise be seen, entertained and resolved only with the greatest difficulty if at all.[29]

I interpret this passage from Plantinga as giving the following answer to the circularity objection. (27) is false because the determination of which world is actual is not logically or explanatorily prior to the determination of the truth value of a counterfactual. The truth value of a counterfactual $A > B$ in the actual world obviously depends on which world is the actual world in one sense of "depends on." But this is not to say that the determination of the actual world as one world rather than another is logically *prior* to the determination of the truth value of $A > B$.

This response is a reasonable one to one version of Adams's objection, but I do not think it avoids the fundamental difficulty. As I see it, the main problem can be expressed without reference to the current manner of assigning a truth value to counterfactuals on the basis of similarity of worlds. On the Molinist theory of middle knowledge adapted by Plantinga, there are true propositions such as (i) to (iii) of Section 1.1, and God knows them. Both Molina and Plantinga would say these propositions are contingent. They are, after all, just big counterfactuals of freedom. To say they are necessary conflicts with the standard semantics, but worse than that, it does not make sense. If there is any doubt about this, consider:

(i) If God created world-germ 1, world w1.2 would be actual.

(i) is, of course, true in world w1.2. But if (i) is a necessary truth, it would also be true in w1.1 and w1.3. But that is absurd. So (i) must be contingent. It is true in some worlds and not others. One of the worlds in which it is true is w1.2. It may also be true in some worlds in other galaxies. Whether the standard interpretation of counterfactuals in terms of world similarity can be used to determine its truth value in worlds in other galaxies is not the question. Perhaps it can and perhaps it cannot. In any case, (i) is true in w1.2 and in no other world in galaxy 1. In w1.1 (i) is false, and it is true instead that

(iv) If God created world-germ 1, world w1.1 would be actual.

And in w1.3 both (i) and (iv) would be false, and it would be true instead that

(v) If God created world-germ 1, world w1.3 would be actual,

and so on.

But there is a problem here. Suppose that the actual world is w1.2. On the Molinist theory, God's knowledge that

(vi) The actual world is w1.2

is explained by his knowledge of (i). So his knowledge of (i) is logically prior to his knowledge of (vi). But how can God know (i) logically prior to his knowledge of (vi)? How can he know that (i) is true and (iv) and (v) are false rather than that, say, (iv) is true and (i) and (v) are false without knowing (vi)? It would seem that the only explanation of his knowledge of (i) is his knowledge of (vi), but then, of course, the explanation is circular.

I understand the Adams and Kenny objections as different versions of this same point. The theory of middle knowledge seems backward. There is no reason or explanation for the truth of (i) other than the fact that the actual world is w1.2. But the theory of middle knowledge was supposed to explain the knowledge that the actual world is w1.2 by the knowledge of (i).

The only way out of this problem for the middle knowledge proponent, as far as I can see, is to admit that there is no explanation for God's knowledge of (i). Since the actual world is w1.2, (i) is true, and since it is true and God is omniscient, God knows (i). And that is all there is to say. But if this is the position, the function of the theory of middle knowledge in solving the foreknowledge problem has been completely abandoned. Why not just say instead that since w1.2 is the actual world (vi) is true, and since (vi) is true and God is omniscient, God knows (vi)? But this is, of course, totally unsatisfactory to those who feel the grip of the fore-knowledge dilemma. There is a problem of seeing how God *can* know certain truths. But that problem is as severe for the knowledge of (i) as it is for (vi). I cannot see, then, that a theory that explains God's knowledge of (vi) by his knowledge of (i) can succeed. I conclude that either the Plantinga position has the order of explanation of the truth of future contingents and counterfactuals of freedom backward, in which case the theory of middle knowledge cannot explain how God knows the absolute contingent future through this knowledge of counterfactuals of freedom, or the truth of conditional future contingents is just as logically primitive as the truth of absolute future contingents, in which case again knowledge of the former cannot explain knowledge of the latter. Either way, middle knowledge cannot explain foreknowledge.

This problem with middle knowledge also affects its ability to solve the problem of evil and the creation in the way outlined by Plantinga. Suppose God wants to see that world w1.2 is actualized. Can he do so by creating world-germ 1 and knowing (i)? It would seem not if he cannot know (i) logically prior to his knowledge that w1.2 is actual. Furthermore, there are problems even with his knowledge of very general counterfactuals, such as:

(vii) If God created world-germ 1, more good than evil would result

which, presumably, could be true in many worlds in galaxy 1. Could it be true in all of them? I do not see how it could if galaxy 1 includes the creation of free creatures, but let us see what would happen if (vii) *is* true in all worlds in galaxy 1. Even then, (vii) is not true in all worlds, since it is contingent. Let us say that it is not true in any of the worlds in galaxy 2. In that galaxy let us suppose it is true instead that:

(viii) If God created world-germ 2, more good than evil would result.

So in galaxy 1 (vii) is true and (viii) is false; in galaxy 2 (viii) is true and (vii) is false. But then how can God use his knowledge of the truth values of these propositions as part of a plan of creation? Plantinga defends the fact that God could use a proposition such as (vii) as a reason for creating what he created.[30] He could reason that if he were to create world-germ 1, (vii) would be true. Since he wants there to be more good than evil, he can use the creation of world-germ 1 as a means to that end since the creation of world-germ 1 also makes (vii) true.

I do not deny that God could reason that way. But I deny that that gives God a reason to create world-germ 1 rather than world-germ 2. If he did the latter, (viii) would be true and (vii) false. And, of course, there are an infinite number of other such alternatives. So even if a proposition such as (vii) is true in all worlds of some galaxy, an assumption I deny, this account would make God's choice of a world-germ to create arbitrary.

This objection to middle knowledge shows that Plantinga's solution to the problem of evil by way of middle knowledge is unsuccessful. My objection is not a general objection to the free will defense, however. In fact, as Plantinga has argued, if God does not have middle knowledge, the problem of evil is less difficult to answer, and Adams has shown that this is so on his position.[31] Furthermore, although my objection shows that middle knowledge cannot explain foreknowledge, it should be noted that even though Plantinga is a proponent of middle knowledge, he does not himself believe that foreknowledge proceeds by way of middle knowledge.[32]

4. Objections to My View on Middle Knowledge

My theory on middle knowledge is a moderate one. I have not denied that there are true counterfactuals of freedom or that God knows the ones there are, as other opponents of middle knowledge have done. What I have argued is that there are not enough of them to do the job of explaining foreknowledge. And I have argued that even if there were enough of them, God's knowledge of them could not be logically prior to his knowledge of the simple future contingents they are supposed to explain.

But some proponents of middle knowledge and even one vocal opponent have argued that foreknowledge without middle knowledge is useless.[33] Apparently what it is useless for is divine providence. Now it seems to me that foreknowledge is not valuable only as a means to the exercise of divine providence. Divine foreknowledge is important because foreknowledge is required by omniscience, and omniscience is essential to deity. But even so, it is important that my view on middle knowledge be consistent with the doctrine of divine providence. In this section I will argue that it is.

David Basinger has discussed a case in which a woman is trying to decide which of two men to marry. Middle knowledge is critical to God's ability to help her, he argues.

> For example, in the case of Sue's marriage proposals, a God with MK is not limited to knowing only what might or will in fact happen. He knows before he gives guidance to Sue exactly what would happen if she marries Tom, exactly what would happen if she marries Fred, and exactly what would happen if she marries neither. He knows, for instance, if Tom would still love her thirty years after their marriage or if Sue would meet someone better if she refused both proposals. Accordingly, Sue can be assured she is getting infallible, long-term advice. To the extent to which she believes she has correctly discerned God's guidance on this issue, and has acted in accordance with it, she need never wonder whether she has made a mistake—i.e., whether things would have been better if she had acted differently. No matter what problems develop, she can steadfastly believe that she is pursuing the best "life-plan" available to her.[34]

There is something appealing about the work of God in Sue's life as described in this passage. Nonetheless, I find myself unable to believe that this is the way it works, even on the assumption that God is inclined to give Sue direct advice. God certainly knows and could advise Sue about the truth of counterfactuals based on natural necessity, and he could also advise her that certain counterfactuals of freedom about Tom and Fred are true; for example, if she married Fred, he would never intentionally bring serious harm to any of their children. But she probably knows most of the important ones in this category already. I do not see that God could tell her that if she married Tom she would be happy in 30 years, or that she would be happier with Tom than with Fred. Presumably, he would tell her that she might be happy with Tom and she might not be. To the extent to which happiness is the result of human choice, it is up to her and Tom, as well as perhaps other persons who would significantly affect their lives, such as their children. To the extent to which happiness is the result of circumstances that occur by natural necessity, God could inform her of those circumstances. So he could tell her that if she married Fred this summer he would develop multiple sclerosis within 3 years. This means that at best he could tell her that she would *probably* be happier with Tom than with Fred, and I would think that that is all the advice she would be looking for.

Of course, whether or not we can expect to be given certain divine guidance is not the deeper issue. Whatever view we have of God's knowledge, it is important to Christian belief that God never lose control of his creation and that he always be able to bring it to the end he has in mind. This includes bringing good out of evil, and probably many other, more particular ends. How can God do this without the full range of middle knowledge?

On the view I have defended in this chapter, God knows that if he creates world-germ N, any one of the worlds in galaxy N might result, but there isn't any particular one that *would* result. God does not intend that, say, world w2.3 be actual and so creates world-germ 2 as a means to that end. He cannot do this because it is not true that if he created world-germ 2, w2.3 would be actual, and it is not true even if w2.3 *is* in fact the actual world. The Plantinga picture is attractive because it describes God as acting in order to see that a particular chain of events, down to every particular, becomes actualized. And it is attractive because God need not fear that some world other than the one he wants becomes actualized instead. Presumably, some of those worlds in galaxy 2 are well worth fearing.

But rather than glorify God's omnipotence, as this picture is intended to do, it seems to me actually to detract from it. Recall that each world in galaxy 2 includes not only all the actions of free creatures, but God's responses to those actions as well. To think it necessary that God be assured that w2.3 result rather than, say, w2.4, is to say that God would somehow be defeated in w2.4. Things would get to such a point in that world that he would be at a loss as to how to respond, so it is much safer if he always knows that a particular chain of events would result from any one of his own creative choices and can count on the actual world being w2.3 rather than w2.4 or something else even worse.

But surely God does not have such worries. Why couldn't an omnipotent and omniscient being have a providential plan for *each* world that might result from his creative choice?[35] If he can do it for one world, he can do it for an infinite number of them. Isn't it likely that God is able to respond to *whatever* free creatures bring about in a way that he can lead to his own ends? To deny this is to deny his omnipotence. And if God is able to do this, middle knowledge would not be necessary for providence. It seems to me that this is, in fact, the way it is.

6

Two More Solutions of My Own

1. Introduction

In Chapter 1 I presented what I think is the strongest version of the foreknowledge dilemma—the Accidental Necessity Version. In Chapters 2, 3, and 5 we looked at a series of attempted solutions to this dilemma. I argued that the Boethian, Ockhamist, and Molinist solutions are unsuccessful as they stand, but I proposed a solution I called Thomistic Ockhamism that I think is successful. In this chapter I will present two more solutions to the dilemma and will argue that they solve both the Accidental Necessity Version of the foreknowledge dilemma and what I have called the Timeless Knowledge Dilemma. I will conclude with a new model of divine foreknowledge.

The argument against free will from accidental necessity was formulated in Chapter 2 as follows:

Argument from Accidental Necessity

(1) God's belief at $t1$ that I will do S at $t3$ is accidentally necessary at $t2$.

(2) If A is accidentally necessary at t and A is strictly equivalent to B, then B is accidentally necessary* at t.

(3) God's belief at $t1$ is strictly equivalent to my act at $t3$.

(4) So my act at $t3$ is accidentally necessary* at $t2$.

(5) If my act at $t3$ is accidentally necessary* at $t2$, I cannot do otherwise than bring about that act at $t3$.

(6) If when I bring about an act I cannot do otherwise, I do not bring it about freely.

(7) Therefore, I do not bring about my act at $t3$ freely.

In Chapter 2 we examined the Boethian solution. This solution denies premise (1) on the grounds that God is not in time. In Chapter 3 we examined the Ockhamist solution. This solution denies that God's past beliefs are accidentally necessary. In this chapter I will propose a solution that denies (6), and one that shows that either (1), (2), or (3) is false. I will then focus in particular on the denial of (2).

2. Free Will and the Ability to Do Otherwise

2.1. First Solution

In this section I will argue that even if all my acts are accidentally necessary*, they can still be done freely in a sense of "free" that is incompatible with determinism. The argument will first involve showing that the following is false:

(6) If when I bring about an act I cannot do otherwise, I do not bring it about freely.

The rejection of (6) is not sufficient to get a solution to the foreknowledge dilemma, however, because accidental necessity* might deprive me of freedom for a reason other than that expressed by (6). Compare, for example, the last three steps of the argument from accidental necessity with the analogous argument from causal necessity.

(5') If my act at $t3$ is causally necessary at $t2$, I cannot do otherwise than bring about that act at $t3$.
(6) If when I bring about an act I cannot do otherwise, I do not bring it about freely.
(7) Therefore, I do not bring about my act at $t3$ freely.

But even though (6) is false, it is still the case that if my act is causally necessary I do not bring it about freely. This is because causal necessity deprives me of freedom, not because it makes it the case that I cannot do otherwise, but for another reason that we will soon address. Similarly, even if (6) is false, accidental necessary* might deprive me of freedom for a parallel reason. The first solution of this chapter, then, must show both that (6) is false and that there is no reason other than (6) to think that accidental necessity* deprives my act of freedom. I think this can be done convincingly and that it can be done in a way that maintains a definition of free will that is incompatible with determinism.

Frankfurt has proposed a class of examples that can be taken to be counterexamples to (6).[1] The focus of his discussion is on the relationship between the ability to do otherwise and moral responsibility, but we can just as well use his examples to illustrate the relationship between the ability to do otherwise and acting freely.

The examples all have the following form:[2] A person is in the process of deciding between *A* and *not-A*. She decides to perform *A* and does *A*. Unknown to her, however, there are conditions present at the time of the choice that would have prevented her from deciding *not-A* if she had been about to decide *not-A*. These conditions played no role in her actual choice, however, since she decided to do *A* anyway.

Fischer describes a simple Frankfurt-style example that presses the point of these cases in an especially vivid way.[3] We are to imagine that Black is an insane neurosurgeon who inserts a mechanism into Jones's brain that enables Black to monitor and control Jones's neurological activities. For example, at the time of the Reagan-Carter election, if Jones's neurological activity indicates that he is on the verge of deciding to vote for Carter, Black's mechanism intervenes and brings it about that he votes for Reagan instead. On the other hand, if Jones decides to vote for Reagan on his own, the control mechanism does not go into operation. It monitors but does not affect Jones's neurological activity.

Now suppose that Jones decides to vote for Reagan on his own without any "help" from the mechanism inserted by Black. Frankfurt would claim, and Fischer agrees, that he is just as responsible for that act as he would have been if there had been no mechanism in his brain. After all, even though the mechanism had the capability of controlling him, in fact it did not. The explanation of his choice is exactly as it would have been without the mechanism. Of course, it *might have turned out* that the mechanism controlled his choice, but his responsibility depends on what actually happens, not on what might have happened. This seems to me to be the right conclusion to draw from this example. I would claim that it shows both that Jones is responsible for the act in question and that he did it freely. It is clear, however, that conditions obtained at the time of the choice that made it impossible for him to choose otherwise. I think, then, that Fischer's example shows the falsity of (6).

This example is a sophisticated variation of a well-known case described by Locke. In Locke's example, a person decides to remain in a room, although, unknown to him, the door is locked and he would not have been able to leave anyway. Again, it looks as if the act is free because the fact that he could not have done otherwise plays no part in the decision, although it might have. The locked door indicates that his act *might not* have been free, not that it *was not* free.[4]

It does not follow, however, that free will is compatible with determinism. Fischer has expressed this point well as follows:

[T]here are two ways in which it might be true that one couldn't have done otherwise. In the first way, the actual sequence compels the agent to do what he does, so he couldn't have initiated an alternate sequence; in the second way, there is no actual-sequence compulsion, but the alternate sequence would prevent the agent from doing other than he actually does. Frankfurt's examples involve alternate-sequence compulsion; the incompatibilist about determinism and responsibility can agree with Frankfurt that in such cases an agent can be responsible even while lacking control, but he will insist that, since determinism involves actual sequence compulsion, Frankfurt's examples do not establish that responsibility is compatible with determinism.[5]

So, according to Fisher, if determinism holds, it deprives my act of freedom because the prior conditions that make me unable to do otherwise play a role in the actual occurrence of my act, whereas the conditions that make Jones unable to do otherwise in the Frankfurt-Fischer case play no role in the actual occurrence of his act.

The difference can be put in another way that Fischer does not mention. What is objectionable about determinism is that in a deterministic world, if the cause of an event had not occurred, the event would not have occurred either. For example, we can truly say that if some match had not been struck, it would not have lit. Give determinism, each choice is counterfactually dependent on the conditions that make it impossible to do otherwise. If those conditions had not obtained, the choice would not have been made.[6] In the Frankfurt-Fischer case, in contrast, Jones seems free because his act would have occurred without the mechanism that prevented it from being otherwise. If Black had not inserted the mechanism into Jones's brain, Jones would have voted for Reagan anyway. Jones's act is counterfactually independent of the mechanism that makes him unable to do otherwise. So if causal determinism holds, my act is counterfactually dependent on previous events that make me unable to do otherwise. But in the case of Jones and related examples, his act is not counterfactually dependent on previous events, or at least need not be. And this difference is crucial to the kind of power necessary for free choice.

If this is right, it has some interesting implications for the foreknowledge problem. First, it shows that even if God's foreknowledge is a condition obtaining at the time of my choice that is incompatible with my choosing otherwise, this fact is not sufficient to show that I do not have free will in a sense that is incompatible with determinism. Second, it shows that if determinism is incompatible with free will for a reason other than the fact that it makes it impossible to do otherwise, accidental necessity* might be incompatible with free will for a parallel reason. So to show that accidental necessity* does not deprive me of freedom for the same reason that causal necessity deprives me of freedom, it must be clear that my choice is counterfactually independent of God's foreknowledge. My choice must be as independent of God's foreknowledge as Jones's choice is independent of Black's mechanism.

I will argue in Section 2.2 that there is an important disanalogy between the foreknowledge case and the Frankfurt-style examples that make it the case that I *can* do otherwise in the foreknowledge case. But for the purposes of the present solution, I will accept the position that God's foreknowledge makes it impossible for me to do otherwise and will argue that even so, I can act freely.

The foreknowledge case, like the Frankfurt-Fischer case, can be understood as a case of modal overdetermination. To see the relationship between the conditions that overdetermine some event, let us consider first causal overdetermination, the familiar variety of modal overdetermination.

Some automobiles have automatic doorlock buttons on both the driver side and the passenger side of the front seat. Suppose the driver presses the button on his side at *t1* and the passenger independently presses the button on her side at *t2* a fraction of a second later. The doors lock at *t3*. The passenger's act is causally sufficient for locking the doors, even though conditions causally sufficient for locking the doors already obtain at *t2*. It is natural to think that the act of the driver is the actual cause of the doors locking because it occurs first. But if, for some reason, the mechanism on the driver's side did not work, the act of the passenger would have caused the doors to lock. Because the acts of the driver and the passenger are independent of each other, we might say it is just an accident that the driver's act caused the doors to lock rather than the passenger's act. The event of the doors locking is causally overdetermined because each of two independent events is causally sufficient for its occurrence.

There are cases similar to this in which we are asked to judge the moral responsibility of an agent who performs an act causally sufficient for a causally overdetermined event. In a puzzle of this sort we suppose that Jack is given a canteen of poison by Jill before his trek into the desert. Jim, who also wants Jack to die and who does not know about the poison, subsequently pokes holes in Jack's canteen. All the poison leaks out and Jack dies of lack of water in the desert. Who is responsible for his death? Jim's act caused him to die of dehydration, but he would have died anyway due to the action of Jill. In this case it is not so easy to say which of the two sufficient conditions for Jack's death is the causally efficacious one. But whichever it is, it is only an accident that that act caused the death rather than the other one, and we might hold Jill and Jim equally blameworthy.

Now if God has foreknowledge, each event is modally overdetermined, but one of the overdetermining events is not a cause. God's belief at $t1$ is logically sufficient for my act at $t3$, although I argued in Chapter 4 that we need not claim that it is causally sufficient. That is, it may play no part in the causal history of my act at $t3$. Suppose that at $t2$ I make a decision to do S at $t3$, and assume that my decision is sufficient for my subsequent act. Nevertheless, at $t2$ conditions sufficient for my act already obtain.

These two examples have some structural features in common with the Frankfurt examples. The driver performs an act that brings about the locking of the car doors. But if he had not chosen to press the lock button, the doors would have locked anyway due to an independent mechanism. The driver seems to be responsible for locking the doors even though *he* could not have made it otherwise than that the doors locked. Now what about the responsibility of the passenger who also presses the door lock? She does not actually cause the locking of the door, but she might have, and it is only an accident that she does not. Similarly, either Jill or Jim brings about Jack's death, and it is only accidental that the one who does not do so does not do so. Also, as long as they act independently, neither of them could have made it otherwise than that Jack died.[7]

Suppose we think of God's forebelief as analogous to the act of the driver in pressing his lock button and my choice as analogous to the act of the passenger in pressing her lock button. The difference is that God's belief is not in the causal history of my act, and so it does not causally necessitate my act, although it does make it accidentally necessary*. So my act is modally overdetermined, but not causally overdetermined. If we can find a clear sense in which my decision occurs independently of God's belief, just as the pressing of the two doorlock buttons can occur independently of each other and Jill and Jim's acts occur independently of each other, we can make a case that my act is accidentally necessary* in a literal sense of "accidental." It is necessary "by accident" and free because it would have occurred in the absence of the accident.

We said that in the Fischer example Jones is free because he would have behaved the same way in the absence of the necessitating condition. If Black had not installed the control mechanism in Jones's brain, Jones would still have voted for Reagan. If we can make a case that if God had not believed at *t1* that I would do *S* at *t2*, I would have done so anyway, then my act would be as free as the act of Jones in voting for Reagan.

Unfortunately, the analysis of the proposition

(8) If God had not believed that I would do *S* at *t3*, I would have done *S* at *t3* anyway

is problematic. There is a tendency to assume all necessary truths as background suppositions in the evaluation of counterfactuals. So if it is a necessary truth that God is omniscient, and if this necessary truth is assumed to hold under all counterfactual conditions, (8) is false.

On the other hand, the standard semantics interprets all counterfactuals with necessarily false antecedents as vacuously true. This means it would be vacuously true that:

(9) If God were not omniscient and had not believed that I would do *S* at *t3*, I would have done *S* at *t3* anyway.

I have argued elsewhere that it is a serious philosophical mistake to consider all counterfactual conditionals with necessarily false antecedents as vacuously true.[8] To do so prevents us from seeing the special connection certain metaphysically necessary truths have with certain contingent truths. To see this, consider the following pair of propositions:

(10) If God had not been good, he might not have created Eve.
(11) If God had not been good, he would have created Eve anyway.

Surely (10) and (11) are not on a par, although both have necessarily false antecedents. (10) seems to me to be true and (11) false. But without any way of distinguishing between (10) and (11) we have no way of indicating what effect God's goodness has on the world. If God is both necessarily existent and essentially good, and if all conditionals with the antecedent of (10) and (11) are vacuously true, then we are prevented by the semantics of counterfactuals from expressing the fact that God's goodness has a special connection to certain contingent events and not others.

Likewise, consider the following pair of propositions:

(12) If God were not omniscient and had not believed that I would do *S* at *t3*, I might not have done *S* at *t3*.
(9) If God were not omniscient and had not believed that I would do *S* at *t3*, I would have done *S* at *t3* anyway.

(12) and (9) also do not seem to me to be on a par, only in this case it is (9) that seems true and (12) that seems false. Again, without any way of

distinguishing between (12) and (9), we have no way of indicating which events in the future depend on God's foreknowledge and which do not. And this is the case whether we take the compatibilist position on foreknowledge and freedom or whether we take the incompatibilist position. If God's foreknowledge interferes with my freedom in a way analogous to the way causes interfere with my freedom, then my act should turn out to be counterfactually dependent on God's foreknowledge, and (12) should be true and (9) false. Since on the standard semantics both (12) and (9) are trivially true, the claim of counterfactual dependency is vacuous. This means that the standard semantics prevents us from expressing *either* the fact that my act is counterfactually dependent on God's foreknowledge *or* the fact that my act is counterfactually independent of God's foreknowledge. Surely it is one or the other. I claim that it is more reasonable to interpret (9) as true and (12) as false. This requires a revision of the standard semantics but, as we have seen, such a revision would be necessary in any case.

The defense of the nontrivial truth of (9) depends on the acceptance of the nontrivial truth of the following propositions:

(13) If God had not been omniscient, he *might* not have believed at *t1* that I would do *S* at *t3*.

(14) I would have done *S* at *t3* even if God had not believed at *t1* that I would.

Taking the Lewis-Pollock definition of the might-counterfactual, we get the following analysis of (13) and (14): (13) is equivalent to:

(13a) ~ (If God were not omniscient then he would forebelieve my act *S*.)

Assuming that it is necessarily false that God is not omniscient, the standard semantics makes (13a) false. But it seems to me that (13) and (13a) are true. How can this be? I suggest that a sentence of the form of (13):

If *P* were false it might be that *Q* is false,

is true as long as there is no *R* that would be true if *P* were false that entails *Q*. If *P* is necessarily true, what might be the case if *P* is false? If certain metaphysically necessary truths are explanations for the truth of other propositions, then it is reasonable to say that if they were false, these other propositions might be false. If God's omniscience is metaphysically necessary and is the explanation of his belief in future truths, it is reasonable to say that if God had not been omniscient he might not have believed such truths. If so, it is reasonable to interpret (13) as true, and nonvacuously so.

Taking the Pollock definition of the "even if" counterfactual, (14) is equivalent to:

(14a) I do S at $t3$ and there is no R that might be true if God did not foreknow my act S and that together with God's not foreknowing S necessitates S.

But surely (14a) is true.

Now if (13) and (14) are both true, then (8) is true. If (8) is true, this means that in considering what states of affairs some event counterfactually depends on, we have every right to ignore some metaphysically necessary truths. That is, we may consider an event E as if these necessary truths were not true. Of course, the falsehood of one of these truths N might affect the occurence of E, but the only way to find that out is to consider in a nontrivial way what would have been the case had N been false. So, for example, God's goodness is metaphysically necessary and is also counterfactually connected to the creation of Eve. So it is nontrivially true that if God had not been good Eve might not have been created. On the other hand, it is nontrivially true that if, *per impossibile*, God had not infallibly believed that I would do what I did, I would have done it anyway.

So it is reasonable to consider (8), (13), and (14) as true. This means my act does not counterfactually depend on God's foreknowledge, and hence accidental necessity* does not deprive my act of freedom for a reason analogous to the reason causal necessity deprives my act of freedom.

I suggest that it is acceptable to adopt the following definition of free choice, one that is satisfied on the view I have proposed in this section, even if God foreknows each and every choice.

Definition of Free Choice

A choice is free if and only if a) it could have not occurred even if the causal history of that choice had been identical to the one that actually obtains and b) it would still have occurred even if non-causally necessitating factors had not obtained.[9]

This definition is incompatible with causal determinism.

I have argued in this section that even if divine foreknowledge makes it the case that all my choices are accidentally necessary* and are such that I cannot do otherwise, it does not follow that my choices are not free. To demonstrate this, I first argued that the inability to do otherwise is compatible with a reasonable notion of free will that is incompatible with determinism. I then argued that the reason causal determinism takes away free will is not that it makes it the case that I cannot do otherwise, but that it makes it the case that my choices counterfactually depend on previous states of affairs. But I suggested that it is reasonable to say that my choices do not counterfactually depend on God's foreknowledge in a way analogous to the way events counterfactually depend on their causes. I pointed out that this claim requires a revision of the standard semantics of counterfactuals, but that such a revision would be necessary to express the contrary position as well. If the argument I have given expresses at least a possible interpretation of the relation between God's foreknowledge and my choices, this is a satisfactory negative solution to the dilemma of this book. To the extent to which this theory is plausible it is, or can be developed into, a positive solution to the dilemma.

2.2. Second Solution

In Section 2.1 I proposed a solution to the dilemma of foreknowledge and freedom that concedes that my acts are all accidentally necessary* due to God's foreknowledge. It also concedes that this means that I cannot act differently than I do, given the conditions that obtain at the time of my act. However, I argued that it is a mistake to conclude from this that my acts are not free in a strong sense of freedom that is incompatible with determinism. The idea was that the conditions that make it the case that I cannot do otherwise have nothing to do with my choice. I do not do what I do because I cannot do otherwise; my act does not counterfactually depend on the conditions that make it such that it cannot be otherwise.

In this section I wish to turn to another solution to the dilemma from accidental necessity. I will argue that an important disanalogy between the foreknowledge case and the Frankfurt-Fischer cases makes it most reasonable to maintain that in the former case I *can* do otherwise. If so, it is not necessary to alter the definition of free choice in the manner suggested in Section 2.1. I will attempt to show that given God's fore-knowledge, I can still do otherwise, and therefore, either (1), (2), or (3) in the argument from accidental necessity (p. 153) must be false. I will conclude the section with an argument supporting the denial of (2). This solution understands the relationship between God's foreknowledge and my act in a way that is closer to the traditional view on that relationship. Unlike the solution of Section 2.1, it will not include the idea that God's knowledge and my choice are independent of each other.

The foreknowledge case is different from the Frankfurt and Locke examples in a critical respect. In the Locke example I choose to remain in the room even though, unknown to me, the door is locked. This means, presumably, that there is a possible world very similar to the actual one in which I choose to leave the room but am prevented from doing so by the locked door. In the Frankfurt-Fischer example an insane neurologist is prepared to prevent Jones from choosing Carter, but he need not intervene, since Jones chooses Reagan anyway. In this case also we assume that there is a similar world in which Jones is about to choose Carter but is prevented from doing so by the neurologist.

But in the case of divine foreknowledge, we assume that in *every* world in which someone makes a choice, God foreknows the correct choice in that world. The analogue in the Locke example would be one in which in every world in which I choose to stay in the room I am, unknown to me, prevented from leaving, and in every world in which I choose to leave I am, unknown to me, prevented from staying. The analogue in the Frankfurt-Fischer example would be one in which in every world in which Jones chooses Reagan the neurologist is prepared to prevent him from choosing Carter, and in every world in which Jones chooses Carter the neurologist is prepared to prevent him from choosing Reagan. We need to fill out the analogy further to see how this can be.

Let us suppose that the Frankfurt neurologist is not insane, but is benign and loving, and is not just powerful, but is more powerful than any human neurologist could be. Assume also that I have less power to choose on my own than I think. In fact, I am actually unable to choose anything completely by my own power. Suppose that what I do by myself is necessary for my choice, but what the neurologist does is necessary for my choice also, and they are jointly sufficient. Neither is sufficient by itself, although each is sufficient in the sense that in every world in which it occurs the choice follows, since the one never occurs in any world without the other.[10]

Let us imagine that what the neurologist actually does is not independent of my action but is supportive and reinforcing of my own activity. The neurologist acts in such a way that when I do as much as I can in the direction of choosing A, he helps me make the choice of A, and this activity prevents me from choosing *not-A*. When I do as much as I can in the direction of choosing *not-A*, he helps me choose *not-A*, and his activity prevents me from choosing A. Furthermore, imagine that the neurologist and his reinforcing mechanism are operative in every world in which I exist and am faced with the choice of A or *not-A*. So there is no world in which the neurologist acts in a direction contrary to my own will. Applied to foreknowledge this model could be taken as an explanation of Aquinas' otherwise puzzling claim that God brings it about that I act freely: "Those words of the Apostle are not to be taken as though man does not wish or does not run of his free choice, but because the free choice is not sufficient for this unless it be helped and moved by God."[11]

So unlike the Frankfurt-style examples, it is not true that I am not free in closely similar worlds. It is not the case that the mechanism that prevents me from choosing differently thwarts my will in any world. Suppose that I choose *not-A* in the actual world. On our new expanded model we need to say that there is no world in which I try to choose *A*, but am prevented from doing so by the mechanism in operation in the actual world. Furthermore, there *are* worlds in which I choose *A* that are just like the actual world except that the will-reinforcing mechanism reinforces the choice of *A* instead of the choice of *not-A*. It is unreasonable, I believe, to describe this scenario as one in which I am not able to do otherwise.

If this is right, then even though God foreknows infallibly everything I will to do and even simultaneously wills everything I will, I can still do otherwise.[12] But if I can do otherwise, then either premise (1), (2), (3), or (5) of the argument for theological fatalism is false. So either (1) it is false that God's past knowledge (and willing) is accidentally necessary, (2) TNP 2 ($Nec_w\ p\ and\ Nec\ (p \longleftrightarrow q), \vdash Nec_w\ q$) is invalid, (3) God's foreknowledge is not strictly equivalent to my choice, or (4) my choice is accidentally necessary* but I can still choose otherwise. Option (4) is probably incoherent. I argued for option (1) on independent grounds in Chapter 3, and I think the preceding argument strengthens the argument of that chapter. In Chapter 3 I also argued on independent grounds for option (3). Again, the argument of this section can be used to strengthen that argument. Here I would like to consider the final option, choice (2). Are there any good reasons to deny premise (2) of the argument from accidental necessity?

Premise (2) is an application for the case of accidental necessity of the following TNP:

Transfer of Necessity Principle 2

$$Nec_w\ p,\ Nec\ (p \longleftrightarrow q) \vdash Nec_w\ q^{13}$$

This principle is on the face of it so plausible that it is difficult to see how anyone could devise a counterexample that is more plausible than the principle. But let us see how far we can shake it.

We saw in Chapter 5, Section 1.2, that part of Molina's solution was to reject, without argument, the following weaker TNP:

Transfer of Necessity Principle 1

$$Nec_w\ p,\ Nec\ (p \rightarrow q), \vdash Nec_w\ q$$

Recently Michael Slote has argued that this principle is false for certain kinds of necessity. He says the principle fails for epistemic and deontic necessity and that the necessity of unavoidability may contain epistemic elements sufficient to unhinge it from the transfer principle. Assuming that accidental necessity is a form of the necessity of unavoidability, Slote's argument may be relevant to our concerns here. Furthermore, Slote argues, the preceding transfer principle fails for nonaccidentality, another type of necessity close to the one relevant to our discussion. Let us briefly consider this argument, since it comes the closest that I know of in the literature to casting doubt on TNP 1 for unavoidability.

Slote argues as follows:

> Nonaccidentality . . . appears not to be closed under entailment. It may be no accident that I am in a certain place right now (I was sent there by a superior in accordance with a routine plan of business operation), yet nevertheless be an accident that I am still alive right now (only an accidental and unintentional swerve on my part has just prevented me from being flattened by a runaway truck). Failing that, it may at least be an accident that I ever exist at all (imagine a suitable tale of contraceptive woes), yet that too is entailed by my being where I am at the present moment. If closure thus fails for nonaccidentality, we can perhaps go on to deny that it is governed by our main modal principle [what I have called TNP 1], on the grounds that in the above cases where it is no accident that I am at a certain place and yet something of an accident that I still (or ever) exist, it is also (on trivial logical grounds) no accident that if I am at that place, then I still (or at some time) exist.[14] (Bracketed note mine.)

The examples in this argument may not be perfectly convincing. Even if they are, they are not sufficient to call into question the stronger TNP 2 that is used in the argument that God's essential omniscience makes our acts accidentally necessary*. However, Slote's examples have helped me see how the argument of this section can be used to deny the stronger transfer principle.

In the story in Section 2.1 the neurologist reinforces and supports each of my choices, and he would have reinforced each of the choices I would have made, no matter what else was the case. Some of my choices I make with the appropriate deliberation, but some choices I may make randomly or in some other way. Suppose, for example, I find myself faced with the choice of several buttons to push on a soft drink machine. Unable to choose in a nonrandom manner, I simply pick one and push. By hypothesis, I am not capable by myself of choosing to push a button, whether or not it is after deliberating. Each time I make a choice of any kind, the neurologist helps me complete the act of choosing after I go as far as I am able to go in the direction of making a choice. Let us call the neurologist's activity in bringing it about that I choose to push the button *Bn*, and my own activity in choosing *Bl*. It is reasonable on this story to say that it is not an accident that *Bn* occurs, that it is not an accident that *Bn* occurs if and only if *Bl* occurs, but it is an accident that *Bl* occurs. It is an accident that I do what I do in the direction of choosing the particular button I choose, but it is not an accident that the neurologist reinforces the choice I make, nor is it an accident that he reinforces whatever choice I make in any world. After all, he has deliberately set up a system to accomplish this. This means, then, that in the case in which necessity is interpreted as nonaccidentality, TNP 2 fails. If so, and if accidental necessity is a type of nonaccidentality, premise (2) of the argument at the beginning of this chapter is false.

I believe we can also find counterexamples to TNP 2 for senses of necessity other than nonaccidentality due to intelligent choice. Let us consider causal necessity. Many people believe there are causally accidental events in nature, by which I mean a physical event whose occurrence is not entailed by the conjunction of causal laws and previous events. If there are such events their causal consequences are themselves causally necessitated, since they are entailed by the conjunction of causal laws and previous events. Some of these causal consequences might also be such that they can be caused only by their actual causes. In these cases the actual cause would be both causally necessary and causally sufficient for the effect. The cause and effect occur in exactly the same worlds with our causal laws.

It might be objected that a causally accidental event makes its immediate causal consequences accidental as well. I have not heard of a good reason for thinking this to be the case but, even if it is, surely it is too much to say that *every* causal descendant on into the indefinite future is rendered accidental, for that would be to make too much of what goes on in an almost-deterministic universe accidental. In fact, eventually it might make everything accidental. It is clear, then, that at some point in the sequence of causal consequences of some causally accidental event the events become causally necessary.

Now let us consider two examples of causally accidental events.[15] In the first example let B be a particular occurrence of a genetic mutation, that is, a change in the nucleotide sequence or structure of a strand of DNA. Such a mutation is a chance event in the sense that we have no way of predicting the occurrence of this event at any time in this organism, nor do we know what the physical factors are that result in this mutation. It is not clear, then, that the mutation occurs as a result of specifiable physical causes at all. Mutations may occur spontaneously, without any assignable cause(s). If so, they are causally accidental in the sense I am considering. Their occurrence is not entailed by the conjunction of previous events and causal laws.

Let A be the phenotypic effect of the mutation B in a descendant of the organism in which B occurs. A might be the inability to discriminate sweet and salty, for example. We will assume a case in which the reproductive processes leading to the existence of the descendant are themselves causally necessary. Now it is the case that in all worlds with our causal laws if B occurs A occurs, and if A occurs B preceded it. This judgment could be empirically supported by investigations that show that there are occurrences of the type A if and only if there are occurrences of the type B. Let C be the conjunction of all causal laws in our world. The conjunction of C and A is strictly equivalent to the conjunction of C and B. That is, it is the case that *Nec* $[(C \text{ and } A) \longleftrightarrow (C \text{ and } B)]$. $(C \text{ and } A)$ is causally necessary, but $(C \text{ and } B)$ is causally contingent, assuming that a conjunction is contingent if any conjunct is contingent. I have purposely chosen for A a nonimmediate causal consequence of B in order to bypass an objection based on the position mentioned before that the immediate consequences of B are also accidental. A is causally necessitated by B and is enough removed from B in time that there is no temptation to say it borrows B's accidentality. We have, then, a counterexample to TNP 2 for the case of causal necessity.

But it might be thought that mutations are not really causally contingent occurrences, that they seem accidental only relative to what we happen to know about them. If so, consider another counterexample. Let B be the decay of an ion from a radioactive substance, say, a lump of Uranium 238. This substance emits a particle completely at random every so often. We know what the half-life of this substance is, but what we do not and cannot know is the exact time of the decay of any given particle. The decay of a particle is the product of physically indeterminate processes occurring at the level of atomic nuclei. Physicists tell us that it is not just that we do not *know* enough to be able to predict when a given particle will decay. Even total information on the physical variables involved would be insufficient to permit us to predict accurately the decay of the particle. Such an event is physically indeterministic if anything is, and in the strongest sense.

Let A be the recording on a meter of the impact of a particle on a spherical screen completely surrounding the lump of Uranium. The meter always reacts if the uranium emits a particle and reacts only when the uranium emits a particle. The spherical screen is, then, a foolproof detector of ionizing radiation. The description so far is enough to give us a counterexample to TNP 2 if it is allowed that A is itself causally necessary. That is, it is entailed by the conjunction of C and B.

But a few paragraphs back we considered the possibility that the immediate causal consequences of causally accidental events may themselves be thought to be causally accidental. If so, A might not be causally necessary after all. As I have said, I see no reason to think that this is correct but, even if it is, an alteration in our case can block this objection. Just let A be a recording of the impact of the particle on a device more remote in space and time than the spherical screen. Perhaps the particle is emitted by a natural body many millions of light-years removed from the recording device. In such a case as well we have a counterexample to TNP 2. (C and A) is causally necessary, $Nec\,[(C\ and\ A) \longleftrightarrow (C\ and\ B)]$, but ($C$ and B) is causally accidental.

If TNP 2 is false, we have reason to doubt premise (2) of the argument from Accidental Necessity. That premise says that if A is accidentally necessary at t, and if A is strictly equivalent to B, then B is accidentally necessary* at t. Recall that accidental necessity* is whatever sort of necessity is transferred from accidental necessity by way of strict equivalence. But what reason do we have to think that this kind of necessity is transferred over strict equivalence? We have just seen that causal necessity is not always transferred over strict equivalence, nor is the necessity of nonaccidentality. I have never heard of an argument supporting a proposition similar to premise (2) other than that it is an instance of the more general transfer principle and that such a principle seems right. I conclude that until a better argument comes along in support of it, we need not accept it.

The solution of this section suggests that we have two other alternatives to the rejection of premise (2). One is to reject (1) and the other is to reject (3). We have already looked at independent reasons for rejecting those premises in Chapters 3 and 4.

3. Solutions to the Timeless Knowledge Dilemma

The two solutions I have just given to the Accidental Necessity Version of
the Foreknowledge Dilemma are also solutions to the Timeless Knowledge Dilemma presented in Chapter 2. I argued in that chapter that the
Boethian solution generates a new dilemma based not on the necessity of
the past, but on the necessity of eternity. Just as it seems as if there is
nothing I can do now about the past, it also seems as if there is nothing I
can do now about eternity. This is because what we know about the realm
of eternity, which is not much, would lead us to say that it is much more
like the past than the future. Like the past and unlike the future it is
ontologically real, and like the past and unlike the future it exists in act
rather than merely in potency. But then if God's knowledge is in eternity,
it would seem that I have no more power over it than I do over the past.

Let us say that some timeless state of affairs is *eternally necessary* at *t* just
in case there is nothing I can do about it at *t*. The intuition here is that all
timeless states of affairs are eternally necessary at all times. But then there is
an argument against my free will from the necessity of eternity that is parallel to the argument we have been considering from accidental necessity.

Argument from the Necessity of Eternity

(1') God's timeless belief that I do *S* at *t3* is eternally necessary at *t2*.

(2') If *A* is eternally necessary at *t* and *A* is strictly equivalent to *B*, then
B is eternally necessary* at *t*.

(3') God's timeless belief is strictly equivalent to my act at *t3*.

(4') So my act at *t3* is eternally necessary* at *t2*.

(5') If my act at *t3* is eternally necessary* at *t2*, I cannot do otherwise
than bring about that act at *t3*.

(6) If when I bring about an act I cannot do otherwise, I do not bring it
about freely.

(7) Therefore, I do not bring about my act at *t3* freely.

In this argument, eternal necessity* is related to eternal necessity as
accidental necessity* is related to accidental necessity. Eternal necessity*
is the kind of necessity that is transferred from the eternally necessary
through strict equivalence. By definition, only timeless states of affairs
have eternal necessity. My acts are not timeless; hence they cannot be
eternally necessary. Nonetheless, we saw in Chapter 1 that TNP 2:

ϕ is *W*-necessary

ϕ is strictly equivalent to ψ

$\vdash \psi$ is *W*-necessary

has considerable intuitive support. If it did not, the foreknowledge dilemmas would be easy to dismiss. Therefore, even if W-necessity is defined in such a way that ψ is precluded from having it, as can happen with both the necessity of the past and the necessity of eternity, it still seems as if there is some kind of necessity transferred over strict equivalence, a necessity that is just as strong as W-necessity. The argument from the necessity of eternity, then, is an argument that my acts all have a necessity just as strong as the necessity of eternity, a necessity we may call eternity necessity*.

The first solution of this chapter denied (6) and argued that there is no reason other than (6) to think that accidental necessity* deprives me of freedom—no reason, at least, that is parallel to the reason causal necessity deprives me of freedom. I argued that causal necessity deprives me of freedom because a causally necessary act counterfactually depends on its cause, whereas even if God's foreknowledge makes my act accidentally necessary*, my act does not counterfactually depend on his foreknowledge of it.

Exactly the same argument can be used as a solution to the argument from the necessity of eternity. (6) is false, and there is no reason to think that my act counterfactually depends on God's knowledge of it, whether or not such knowledge is outside of time. I believe, then, that the argument of Section 2.1 is a solution to both the Accidental Necessity Version of the foreknowledge dilemma and the Timeless Knowledge Dilemma. Even though the Boethian solution does not solve the foreknowledge problem, it is a permissible option when combined with the first solution of this chapter.

Next let us look at the second solution as a way out of the argument from the necessity of eternity. On that solution an interesting disanalogy with the Frankfurt/Fischer examples was used to produce a model on which it is reasonable to say I can do otherwise, even if all my acts are foreknown. I concluded that this means that either (1), (2), or (3) is false. Can we use the same argument to show that either (1'), (2'), or (3') is false?

I think we can do so easily. The story of the reinforcing neurologist can be amended so that the neurologist is outside of time. Otherwise, the story can remain exactly as it was presented in Section 2.2. I concluded that section by claiming that either (1), (2), or (3) is false and discussed in detail the rejection of (2), the Transfer of Necessity Principle. I think we should conclude from the parallel story about the timeless neurologist that either (1'), (2'), or (3') is false.

It is easier to defend the falsehood of (1'), I believe, than it is to defend the falsehood of (1). The intuitive notion of time and its asymmetry is so firmly entrenched in common sense that any alteration of it cannot help but meet with strong and, I think, well-founded resistance. My argument against it in Chapter 3 required a rather elaborate theory on the distinction between essential and nonessential temporality, a theory that I would never claim fits smoothly with ordinary beliefs. The fact that we have so little idea of the nature of eternity and certainly have nothing comparable to commonsense intuitions about it is advantageous for the denial of (1'). I argued in Chapter 2 that the timeless realm does seem to have an ontological and modal status more like the past than the future. It seems to be fixed and beyond our power. However, we have no sayings such as "There is no use crying over the eternal truths," so the denial of the necessity of eternity in some case does less violence to our intuitive sensibilities than the analogous denial of the necessity of the past.

The case for denying (2') is about equal to the case for denying (2). Most of the argument I gave in Section 2.2 for doubting (2) can be straightforwardly adapted to the denial of (2'). Since both (2) and (2') are instances of TNP 2, any argument against the latter gives us reason to doubt both (2) and (2'). Similarly, the argument about the neurologist given in that section can be amended so that the neurologist is timeless rather than temporal.

Proposition (3') is at least as easy to deny as (3), and probably more so. I argued in Chapter 3 that on a Thomistic account of God's knowing, God does not know distinct propositions but knows by a simple, direct awareness of his own essence in which is contained everything knowable, and that does not change over time. God's awareness at $t1$ of my act at $t3$ is contained in that single epistemic state. He does not have one epistemic state that consists in being aware of my act at $t3$ and another epistemic state that consists in being aware of some other state of affairs at, say, $t14$. But this means that it is quite misguided to say that God's belief at $t1$ that I will do S at $t3$ is strictly equivalent to my act at $t3$. The state of affairs of God's believing that I will do S at $t3$ is not distinct from the state of affairs of God's believing Jane Smith will do R at $t14$. But obviously his belief that Jane Smith will do R at $t14$ is not strictly equivalent to my act at $t3$. Therefore, neither is God's belief at $t1$ that I will do S at $t3$ strictly equivalent to my act at $t3$.

If God is outside of time this point is even more obvious. God's foreknowledge of my act could not be strictly equivalent to my act unless the very same act of foreknowledge was also strictly equivalent to every other object of God's knowledge. But, since strict equivalence is transitive, this would mean that every proposition God knows is strictly equivalent to every other proposition God knows. Since this cannot be, we must conclude that God's foreknowledge and my act are not related by strict equivalence.

I think the arguments of this section show that even though the Boethian move is not sufficient to solve the foreknowledge/timeless knowledge dilemma, it can be combined easily with other solutions. If there are good metaphysical reasons for preferring the view that God is timeless, the dilemma can be solved at least as well as it can if God is temporal.

4. A Model of Foreknowledge: The Fourth Dimension

Some compatibilists are content with showing that foreknowledge and freedom have not yet been proven logically inconsistent. I have argued in this book that such a position is only the weakest compatibilist position. People expect to be shown that foreknowledge and freedom are coplausible, not just copossible, and I think they are right to do so. After all, a demonstration of logical inconsistency is only the worst sort of attack a position can face, not the only worrisome one. It is not terribly hard to show that the conjunction of divine foreknowledge and human free will can survive the worst attack. As remarked in Chapter 1, propositions A and B can be shown successfully to be logically consistent if we can find a contingent proposition C, consistent with A, and that together with A entails B. C does not even have to be known to be true. In fact, it can be known to be false. I suggested that backward-causation solutions might fit into this category. If the proposition that there is backward agent causation is contingent, even if false, since it is consistent with a proposition expressing the performance of a free act and together with such a proposition (suitably worded) entails God's foreknowledge, then this shows foreknowledge and freedom to be consistent. That is, they are copossible. This is what I have called a negative solution to the dilemma. But few people would be happy with such a "solution." This is because it is still the case that even if some pair of propositions A and B are copossible, A may still make B very improbable, and B may likewise make A improbable. The backward-causation solution is clearly not adequate to showing the coplausibility of foreknowledge and freedom if backward causation is known or justifiably believed to be false. Even the solutions I have defended in this book are not much more than negative solutions. This is because I have concentrated on finding reasons for rejecting one or another of the premises in the argument that foreknowledge takes away freedom. These arguments show that the most compelling attempt to demonstrate the inconsistency of foreknowledge and freedom is unsuccessful, but they do not by themselves give us good reason to think that both divine foreknowledge and human freedom actually exist.

As I argued in Chapter 1, there are preexisting reasons for accepting divine foreknowledge and human free will in the Christian tradition, and these reasons strengthen the compatibilist position. But regardless of the history of these two claims, and in spite of everything already said, it still may not seem plausible that God can know future contingents because it is so hard to see *how* he could come by such knowledge. An argument for the coplausibility of foreknowledge and freedom would be aided by a model of the way in which God knows the future. In Chapter 3 we looked at Aquinas' model of God's knowing all contingent truths, including future contingents, by a simple and direct knowledge of his own essence. That model represents God as knowing the future in roughly the same way we know our own mental states. To the extent that the Thomistic account is defensible, we have a good start on a positive solution to the foreknowledge dilemma, but there is no doubt that many Christian philosophers will find it unacceptable. In this section I will give an entirely different model, one in which God knows the future by observing it. My intent is to let this be a start toward the construction of a much different positive solution to the foreknowledge problem, one that may be more palatable to those who have a distaste for Thomistic metaphysics.

First, let us be clear on what such a model should do if it is to make foreknowledge and freedom coplausible. I do not think it is important that the model be believed to actually fit the way God knows. What is important is that the model show at least one way an omniscient being might know the future that violates no Christian beliefs about God or other beliefs firmly held, nor is made improbable by those beliefs. The more such models we can invent, the more likely it is that there are others we have not yet considered. So even if the model is ultimately rejected, its usefulness may be in its capacity to help us imagine how infallible foreknowledge of free acts can occur, and that would be enough to overcome the major stumbling block in the acceptance of the coplausibility of divine foreknowledge and human freedom.

In the early 1880s a delightful little book called *Flatland* was published by the English scholar and theologian, Edwin Abbott Abbott. In this book Abbott describes an imaginary two-dimensional world (Flatland), where all the inhabitants are plane figures—lines, squares, hexagons, circles, and so on. The narrator, a square, describes his vision of what it would be like for a visitor from the three-dimensional world (Spaceland) to visit Flatland, and for him to visit Spaceland. The book ends with speculation about worlds of more dimensions than three.

Flatland apparently did not attract much attention when it was first published, but on February 12, 1920, an anonymous letter appeared in *Nature* entitled "Euclid, Newton, and Einstein." The author of the letter presented a vivid description of the way in which Abbott's book can help us imagine a fourth dimension.

> Dr. Abbott pictures intelligent beings whose whole experience is confined to a plane, or other space of two dimensions, who have no faculties by which they can become conscious of anything outside that space and no means of moving off the surface on which they live. He then asks the reader, who has consciousness of the third dimension, to imagine a sphere descending upon the plane of Flatland and passing through it. How will the inhabitants regard this phenomenon? They will not see the approaching sphere and will have no conception of its solidity. They will only be conscious of the circle in which it cuts their plane. This circle, at first a point, will gradually increase in diameter, driving the inhabitants of Flatland outwards from its circumference, and this will go on until half the sphere has passed through the plane, when the circle will gradually contract to a point and then vanish, leaving the Flatlanders in undisturbed possession of their country. . . . Their experience will be that of a circular obstacle gradually expanding or growing, and then contracting, and they will attribute to *growth in time* what the external observer in three dimensions assigns to motion in the third dimension. Transfer this analogy to a movement of the fourth dimension through three-dimensional space. Assume the past and future of the universe to be all depicted in four-dimensional space and visible to any being who has consciousness of the fourth dimension. If there is motion of our three-dimensional space relative to the fourth dimension, all the changes we experience and assign to the flow of time will be due simply to this movement, the whole of the future as well as the past always existing in the fourth dimension.[16]

A copy of Abbott's diagram of the movement of the sphere through Flatland is given in Figure 1.

Now let us change Abbot's story a bit. Imagine that the Flatlanders perceive themselves and their world just as Abbott describes, except that the dimensions of the plane figures are perceived to expand and then contract gradually. Circles, squares, triangles are infinitesimally small at first, gradually increase until they reach a certain size, and then diminish is size until they disappear.[17] Assume also that each Flatlander is really three dimensional. The circles are really spheres, the squares are really cubes, and so on. By hypothesis they do not know they are three dimen-

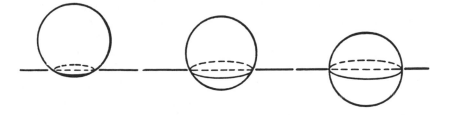

FIGURE 1

sional and would not understand what it means to be three dimensional if so informed by a Spaceland visitor. Flatland, then, is the world as perceived by them, not the world as things actually exist. Of course, this is not to say that the Flatlanders' experience of the world is totally illusory. After all, Flatland *is* what three-dimensional space looks like in two dimensions. It is an actual two-dimensional slice of three-dimensional space, and the perception of it is the best that beings with consciousness of only two dimensions can do in experiencing spatial objects.

If this were so, the way Abbott describes the Flatlanders' experience of a visitor from Spaceland would describe the Flatlanders' experience of themselves and their compatriots. Their experience of a Flatland "circle" expanding and contracting would be seen in Spaceland as a sphere moving in the third dimension. Even the "circle" himself would only be able to understand himself as expanding and contracting in time rather than as moving in a dimension he cannot imagine. Only the Spaceland observer would see the Flatland "circle" as a sphere moving in space rather than as changing in time.

In the story as told by Abbott the Flatlanders are intelligent creatures who can act and choose and, of course, they perceive these events, both in themselves and in others, as involving change through time. Let us suppose that whenever a Flatlander acts a spot of color appears on its surface, with a difference in color determining a difference in the nature of the act. Of course, the spot disappears again momentarily, since the portion of the surface of a three-dimensional object perceptible in Flatland continually changes. Since events perceived in the two-dimensional world as change through time are perceived in the three-dimensional world as movement through a third spatial dimension, the acting and choosing of the Flatlanders would be perceived by the Spacelanders as movement in space rather than as change through time. Acting and choosing would be perceived as enduring properties of a three-dimensional being rather than as fleeting properties of a two-dimensional being. We can compare the way an act of a sphere-circle appears to the Flatlander with the way it appears to a Spacelander by modifying the Abbott diagram as it is in Figure 2. In this diagram a black dot represents the sphere's act.

So the acting of the sphere-circle is perceived by himself and his fellow Flatlanders as the momentary appearance of a black dot on his surface, whereas it is perceived by the Spacelanders as the movement of the black dot through space. The Spacelanders would be able to perceive the black dot long before its appearance to the Flatlanders, even before it appears to the sphere-circle himself. This is because the sphere-circle's perception of his own act is limited by his nonability to perceive his own third dimension.

This model is completely neutral on the question of whether the sphere-circle produces his act (the black dot) freely. The Spaceland philosophers, of course, give a different analysis of such concepts as cause, choice, and action than the Flatland philosophers do, since the latter perceive change in time where the former perceive movement in space. But there is nothing in *this* difference that precludes the Space-landers from attributing the existence of the black dot to the sphere-circle himself. There is no reason why the sphere-circle himself cannot cause or bring about or be otherwise responsible for the existence of the black dot. The sphere-circle, like all of us, is no doubt used to thinking that the way he perceives himself making choices in time is the way they actually occur and would be perceived by an external observer of whatever nature. So he will probably resist the Spaceland visitor who informs him that his black dot was perceptable by Spacelanders, along with everything else on his spherical surface, long before the Flatlander observed them himself. "Surely," the Flatlander will say, "if I perceive my acting as involving change in time, it *does* involve change in time. After all, I know what I'm doing, don't I?" But the Flatland sphere-circle has not considered the possibility that even though he may be right about the fact that his act is of a certain kind and that it is done freely, his perception of himself doing

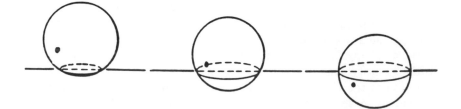

FIGURE 2

it might not be the way it is perceived by a higher creature (i.e., one who has the capacity to observe more spatial dimensions).

If we were really four-dimensional beings whose perceptual faculties were limited to three dimensions, our position would be analogous to that of the sphere who perceives himself and everything around him in two spatial dimensions. A being who has the ability to perceive the fourth dimension would see everything we perceive as change in time as movement relative to the fourth dimension. The fourth dimensioner would also perceive such movement as occurring in time, but it would still be the case that everything we perceive as change in ourselves through time would be perceived by the fourth dimensioner as enduring properties of ourselves in time. Some of these properties could still be freely chosen by ourselves, but we would not perceive the instantiation of these properties the way they would be perceived by a being who can see the fourth dimension.

If the universe has four spatial dimensions, as just described, then a divine and omniscient being perceives it in four dimensions. In this case, presumably, the capacity to observe only three dimensions is a limitation and, by hypothesis, God has no limitations in perception. This model obviously requires that we allow that four-dimensional space is not implausible, and it also requires that we accept the limitations in our own powers to know and to observe that follow from it. There does not seem to me to be anything unreasonable in these requirements. So even if we are not convinced that the spatio-temporal realm is structured just as described in this model, it taxes our imagination very little to consider it, and it does describe a way an omniscient being might know the future that answers the nagging query, "*How* does he do it?"

This model of foreknowledge has some of the advantages of the view that God is timeless without the objections that view encounters. One of the attractions of the timelessness view is that it permits God to have a perspective on reality from which all things are present to him at once. This has been traditionally considered a superior mode of knowing, as we saw in Chapter 2. As Augustine puts it:

> For He does not pass from this to that by transition of thought, but beholds all things with absolute unchangeableness; so that of those things which emerge in time, the future, indeed are not yet, and the present are now, and the past no longer are; but all of these are by Him comprehended in His stable and eternal presence.[18]

But the Abbott model is also a model in which God, or any being with the perspective of the fourth dimension, can know what we know all at once. Everything that has been, is now, or will be from the viewpoint of three dimensions is already present to be observed in the fourth dimension. This model, then, has the advantage of preserving a very strong notion of omniscience, one that would have been agreeable to Augustine, but without the problems we investigated in Chapter 2 that arise from the view that God transcends space-time. For example, we need not worry about whether God knows it is *now* 4 o'clock, or that the War of 1812 is already past. If time as we know it is perspectival, indeed, dependent on a *limited* perspective, we could not very well insist that God should know things from *that* perspective.

Foreknowledge is most fundamentally a problem about the structure of time. In its most forceful form it assumes there is a single absolute temporal order embracing all events and roughly described by McTaggart's A-theory. I argued in Chapter 1 that this view is supported both by a long metaphysical tradition and by common sense. I also pointed out in Chapter 1 that contemporary views on the physics of time might aid the compatibilist's position by requiring us to give up the view that time is absolute and to revise the distinction between past and future. I have not made use of any such models in this book, however, since I have aimed to keep as close as possible to the commonsense view of time. The model I have just given requires an imaginative *addition* to such a view, but not a fundamental restructuring of it. It is compatible with my model that there is a single absolute temporal order, that the A-series is not reducible to the B-series, that the past has a necessity that the future lacks, and that the human perception of temporal succession is nonillusory, albeit incomplete. In spite of all this, we can see in this model how a being with a more complete awareness of temporal succession can know the course of our entire temporal existence in a single moment from his temporal perspective.

In Section 4 I have argued that we want the compatibilist view that God has foreknowledge of our free acts to be plausible, not just logically consistent. If it is not plausible, it may not be rational to believe it, even if it is not logically inconsistent. After all, there are many propositions that are not logically inconsistent that it is irrational to believe, and some of these may even have support in the religious tradition.

How can the plausibility of the compatibilist position be supported? The difficulty in seeing *how* God can know the contingent future is probably the single most difficult problem for the foreknowledge issue. The most complete answer to this question would probably have to involve an extensive theory on the relation between the necessary and the contingent and between God and the creation within which God's knowing mechanism is explained. Short of an elaborate theory on God, the creation, time, and the necessary and the contingent, little models of foreknowledge can be helpful. I have just made up one myself, and even though I am not proposing that we adopt this model of time consciousness, I think that it can lead us to see that we could go on indefinitely inventing such models. There are probably so many ways of understanding the relation between God and time and ourselves and time that it is not only possible, it is even probable, that God's relation to time is enough unlike ours that we need not worry that the compatibilist position is unjustified.

5. Conclusion

In this book I have examined a number of solutions to the dilemma of freedom and foreknowledge. I have argued that the three major traditional solutions are inadequate in their usual forms. This includes the Boethian, Ockhamist, and Molinist solutions. I have also proposed three original solutions, one in Chapter 3 that I call Thomistic Ockhamism, and two others in this chapter. I believe each of these is a successful negative solution to the strongest form of the dilemma, the Accidental Necessity Version. In Chapter 4 I proposed a solution to the Causal Necessity Version as well.

I have said repeatedly that a negative solution is not enough. It is not sufficient to be shown that God's foreknowledge and human free will are not logically inconsistent. Logical inconsistency is only the worst sort of incompatibility there can be between two states of affairs. To show that the worst sort does not obtain is not to show that there is no incompatibility at all, and so reasonable people are not yet satisfied. We still desire a positive solution, one that would show that divine foreknowledge and human free will are coplausible. In Section 4 of this chapter I suggested a model of foreknowledge that I hope reduces the implausibility of the compatibilist position, but it is only a start. A complete positive solution to the dilemma of this book would need to do much more. Metaphysical theories gain the power to convince partly through scope, partly through simplicity, and partly through subtlety. A position on the relation between God's knowledge and human acts will not get very far unless it is part of a general theory of great explanatory power. This means we ultimately need to tell a metaphysical story about the larger relation between God and creation within which divine knowledge and human choice both have their place. The persuasiveness of the foreknowledge solution would be a by-product of the persuasiveness of the big theory. I am confident that it is possible to do this.

It seems to me that the intuition of the necessity of the past is virtually intractable. Even modern physics has not shaken it, at least not yet. Fatalistic arguments lead to a collapse of our intuitive distinctions between past and future and between what we can control and what we cannot control. These arguments purport to show that some of our most basic attitudes are rationally indefensible. This is good reason to think there is something wrong with such arguments, but it is surprisingly difficult to locate the problem. Some religious philosophers have wanted to opt for foreknowledge over the commonsense notion of time because they think that that is what they should do as religious philosophers. In my opinion it is misplaced reverence to think that a religious belief takes precedence over common sense. When faced with a dilemma, I do not see why we should opt for one belief over another either because its content is religious as opposed to metaphysical, or because of its importance. We should opt for one belief over another to the extent to which it seems more likely to be true. It is no less a praise of God to retain what we have come to believe about the structure of time and principles of necessity, whose truth is due to God, than to retain what we have come to believe about God himself. I suggest that we should not deny the necessity of the past until such time as it has been demonstrated to be incoherent. Of course, as long as all the premises in the argument for incompatibilism have strong intuitive support, *any* solution will be counterintuitive up to a point, but we should aim to reduce that to a minimum.

A truly satisfying solution to the dilemma of divine foreknowledge should be as thrilling as the dilemma itself is disturbing. The divine foreknowledge dilemma is so disturbing, it has motivated a significant amount of philosophical work on the relation between God and human beings since at least the fifth century. A really good solution should lay to rest the gripping worries that have motivated all this work. Sadly, none of the solutions I have proposed in this book really do that, and I have never heard of one that does.

APPENDIX

A New Foreknowledge Dilemma

The dilemma of divine foreknowledge and human free will is difficult enough. But I have discovered an even deeper dilemma, one that purports to show that the foreknowledge of an essentially omniscient being is inconsistent with the very notion of temporal asymmetry described in this book and at least indirectly defended. This new dilemma is entirely independent of the issue of free will.

I have claimed repeatedly that the commonsense notion of time involves the idea that there is both an ontological and a modal asymmetry between past and future. The past is real; the future is not. The past is not related to the present as the present is related to the future, since the future does not exist. The present contains traces of the past, but no traces of the future. There is only one possible past, but many possible futures. There are no events that now are such that they may have obtained in the past and may not have obtained in the past. But there are events that now are such that they may obtain in the future and they may not obtain in the future. For example, it is now possible that I go to Santa Barbara next Thursday and it is now possible that I do not go to Santa Barbara next Thursday, and this is the case because my going or not going to Santa Barbara is both causally contingent and future.

We also saw in Chapter 1 that Ockham associates the temporal asymmetry just described with the Aristotelian act/potency distinction. Consider a true proposition p about a contingent event at t. p is true at all times. Nonetheless, there exists a potency in things both for p and for not-p until t when the potency for p is reduced to act and the potency for not-p is lost forever. After t, then, there is a sense in which p is necessary. It is necessary in that there is no longer any potency in things for its negation. This is the basis for the idea that there is a kind of necessity independent of logical and causal necessity that the past has and the future lacks.

I assume that an essentially omniscient being is such that it is impossible that that being exist and fail to know at any time the truth value of every proposition. But a contradiction can be derived from the assump-

181

tion that there is an essentially omniscient foreknower, the view of time just described, and the Law of Excluded Middle.

New Foreknowledge Dilemma

Assume:

> (1) There is (and was in the past) an essentially omniscient foreknower.
> (2) It is now possible that I will go to Santa Barbara next Thursday and it is now possible that I will not go to Santa Barbara next Thursday.

Since the proposition *I will go to Santa Barbara next Thursday* is strictly equivalent to the proposition *The essentially omniscient foreknower believes I will go to Santa Barbara next Thursday*,[1] (1) and (2) strictly imply:

> (3) It is now possible that the essentially omniscient foreknower believed before now that I will go to Santa Barbara next Thursday and it is now possible that the essentially omniscient foreknower believed before now that I will not go to Santa Barbara next Thursday.

From (1) and the Law of Excluded Middle we know that:

> (4) Either the essentially omniscient foreknower did believe I will go to Santa Barbara next Thursday before now or he did not.

But the Principle of the Necessity of the Past entails:

> (5) If he did, it is not now possible that he did not, and if he did not, it is not now possible that he did.

(4) and (5) entail:

> (6) Either it is not now possible that he did not or it is not now possible that he did.

But (6) contradicts (3).

I assume that the Law of Excluded Middle is unassailable, so it seems that (1), (2), and (5) are inconsistent. So either one of two very common intuitions about time is false or there is no essentially omniscient foreknower. In fact, the two intuitions about time, (2), and (5), are not independent of each other. (2) is an intuition about the future and (5) is an intuition about the past, but both are intuitions about the modal asymmetry between past and future described here and throughout this book. (5) expresses a necessity that the past has and the future lacks. (2)

expresses a possibility that the future has and the past lacks. So (2) and (5) are both connected to a particular way of looking at time and the asymmetry between past and future.

Notice that if both (2) and (5) are true, the preceding argument shows that there is no essentially omniscient being who has *any* beliefs about the contingent future, and this is not limited to future human free acts. Further, if (2) and (5) are necessary truths, (1) is not only false, but necessarily false.

This new foreknowledge dilemma suggests some very interesting things. First, it shows that opting out of free will to save the foreknowledge of God (e.g., Anthony Kenny) does nothing to solve this other, more basic dilemma. Essentially omniscient foreknowledge is more fundamentally a threat to a certain view of time, and only indirectly to human freedom. Second, it makes the denial of God's foreknowledge by those who want to save free will (e.g., Richard Swinburne, John Lucas, William Hasker) look unappealing. This is especially so for those who say that although an essentially omniscient God cannot know our future free acts, God could have had foreknowledge if he was willing not to make us free, and he does have foreknowledge of a lot of things. He just makes the choice to forego knowing our future choices for the sake of our freedom; to do so is presumably a gesture of magnanimity. But the preceding argument seems to show that God literally cannot know any of the contingent future in the manner of an essentially omniscient being because of the structure of time itself.

So those who maintain that freedom and foreknowledge are incompatible are in a predicament. The typical moves of grasping either horn of the foreknowledge/freedom dilemma are unconvincing or ineffective against this new dilemma. But the compatibilist about freedom and foreknowledge is in a predicament also. Some solutions to the foreknowledge/freedom dilemma do not solve the new dilemma at all, and that includes the first solution I presented in Chapter 6. In that chapter I attempted to block the argument from divine foreknowledge to lack of freedom at the step that says that if I lack the ability to do otherwise, I lack incompatibilist free will. This solution is irrelevant to the present dilemma since free will does not enter into it at all.

The new dilemma narrows our options considerably. Consider first the option of denying (5). I have argued in this book that (5) is very well grounded in our most basic ideas about time. I argued in Chapter 3 that no version of Ockhamism I know of in the contemporary literature succeeds in showing it is even possible that God's foreknowing is outside the category of the necessity of the past, so no such argument shows that

(5) is false. However, I proposed my own way to do this by presenting a theory on the relation between God's beliefs and time that has as a consequence that those beliefs cannot be accidentally necessary. I called this solution Thomistic Ockhamism. If it works, we could also get out of the present dilemma by denying (5). This solution involves making some rather elaborate Thomistic assumptions about the divine nature. I believe the solution is successful in solving the present dilemma if we make those assumptions, but it is unhelpful for the case of the foreknowledge of an essentially omniscient being who does not know in the manner described by Aquinas. This might be taken to be an argument that an essentially omniscient being *must* know in that manner if the dilemma is not otherwise solvable.

What about the option of denying (2)? This option is highly unappealing for many reasons, only one of which is that it denies the modal asymmetry between past and future.

What about the option that there is an essentially omniscient *atemporal* foreknower? Is the new dilemma solved if God is timeless, as Boethius thought? It seems to me that it is not because a parallel dilemma can be produced even by the assumption that God is timeless. As I argued in Chapter 2, it is very likely that there is a principle of the Necessity of Eternity that is the analogue of the Necessity of the Past. Both ontologically and modally the realm of the eternal seems to be much more like the realm of the past than of the future. It is ontologically real, like the past and unlike the future, and if p is some proposition about a timeless state of affairs, it is not very likely that there exists (timelessly) a potency for *not-p*. Again, this makes the timeless realm seem to be more like the past than the future, and so one would expect that like the past it is modally fixed, which is to say, unaffected by us. But this generates a parallel dilemma.

New Timeless Knowledge Dilemma

Assume:

(1') There is an essentially omnisicient, timeless knower.

(2) It is now possible that I will go to Santa Barbara next Thursday and it is now possible that I will not go to Santa Barbara next Thursday.

(1') and (2) entail:

(3') It is now possible that the essentially omniscient, timeless knower timelessly believes I go to Santa Barbara next Thursday and it is now possible that the essentially omniscient, timeless knower timelessly believes I do not go to Santa Barbara next Thursday.

From (1') and the Law of Excluded Middle we know that:

(4') Either the essentially omniscient, timeless knower timelessly believes I go to Santa Barbara next Thursday or he does not.

But the principle of the Necessity of Eternity entails:

(5') If he does, it is not now possible that he does not, and if he does not, it is not now possible that he does.

(4') and (5') entail:

(6') Either it is not now possible that he does not or it is not now possible that he does.

But (6') contradicts (3').

Since the intuition of the Necessity of Eternity is no doubt weaker than the intuition of the Necessity of the Past, (5') is less well grounded than (5), and so this dilemma is weaker than the comparable foreknowledge dilemma. Furthermore, (2) and (5') are not both aspects of the same intuition about time as (2) and (5) are. So it is somewhat easier to maintain (2) and reject (5') than to maintain (2) and reject (5). Still, I have argued that the main reason (5') is not so strong in ordinary intuitions is just that we have few intuitions at all about eternity, a reason that is not very flattering to the Boethian move.

In Chapter 6 I argued that the two solutions of that chapter are also adequate solutions to the Timeless Knowledge Dilemma of Chapter 2. It is clear, however, that the first of those solutions will not work against this new timeless knowledge dilemma any more than it works against the new foreknowledge dilemma. What about the second solution? That solution involved denying TNP 2 [$Nec_w A, Nec (A \longleftrightarrow B) \vdash Nec_w B$]. But if that principle is false, so also is a principle we might call the Transfer of Possibility Principle, which allows us to derive (3) from (1) and (2) or (3') from (1') and (2).[2] That principle can be formulated as follows:

Transfer of Possibility Principle

$$Poss_w A, Nec (A \longleftrightarrow B) \vdash Poss_w B$$

The counterexamples to the Transfer of Necessity Principle given in Chapter 6, Section 2.2, apply to this principle as well. To take one example from that section for the case of causal possibility and necessity, suppose that we have a radioactive substance such as a lump of Uranium 238. This substance emits a particle completely at random every so often. Let *A* be the emission of a particular particle at a particular time. Such an event is causally indeterministic if anything is. But if *A* is not causally necessary, *not A* is causally possible. Let *B* be the recording on a meter of the impact of a particle on a spherical screen completely surrounding the lump of Uranium. The meter reacts if and only if the Uranium emits a particle. *B* is causally necessary, so *not-B* is not causally possible. Let *C* be the conjunction of all causal laws. In this case (*A and C*) is strictly equivalent to (*B and C*). And (*not-A and C*) is strictly equivalent to (*not-B and C*). So (*not-A and C*) is causally possible, *Nec [(not-A and C)* ⟷ *(not-B and C)*], but (*not-B and C*) is not causally possible. We have, then, a counterexample to the Transfer of Possibility Principle for causal possibility.

A denial of this principle would block the move to (3) or (3') from (1) or (1') and (2). If this principle is not rejected, the only way to solve the dilemma, as far as I can see, is to deny (5) or (5').

Every foreknowledge dilemma has an analogue in a dilemma about future truth, and my new dilemma is no exception.

New Dilemma of Future Truth

Assume:

(2) It is now possible that I will go to Santa Barbara next Thursday and it is now possible that I will not go to Santa Barbara next Thursday.

(2) entails:

(7) It is now possible that it was true in the past that I will go to Santa Barbara next Thursday and it is now possible that it was true in the past that I will not go to Santa Barbara next Thursday.

From the Law of Excluded Middle we get:

(8) Either it was true in the past that I will go to Santa Barbara next Thursday or it was not true in the past that I will go to Santa Barbara next Thursday.

From the Principle of the Necessity of the Past it follows that:

(9) If it was true it is not now possible that it was not, and if it was not true, it is not now possible that it was.

(8) and (9) entail:

> (10) Either it is not now possible that it was true in the past that I go to Santa Barbara next Thursday or it is not now possible that it was not true in the past that I go to Santa Barbara next Thursday.

But (10) contradicts (7).

This dilemma involves applying the principle of the Necessity of the Past to the past truth of propositions to get (9). But as I argued in Chapter 1, the Necessity of the Past makes much more sense when it is applied to past events such as the past beliefs of persons than when it is applied to the past truth of propositions. This is clearly so if propositions are timeless entities, since then their truth is a timeless property and it was not the case *in the past* that a certain proposition about the future was true. But even if propositions *are* temporal entities, it still does not seem reasonable to say that the past truth of a proposition now has the Necessity of the Past, since that is incompatible with Ockham's association of this kind of necessity with the act/potency distinction described above. Assuming that the future is not real, it is not reasonable to say that the potency for its being 20 years before some event in 1998 is reduced to act in 1978. This means that even if propositions about the future are true in the past, it is not very plausible to ascribe to them the necessity of the past. So the threat of logical fatalism arising from the various dilemmas of future truth is not as serious as the threat of theological fatalism arising from the foreknowledge dilemmas.

We might consider my new dilemma as midway between the dilemma of future truth and the dilemma of freedom and foreknowledge. It is like the latter in that it is based on the necessity of the past belief of an essentially omnisicient being rather than the past truth of a proposition, but it is like the former in that free will does not enter into it at all. It therefore has the strengths of both dilemmas without as many ways out as either one. There are fewer ways out than the freedom/foreknowledge dilemma since there are no premises at all about human free will. At the same time the way out of the dilemma of future truth just sketched does not work because it is much more plausible to ascribe the necessity of the past to the past beliefs of persons than to the past truth of propositions.

I think the puzzle I have presented leaves us with few choices. As far as I can see, there are only five options. Option 1 is that God knows no future contingent events at all, even those that are not produced by free choice. If we take this option, then God's omniscience is limited not only by human free choice, but by the general category of future contingency, and that is surely unattractive. Option 2 is that God does know future contingents, but is not essentially omniscient. Both of the first two options require that we deny a very important attribute of the divinity. Option 3 is that God is in time, and (5) is false. If we take this option, we must deny part of the commonsense notion of time and the modal distinction between past and future. This is the Ockhamist move. I argued in Chapter 3 that there is a way to make this work, but not by any of the moves in the contemporary literature on Ockhamism. Option 4 is that God is timeless, and (5') is false. This is the Boethian move. It involves the rather difficult claim that God is outside of time, and yet the timeless realm is not a fixed realm. This position might be made out coherently, but I think it would take more explanation of the ontological status of the timeless realm that I have seen to date. The final option is that the Transfer of Possibility Principle is false. I think this principle can be plausibly denied, but it must be admitted that it means that the logic of necessity and possibility is much more complicated than generally believed.

How do these two new dilemmas affect the other foreknowledge solutions? The solutions that do not solve the new dilemma are certainly not useless. I suspect that the argument from foreknowledge to lack of free will is a tangle of confusions and problems, and there is probably more than one mistake in it. To show that foreknowledge and freedom are compatible, it is enough to find only one such mistake, but I have suggested several places where I think the argument goes astray. If I am right that there are mistakes in the argument from the accidental necessity of an act to its lack of freedom, it should be illuminating to point that out even though it may also be the case that God is not in time or God's past beliefs do not have the necessity of the past.

NOTES

Chapter 1

1. Christian forms of the dilemma date at least to the time of the third-century philosopher Origen, who is quoted by Aquinas in *ST* IA, Q. 14, A. 8, obj. 1. Richard Sorabji, in *Necessity, Cause, and Blame* (Ithaca, N.Y.: Cornell University Press, 1980), Chaps. 6 and 7, traces back early forms of the foreknowledge dilemma through Proclus and Ammonius to the Neo-Platonist Iamblichus, who died around 330 A.D. Even earlier, the Stoics and Cicero (*De Fato* and *De Divinatione*) examined foreknowledge as part of their general fascination with fate. Carneades, head of the Platonic Academy from 137 to 131 B.C., denied that it is possible to foreknow something without knowing its causes. Sorabji remarks that many of the ancients did not clearly distinguish the foreknowledge dilemma from the still earlier problem of future truth, deriving from Aristotle's Sea Battle Argument of *De Int* IX.

2. *Predestination of the Saints*, 5, trans. Dods, reprinted in Oates, *Basic Writings of St. Augustine*, 2 vols. (New York: Random House, 1948).

3. Nelson Pike, "Divine Omniscience and Voluntary Action," *Philosophical Review*, 74 (January 1965), pp. 27–46.

4. *Summa Theologiae* Ia, Q. 14, A. 13.

5. Calvin Normore says that the majority opinion among major religious traditions is that God knows what will happen because he makes whatever happens happen and so he knows the history of the world by knowing his own intentions. ["Divine Omniscience, Omnipotence and Future Contingents: An Overview," in *Divine Omniscience and Omnipotence in Medieval Philosophy* (Dordrecht, Netherlands: D. Reidel), 1985, pp. 14–15]. Alfred J. Freddoso stresses this point in his defense of the Molinist way out in the introduction to *On Divine Foreknowledge: Part IV of the Concordia* (Ithaca, N.Y.: Cornell University Press, 1988).

6. A failure to appreciate the need for a theological premise in the statement of the divine foreknowledge dilemma seems to be true of Arthur Prior, "The Formalities of Omniscience," *Philosophy*, 37 (April 1962), pp. 114–129; Susan Haack, "On a Theological Argument for Fatalism," *Philosophical Quarterly*, 25 (April 1975), pp. 159–161; and Steven Cahn, *Fate, Logic, and Time*, (New Haven: 1967), Chap. 5. Gary Iseminger, "Foreknowledge and Necessity," *Midwest Studies in Philosophy*, I (Minneapolis: University of Minnesota Press, 1976), pp. 5–11, explicitly states that the problem of foreknowledge is really just the

problem of foretruth, and two of his commentators in the same issue, Edward Langerak and George Mavrodes, agree with him. More recently, William Craig has said in *The Only Wise God* (Grand Rapids: Baker Book House, 1987), pp. 67–68, that he sees no difference between the problem of future truth and foreknowledge. Nelson Pike clearly stated the need for a theological premise of infallibility in "Divine Omniscience and Voluntary Action," op. cit., and the need for it is stressed by Richard Sorabji, op. cit., Chap. 6, pp. 112–113.

7. Norman Kretzmann, *William of Sherwood's Introduction to Logic* (Minneapolis: University of Minnesota Press, 1966), p. 41.

8. *Predestination, God's Foreknowledge, and Future Contingents*, trans. by Marilyn Adams and Norman Kretzmann, 2nd ed. (Indianapolis: Hackett, 1983), Assumption 3, p. 46.

9. *Ordinatio*, Prologus, q.6.

10. Sorabji, Chap. 5, pp. 91–92.

11. *Summa Theologiae* I, Q. 25, A. 4, reply obj. 1, 2. The same idea can be found in *De Veritate* II, 12, and *Summa Contra Gentiles*, I, 67, 2.

12. *Counterfactuals* (Cambridge, Mass. Harvard University Press, 1973), p. 7.

13. It is difficult to find supporters of backward causation, but those who do generally seem to be aware of the connection between their view and a denial of the ontological asymmetry between past and future. They are simply willing to pay the price. Those supporters of backward causation who explicitly mention this connection include Graham Nerlich, "How to Make Things Have Happened," *Canadian Journal of Philosophy*, IX (1979), 2, p. 21; John Earman, "Causation: A Matter of Life and Death," *Journal of Philosophy*, 73 (1976) 6, pp. 21–2; and Bob Brier, "The Metaphysics of Precognition," *Philosophy and Psychical Research*, ed. by Shivesh C. Thakur (London: George Allen & Unwin, 1976), p. 56. Those who reject backward causation at least in part because of its commitment to the claim that the future is as real as the past include Sarah Waterlow, "Backwards Causation and Continuing," *Mind*, 83 (1974), pp. 372–387; William Craig, "The Alleged Logical Impossibility of Backwards Causation," unpublished, and Andros Loizou, *The Reality of Time* (Brookfield, VT: Gower Publishing, 1986).

14. David Lewis, "Counterfactual Dependence and Time's Arrow," *Nous*, 13 (4) (November 1979), pp. 455–477. This point will be examined in Chapter 3.

15. The saying "There is no use crying over spilt milk," although the most commonly used one for this point, is unfortunate, since people are much more inclined to cry over what they can no longer prevent than over what they can do something about.

16. My interpretation of Ockham in this paragraph owes much to the useful commentaries by Marilyn Adams, both in the introduction to the second edition of *Predestination, God's Foreknowledge, and Future Contingents*, op. cit., and *William Ockham* (Notre Dame, Indiana: University of Notre Dame Press, 1987), Chap. 27.

17. This argument could no doubt be extended to show that the present has the same necessity as the past, since it is reasonable to think that the reduction of the potency for *A* to act is simultaneous with the loss of the potency for *not A*.

18. Lukasiewicz, in Storrs McCall (ed.), *Polish Logic 1920–1939* (Oxford: Oxford University Press, 1967), pp. 38–39.

19. Anthony Kenny, "Divine Foreknowledge and Human Freedom," in Baruch A. Brody, ed., *Readings in the Philosophy of Religion* (Englewood Cliffs, N.J.: Prentice-Hall, 1974), p. 411.

20. See Raymond Flood and Michael Lockwood, introduction to *The Nature of Time* (Oxford: Basil Blackwell, 1986).

21. John Lucas, "The Open Future," in Flood and Lockwood, pp. 125–134.

22. Lucas, pp. 126–127.

23. Lucas, p. 133.

24. Sorabji, p. 112.

25. From the discussion of accidental necessity in Section 2.1, it follows that to say that a proposition *p* is now accidentally necessary is the same as to say the *truth* of *p* is now accidentally necessary.

26. This point will be discussed in Chapter 3.

27. "On Ockham's Way Out," *Faith and Philosophy*, 3 (3) (July 1986), p. 239.

28. Ibid., p. 237.

29. Other philosophers have called attention to the distinction between showing the copossibility and the coplausibility of God and evil. Alvin Plantinga's distinction between a "solution" to the problem of evil and a "theodicy" coincides with my distinction between a negative and a positive solution to a dilemma. John Hick also makes such a distinction in the revised *Evil and the God of Love* (New York: Harper and Row, 1978), and Chapter Four of *Philosophy of Religion*, 3rd. edition (Englewood Cliffs, N.J.: Prentice-Hall, 1983). Hick focuses his attention on a positive solution, and I think he is quite right to do so.

30. George Mavrodes, "Is the Past Unpreventable?", *Faith and Philosophy*, 1 (2) (April 1984), pp. 131–146.

31. Some who take this way out include Richard Purtill, "Fatalism and the Omnitemporality of Truth," *Faith and Philosophy*, 5 (2) (April 1988), pp. 185–192, and Joseph Runzo, "Omniscience and Freedom for Evil," *International Journal for the Philosophy of Religion*, 12 (1981), pp. 131–147. According to Calvin Normore, the first serious medieval attempt to abandon the view that future contingents have a truth value was Peter Aureoli at the beginning of the fourteenth century and, of course, many commentators on Aristotle have interpreted him as doing that in his Sea Battle Argument (*De Int.*, IX).

32. Richard Swinburne, *The Coherence of Theism* (Oxford: Clarendon Press, 1977).

33. Anthony Kenny, *The God of the Philosophers* (Oxford: Clarendon Press, 1979).

34. *ST* I, Q. 57, A. 3, sed contra.

Chapter 2

1. Chapter 1, Section 4.
2. *Summa Theologiae* Ia, Q. 14, A. 13, ad. 2.
3. *The Consolation of Philosophy*, Book V, Prose Vi.
4. Ibid.
5. Ibid.
6. Ibid.
7. Ibid.
8. Richard Sorabji, *Necessity, Cause, and Blame* (Ithaca, N.Y.: Cornell University Press, 1980), p. 125.
9. *I Sent.*, d. 38, q. 1 a. 5, (Parma VI, 317). Quoted in Marilyn Adams, *William Ockham* (Notre Dame, Ind.: University of Notre Dame Press, 1987), p. 1120.
10. *ST* Ia, Q. 14, A. 13, reply obj. 3.
11. *Consolation*, Bk IV, prose 6, and *De Trinitate*, 354.78–366.82.
12. Eleonore Stump and Norman Kretzmann, "Eternity," *Journal of Philosophy*, 78 (8) (August 1981), pp. 429–458; reprinted in *The Concept of God*, Thomas V. Morris, ed. (Oxford: Oxford University Press, 1987), pp. 219–252. Subsequent page references are to the Morris edition.
13. See Paul Fitzgerald, "Stump and Kretzmann on Time and Eternity," *Journal of Philosophy*, 82 (5) (May 1985), pp. 260–269.
14. Fitzgerald, ibid.
15. I assume that an atemporal being is the same as a timeless one. Both atemporality and timelessness are defined as lacking temporal location.
16. Stump and Kretzmann, p. 231.
17. What Stump and Kretzmann mean by "observer" does not seem to have much to do with observation. In a footnote in Morris, p. 229, they say: "It is important to understand that by 'observer' we mean only that thing, animate or inanimate, with respect to which the reference frame is picked out and with respect to which the simultaneity of events within the reference frame is determined."
18. Ibid., p. 231.
19. Ibid., p. 247.
20. Robert C. Coburn, "Professor Malcolm on God," *Australasian Journal of Philosophy*, 41 (1963), pp. 155–156; Nelson Pike, *God and Timelessness* (New York: Schocken, 1970), pp. 121–129.
21. Anthony Kenny, "Divine Foreknowledge and Human Freedom," in Baruch A. Brody (ed.), *Readings in Philosophy of Religion* (Englewood Cliffs, N.J.: Prentice-Hall, 1974), p. 409. William Hasker attempts an answer to Prior in "Concerning the Intelligibility of 'God is Timeless,'" *The New Scholasticism*, 57 (2) (Spring 1983), pp. 170–195.
22. Nicholas Wolterstorff, "God Everlasting," in C. Orlebeke and L. Smedes (eds.), *God and the Good: Essays in Honor of Henry Stob* (Grand Rapids:

William B. Eerdmans, 1975); reprinted in S. Cahn and D. Shatz (eds.), *Contemporary Philosophy of Religion* (Oxford: Oxford University Press, 1982), pp. 77–98.

23. Richard Swinburne, *The Coherence of Theism* (Oxford University Press, 1977), p. 221.

24. Wolterstorff, op. cit.

25. William Hasker, *God, Time, and Knowledge* (Ithaca, N.Y.: Cornell University Press, 1989), Chaps. 8 and 9.

26. Alvin Plantinga, "On Ockham's Way Out," op. cit.; Linda Zagzebski, "Divine Foreknowledge and Human Free Will," *Religious Studies*, 21 (Fall 1985), pp. 279–298. This objection is also supported by Edward Wierenga in *The Nature of God* (Ithaca, N.Y.: Cornell University Press, 1989), p. 115.

27. "On Ockham's Way Out," *Faith and Philosophy*, 3 (3) (July 1986), p. 240.

28. Marilyn Adams, *William Ockham* (Notre Dame, Ind.: University of Notre Dame Press, 1987), p. 1121. William Craig, "Was Thomas Aquinas a B-Theorist of Time?," *The New Scholasticism*, 59 (4) (1985), pp. 475–83. Craig does not object to the B-theory in this paper, but he does in "The Alleged Logical Impossibility of Backwards Causation," unpublished.

29. Adams, p. 1121.

30. *ST* Ia, Q. 14, A. 13.

31. Craig, pp. 482–483.

32. *Divine Impassibility* (Cambridge: Cambridge University Press, 1986), p. 96.

33. Ibid., p. 483.

34. Stump and Kretzmann, pp. 235–236.

35. In a much earlier paper, however, Kretzmann did express an interpretation of the timelessness doctrine that commits it to tenet c: "(F)rom a God's-eye view there is no time, that the passage of time is a universal human illusion." ("Omniscience and Immutability," *Journal of Philosophy*, 63 (1966), p. 415.

36. Note that the doctrine of divine eternity as expressed by Boethius includes something close to the doctrine of omniscience, since it includes the view that God is eternally aware of all temporal occurrences.

37. Anthony Kenny, "Divine Foreknowledge and Human Freedom," in Brody, op. cit., p. 409, and A. N. Prior, "The Formalities of Omniscience," in Brody, pp. 415–416.

38. Sorabji, pp. 125–126.

39. P. 126.

40. William P. Alston, "Does God Have Beliefs?", *Religious Studies*, 22 (1986), p. 305.

41. A solution something like this has been suggested to me by Stump in correspondence.

42. See Jonathan Kvanvig, *The Possibility of an All-Knowing God* (New York: St. Martin's Press, 1986), Chap. 6.

43. Wierenga, pp. 180–186.

44. Arthur Prior, "The Formalities of Omniscience," in *Papers on Time and Tense* (Oxford: Oxford University Press, 1968), p. 29.

45. Alfred J. Freddoso, introduction to *On Divine Foreknowledge: Part IV of the Concordia* by Luis de Molina (Ithaca, N.Y.: Cornell University Press, 1988), p. 6.

46. Ibid., p. 8. Passages cited by Freddoso from Aquinas supporting this point include *ST* I, Q. 14, A. 5, 8, and 16; *De Veritate*, Q. 2, A. 3 and 14; *SCG* I, Chap. 65 and II, Chap. 24.

47. For example, Stephen T. Davis uses the vision model in *Logic and the Nature of God* (Grand Rapids: Eerdmans, 1983), pp. 52–67, even though he denies God exists outside of time. This point has already been observed by Freddoso, ibid., n. 8, p. 6.

48. Many philosophers, of course, maintain that God's beliefs *do* cause events in time, and they say this is required by the doctrine of divine providence. I am not here denying this view, but simply pointing out that since the Causal Necessity Version of the foreknowledge dilemma is a serious worry, that problem is eliminated if God's beliefs are outside of time. It is still open to the foreknowledge compatibilist to maintain a causal relation between God and human acts on his own terms.

49. Adams, *William Ockham*, op. cit., p. 1135.

50. In his book, *God, Time, and Knowledge* (Ithaca, N.Y.: Cornell University Press, 1989), p. 165, William Hasker has argued that "is observed as present" must not mean "is observed as, and is in fact present," but rather "is observed as and is *not* in literal fact present" because of problems in explaining how something eternal can really be present in time.

51. Wierenga, *The Nature of God*, p. 172.

Chapter 3

1. Marilyn Adams, "Is the Existence of God a 'Hard' Fact?," *Philosophical Review* 76 (October 1967), pp. 492–503.

2. Defenders of the Ockhamist move include Anthony Kenny, "Divine Foreknowledge and Human Freedom," in *Aquinas: A Collection of Critical Essays*, ed. by Anthony Kenny (Garden City, N.Y.: Anchor Books, 1969), and *The God of the Philosophers* (Oxford: Oxford University Press, 1979), pp. 51–87; William Rowe, *Philosophy of Religion* (Encino: Dickenson, 1978), pp. 154–169; Alfred J. Freddoso, "Accidental Necessity and Logical Determinism," *Journal of Philosophy*, 80 (May 1983), pp. 257–278, and "Accidental Necessity and Power Over the Pat," *Pacific Philosophical Quarterly*, 63 (1982), pp. 54–68; Alvin Plantinga, "On Ockham's Way Out," *Faith and Philosophy*, 3 (3) (July 1986), pp. 235–269; Jonathan Kvanvig, *The Possibility of an All-Knowing God* (New York:

St. Martin's Press, 1986), Chap. 3; David Widerker and Eddy M. Zemach, "Facts, Freedom, and Foreknowledge," *Religious Studies*, 23, pp. 19–28; Thomas Talbott, "On Divine Foreknowledge and Bringing About the Past," *Philosophy and Phenomenological Research*, 46 (March 1986), pp. 455–469; Larry Hohm, "Foreknowledge and Unavoidability," unpublished; and Paul Tidman, "Soft-type Hard Facts," unpublished. Note, however, that Alfred Freddoso now rejects the Ockhamist solution in favor of Molinism.

3. "On Ockham's Way Out," op. cit.

4. Marilyn Adams and Norman Kretzmann, Introduction to second edition of Ockham's *Predestination, God's Foreknowledge, and Future Contingents*, pp. 6–10. An extended discussion of this and related points is contained in Marilyn Adams' *William Ockham* (Notre Dame, Ind.: University of Notre Dame Press, 1987), Chap. 27.

5. *Predestination, God's Foreknowledge, and Future Contingents*, trans. by Adams and Kretzmann, q. 2, a. 4, p. 67.

6. Adams and Kretzmann, 46–47.

7. Ibid., p. 50.

8. Nelson Pike, "Divine Omniscience and Voluntary Action," *Philosophical Review*, 74 (January 1965), pp. 27–46.

9. Fischer, "Foreknowledge and Freedom," *Philosophical Review*, 92 (1983), pp. 67–79. In the introduction to the collection *God, Foreknowledge, and Freedom* (Stanford University Press, 1989), p. 6, Fischer refines this principle and calls it the Principle of the Fixity of the Past: (FP) For any action Y, agent S, and time T, if it is true that if S were to do Y at T, then some hard fact about the past (relative to T) would not have been a fact, then S cannot do X at T.

10. Introduction to *God and Freedom*, pp. 35–36.

11. Fischer, p. 36.

12. Fischer, pp. 37–38. Fischer calls soft facts the falsification of which requires falsifying some hard fact "hard-core soft facts" in the introduction to *God and Freedom*.

13. Alfred J. Freddoso, "Accidental Necessity and Logical Determinism," *Journal of Philosophy*, 80 (1983), pp. 257–278.

14. Ibid.

15. Joshua Hoffman and Gary Rosenkrantz, "Hard and Soft Facts," *Philosophical Review*, 93 (July 1984), pp. 419–434.

16. Pp. 102–109.

17. In the case of Hoffman and Rosenkrantz the solution hits a further snag, since softness is merely a necessary condition, not a sufficient condition for nonfixity. Freddoso, Kvanvig, and Widerker intend the solution to go through.

18. John Turk Saunders, "Of God and Freedom," *Philosophical Review*, 75 (April 1966), pp. 219–225.

19. Alvin Plantinga, *God, Freedom, and Evil* (New York: Harper and Row, 1974), pp. 70–71.

20. "On Ockham's Way Out," p. 253.

21. Philip L. Quinn, "Plantinga on Foreknowledge and Freedom," in *Alvin Plantinga, Profiles*, Vol. 5, (Dordrecht: D. Reidel, 1985), pp. 271–287. See also William Craig, "Temporal Necessity: Hard Facts/Soft Facts," *International Journal for Philosophy of Religion*, 20 (1986), pp. 65–91.

22. "On Ockham's Way Out," p. 253.

23. Ibid., p. 252.

24. Fischer has proposed counterexamples to several interpretations of dependency in "Freedom and Foreknowledge," loc. cit.

25. See especially Edward Wierenga, *The Nature of God: An Inquiry into Divine Attributes* (Ithaca, N.Y.: Cornell University Press, 1989), pp. 108–113.

26. "On Ockham's Way Out," p. 254.

27. Ibid.

28. Ibid., p. 259. The exceptions have to do with problems arising from the difference between direct and indirect action (p. 260) and cooperative action (p. 261).

29. Ibid., p. 259.

30. "Counterfactual Dependence and Time's Arrow," *Nous*, 13 (4) (November 1979), pp. 455–477.

31. William Hasker says Quinn now agrees that one of his Power Entailment Principles is true. This will be discussed in Chapter 4.

32. I will examine the relevant subjunctive conditionals in detail in Chapter 4, since I think that the typical examples of true backward-looking subjunctive conditionals do not really express what I am calling a counterfactual dependency of past on future.

33. Jonathan Kvanvig makes this same point in *The Possibility of An All-Knowing God* (New York: St. Martin's Press, 1986), p. 100.

34. "On Ockham's Way Out," p. 248.

35. Ibid., p. 248.

36. See Chapter 1, Section 1.1.

37. William P. Alston, "Does God Have Beliefs?", *Religious Studies*, 22 (1986), pp. 287–306.

38. *Summa Contra Gentiles* I, Chaps. 51–53.

39. Alston, p. 291.

40. Ibid., p. 298.

41. Ibid., pp. 303–304.

42. This point has been made by John Martin Fischer, *Foreknowledge and Freedom*, loc. cit., pp. 76–78.

43. *SCG*, I. Chap. 48.

44. *SCG*, I. Chap. 49.

45. If the proposition *If there was no such thing as time, God would still have beliefs* has an impossible antecedent, it is trivially true on the standard semantics for counterfactuals. I have argued that some of these propositions are true in a nontrivial sense in "What If the Impossible Had Been Actual?," in *Christian*

Theism and the Problems of Philosophy, ed. by Michael Beaty (Notre Dame, Ind.: University of Notre Dame Press, 1990).

Chapter 4

1. Both (1) and (2) can be rewritten for cases in which *S* is still future: (1') If I were to do *S* at *t*, then God would believe prior to *t* that I would do *S* at *t*; (2') If God were to believe prior to *t* that I would do *S* at *t*, then I would do *S* at *t*.

2. Chapter 3, Section 3.2.

3. David Lewis, "Counterfactual Dependence and Time's Arrow," *Nous*, 13 (4) (November 1979), pp. 455–477. In this article Lewis speaks of counterfactual conditionals instead of the more general category of subjunctive conditionals. Since nothing I will say in this chapter depends on the fact that the antecedents of (1) and (2) are *counter*factual, I will usually refer to them as subjunctive conditionals, even though it is most natural to use them in cases in which the antecedents are contrary to fact.

4. Lewis, pp. 459–462. He agrees that there is also the asymmetry of causal direction but, since he prefers to analyze the causal relation in terms of counterfactuals, it is the asymmetry of counterfactual dependence that is basic.

5. Lewis assumes a deterministic world in his discussion of backtracking counterfactuals, but it is not necessary to do so for the point in this section. Even under the assumption that Jim's asking for help is not causally determined, it is reasonable to say that there are circumstances in the past that are causally relevant to his asking or not asking.

6. Lewis, p. 457.

7. Lewis, p. 469.

8. John Pollock, *The Foundations of Philosophical Semantics* (Princeton University Press, 1984), p. 118.

9. John Turk Saunders, "Of God and Freedom," *Philosophical Review*, 75 (April 1966), pp. 100–108.

10. William P. Alston, "Divine Foreknowledge and Alternative Conceptions of Human Freedom," *International Journal for Philosophy of Religion*, 18 (1) (1985), pp. 19–32.

11. In "Power Over the Past," *Pacific Philosophical Quarterly*, 65 (4) (October 1984), pp. 335–350, John Martin Fischer gives an argument that seems to take Lewis's position on backtracking counterfactuals. He analyzes an example structurally similar to (5) and (6) and claims that these examples do not support the truth of (1) in a way that aids the incompatibilist. I think there is no doubt he is right in this claim.

12. P2 and P3 were introduced in Chapter 3, Section 3.2.

13. William Hasker, *God, Time, and Knowledge* (Ithaca, N.Y.: Cornell University Press, 1989), pp. 109–110. Hasker labels these principles PEP 3 and PEP 4, respectively. Note minor stylistic changes to maintain consistency.

14. Hasker, p. 109.

15. Hasker, p. 110.

16. Hasker, p. 112.

17. Hasker, p. 113.

18. E. M. Curley, "Descartes on the Creation of the Eternal Truths," *Philosophical Review*, 92 (4) (October 1984), pp. 569–597. Problems with this position are mentioned by Curley at the end of his article. Other objections have been given by Alvin Plantinga in "Does God Have a Nature?" (Milwaukee: Marquette University Press, 1980), p. 109.

19. Hasker agrees with Talbott that the sense of "necessary condition" intended in clause (c) of PEP 2 is not logical necessity (Hasker, p. 110).

20. Thomas Talbott has recently argued that God has the power to bring about the logically impossible in "On the Divine Nature and the Nature of Divine Freedom," *Faith and Philosophy* 5 (1) (January 1988), pp. 3–24. His argument there is quite different from mine, since he does not question what I have called the traditional picture of modal structure.

21. See Hugh Chandler, "Plantinga and the Contingently Possible," *Analysis*, 36 (1976), pp. 106–109; Nathan Salmon, *Reference and Essence* (Princeton, N.J.: Princeton University Press, 1981), Section 28, pp. 229–259; and Nathan Salmon, "The Logic of What Might Have Been," *Philosophical Review*, 98 (1) (January 1989), pp. 3–34.

22. Lewis claims in *Counterfactuals*, p. 9, that counterfactuals are strict conditionals corresponding to an accessibility assignment determined by similarity of possible worlds.

23. David Basinger has argued in "Divine Omniscience and Human Freedom: A Middle Knowledge Perspective," *Faith and Philosophy* I (1984), pp. 291–302, that the proponent of middle knowledge should not maintain that the agent brings about the truth of a counterfactual of freedom. Like Molina, he claims that no one is responsible of its truth. Its truth is something like a brute fact. In response, William Hasker has pointed out that if the agent is not responsible for the truth of the antecedent A, nor is she responsible for the truth of $A > B$, it is difficult to see how she could be responsible for the truth of the consequent B, where B describes some alleged free act (Hasker, p. 49).

24. John Pollock, *The Foundations of Philosophical Semantics* (Princeton, N.J.: Princeton University Press, 1984), p. 150.

25. Pollock, p. 160.

26. Pollock, p. 118.

27. Pollock, p. 141.

28. Pollock, pp. 153–158.

29. Pollock, p. 171.

30. This criterion does not deny alternative causal routes leading up to the same event, since the worlds in which those routes occur are farther removed from the actual world than the worlds relevant to the question of the causal contingency of this act.

Chapter 5

1. Some of the recent defenders of middle knowledge include Alvin Plantinga, *The Nature of Necessity* (Oxford: Oxford University Press, 1974), Chap. 9, and "Reply to Robert Adams," in Tomberlin and van Inwagen (eds.), *Alvin Plantinga, Profiles*, Vol. 5 (Dordrecht: D. Reidel, 1985): Alfred Freddoso, introduction to *On Divine Foreknowledge: Part IV of the Concordia* by Luis de Molina (Ithaca, N.Y.: Cornell University Press, 1988); Jonathan Kvanvig, *The Possibility of an All-Knowing God* (New York: St. Martin's Press, 1986); William Craig, *The Only Wise God* (Grand Rapids: Baker Publishing House, 1987); Edward Wierenga, *The Nature of God* (Ithaca, N.Y.: Cornell University Press, 1989), Chap. 5; David Basinger, "Divine Omniscience and Human Freedom: A Middle Knowledge Perspective," *Faith and Philosophy*, 1 (1984), pp. 291–302. Vocal opponents include Robert Adams, "Middle Knowledge and the Problem of Evil," *American Philosophical Quarterly*, 14 (April 1977), pp. 109–117, and "Plantinga on the Problem of Evil," Tomberlin and van Inwagen (eds.), *Alvin Plantinga*; and William Hasker *God, Time, and Knowledge* (Ithaca, N.Y.: Cornell University Press, 1989), Chap. 2.

2. Alfred Freddoso, Introduction to Molina's *On Divine Foreknowledge: Part IV of the Concordia* (Ithaca, N. Y.: Cornell University Press, 1988), pp. 23–24.

3. (1) was discussed by Molina, while (2) is an example of Hasker.

4. It might be thought that since transitivity fails for the counterfactual, $\psi 1 >$ *Peter denies Christ is false.* But transitivity does not fail for subjunctive conditionals with true antecedents and true consequents, the kind we are considering. Also, even if transitivity does fail, this theory still explains how God could know *Peter denies Christ* by knowing nothing but $\psi 1$, counterfactuals of freedom, and his own will.

5. Freddoso, introduction to Molina, pp. 23–24.

6. Molina, *On Divine Foreknowledge: Part IV of the Concordia*, trans. by Alfred J. Freddoso, disputation 52, para. 9, p. 168.

7. Freddoso, pp. 2–7.

8. William Lane Craig, *The Only Wise God*, op. cit., p. 135.

9. Plantinga, *The Nature of Necessity*, Chap. 9. Plantinga's free will defense does not depend on the doctrine of middle knowledge, although it is somewhat more interesting if that doctrine is true. For his version of the defense without middle knowledge, see *The Nature of Necessity*, op. cit., pp. 182–184, and "Reply to Robert M. Adams," *Alvin Plantinga, Profiles*, pp. 379–380.

10. Plantinga calls those states of affairs God directly brings about in the world, both in the creation and as a response to human acts, states of affairs *strongly actualized* by God. Those states of affairs brought about by human free choices but permitted by God are states of affairs *weakly actualized* by God. I have not used this distinction in my version of the theory, since the states of affairs brought about in the creation, together with counterfactuals of freedom,

should be sufficient on this theory to determine that the actual world be what it is. This is because those things God strongly actualizes other than the original creation—responses to prayer and the like—are presumably explainable by counterfactuals of freedom about God's choices. If this amendment to the theory is unsatisfactory, my presentation can be easily read in Plantinga's way. What I call world-germ 1 would be identified with what God strongly actualizes in galaxy 1, world-germ 2 would be identified with what God strongly actualizes in galaxy 2, etc.

11. Freddoso, pp. 53–62.

12. Freddoso, pp. 57–58.

13. Disputation 52, paragraph 34; discussed by Freddoso, introduction, p. 58.

14. Freddoso, p. 60.

15. For the possible worlds interpretation of a counterfactual conditional $A > B$ to work, it must make similarity of worlds to the actual world before the event expressed by A much more important than similarity afterward. In fact, there are cases in which similarity afterward does not seem to matter at all (*If the nuclear button had been pushed, ...*). I think the possible worlds interpretation of counterfactuals can be used in a way that is compatible with the intuitions I am discussing in this chapter, but it need not be. Since my objections to middle knowledge do not require the use of the current semantics, I prefer not to discuss the problems with it here.

16. Note that this argument is the exact parallel of Plantinga's argument that he is more sure of the truth of certain counterfactuals of freedom than he is of the possible worlds semantics for counterfactuals.

17. Robert Adams, "Middle Knowledge and the Problem of Evil," op. cit.

18. David Lewis, *Counterfactuals* (Oxford: Oxford University Press, 1973), p. 79f; John Pollock, "Four Kinds of Conditionals," *American Philosophical Quarterly*, 12 (1975), p. 53.

19. Jonathan Kvanvig, *The Possibility of an All-Knowing God* (New York: St. Martin's Press, 1986); Edward Wierenga, *The Nature of God: An Inquiry into Divine Attributes* (Ithaca, N.Y.: Cornell University Press, 1989).

20. Kvanvig, pp. 147–148; Wierenga, Chap. 5, pp. 134–139.

21. *Alvin Plantinga, Profiles*, p. 373.

22. Hasker says in his new book, *God, Time, and Knowledge* (Ithaca, N.Y.: Cornell University Press, 1989), that he assumes that the position of the opponent of middle knowledge is that all counterfactuals of freedom are false (p. 28).

23. Hasker, pp. 35–39.

24. Adams, p. 112.

25. Adams, pp. 113–114.

26. Anthony Kenny, *The God of the Philosophers* (Oxford: Oxford University Press, 1979), pp. 68–71.

27. *Alvin Plantinga, Profiles*, p. 376.

28. Wierenga, p. 150.

29. *Alvin Plantinga, Profiles*, p. 378.

30. Profiles, p. 377.

31. Adams, p. 117.

32. Plantinga has told me this in conversation.

33. The proponents who have so argued include Craig and Basinger. The opponent is Hasker.

34. David Basinger, "Middle Knowledge and Classical Christian Thought," *Religious Studies*, 22 (1986), pp. 412–413.

35. Since a possible world includes God's own action in that world, I should not say that God could have a providential plan for each complete world. Rather I mean to say that he could have such a plan for each world minus that part of it that consists in his carrying out such a plan.

Chapter 6

1. Harry Frankfurt, "Alternative Possibilities and Moral Responsibility," *Journal of Philosophy*, 66 (December 1969), pp. 828–839; reprinted in *Moral Responsibility*, ed. by John Martin Fischer (Ithaca, N.Y.: Cornell University Press, 1986), pp. 143–152.

2. For simplicity, I will assume that each choice involves only two alternatives. The structure of the example can easily be amended to accommodate choices involving more than two alternatives.

3. John Martin Fischer, "Responsibility and Control," *Journal of Philosophy*, 89 (January 1982), p. 26. The article is reprinted in Fischer, op. cit.., pp. 174–190.

4. Peter van Inwagen argues that Frankfurt has not succeeded in dissociating responsibility from the ability to do otherwise in "Ability and Responsibility," *Philosophical Review*, 87 (2) (April 1978), pp. 201–224; reprinted in Fischer, op. cit., pp. 153–173. I will not go through his arguments and the replies that have appeared in the literature. See especially Fischer, "Responsibility and Control," ibid., and Edward Wierenga, *The Nature of God*, pp. 74–85. I am convinced by the Fischer and Wierenga arguments that free will does not entail the ability to do otherwise, given all the conditions which obtain at the time of the choice. Wierenga, however, presents a variant of the principle connecting free will and the ability to choose otherwise that he says is true (p. 85). As far as I can see, the truth of this principle is not a problem for my point in this section.

5. Fischer, pp. 33–34.

6. This is not to deny the possibility that given determinism, the choice might have occurred as the result of a different causal path. But this does not prevent its being the case that if the cause had not occurred the effect would not have either because the worlds in which the effect occurs due to a different causal sequence are no doubt farther removed from the actual world than those worlds in which neither the cause nor the effect occurs. Hence, in the standard semantics of

202 NOTES

counterfactuals, the counterfactual that makes determinism objectionable is still true.

7. William L. Rowe takes a position similar to the one here in "Causing and Being Responsible for What Is Inevitable," *American Philosophical Quarterly*, 26 (2) (April 1989), pp. 153–159. He argues in that paper that there is a class of cases in which a person is responsible for a state of affairs and can be said to have caused the state of affairs to obtain, even though that state of affairs would have obtained regardless of what he did.

8. Linda Zagzebski, "What if the Impossible Had Been Actual?," in *Christian Theism and the Problems of Philosophy*, ed. by Michael Beaty (Notre Dame, Ind.: University of Notre Dame Press, 1990).

9. It has been pointed out to me by Eleonore Stump that the second clause of this definition is open to the objection that internal factors may necessitate my act, though noncausally, and still not preclude my acting freely. For example, a woman's love for her daughter might make it inconceivable that she would permit her daughter to be tortured for a dime, and yet we might still say she rejects the offer of the dime freely. In this case the second clause of my definition would not be satisfied. To block this objection we can weaken the second clause so that it applies only to external, noncausally necessitating factors. Since God's foreknowledge is an externally necessitating factor, the revised definition would still permit my acts to be free in the foreknowledge case.

10. We must assume for this model that the neurologist exists in every world in which I exist. This does not seem to me to be a serious difficulty. For example, if we accept the Kripkean idea that the origin of a being is essential to it, we can avoid this problem by making the neurologist my mother.

11. *ST* I, Q. 83, A. 1, reply obj. 2.

12. As in previous chapters, I am taking "wills" here in a very broad sense that includes permits.

13. Michael Slote, "Selective Necessity and the Free Will Problem," *Journal of Philosophy*, 79 (1) (January 1982), pp. 5–24; and review of Peter van Inwagen's book, *An Essay on Free Will, Journal of Philosophy*, 82 (6) (June 1985), pp. 327–330. There have even been doubts expressed about the transfer principle when the type of necessity in question is logical necessity. See Martin Davies, "Weak Necessity and Truth Theories," *Journal of Philosophical Logic*, 7 (4) (November 1978), pp. 415–439.

14. Slote, "Selective Necessity and Free Will," p. 16.

15. Ideas for these two examples were suggested to me by Timothy Shanahan.

16. Quoted by William Garnett in introduction to *Flatland* by Edwin Abbott Abbott, 5th. ed. (New York: Harper and Row, 1963). p. ix.

17. For the purposes of my use of Abbott's story, we will assume that none of the Flatlanders are lines.

18. *The City of God*, XI, 21, trans. by Marcus Dods (New York: The Modern Library, 1950), p. 364.

Appendix

1. These propositions are strictly equivalent provided that the essentially omniscient foreknower exists in every world in which I go to Santa Barbara next Thursday, a reasonable assumption if such a foreknower is identified with God.

2. The idea that a TNP is involved in this new dilemma was suggested to me by Hasker.

BIBLIOGRAPHY

Adams, Marilyn McCord. 1967. "Is the Existence of God a 'Hard' Fact?" *Philosophical Review*, 76 (October), 492–503.

———. 1987. *William Ockham*. Notre Dame, Ind.: University of Notre Dame Press.

Adams, Robert. 1977. "Middle Knowledge and the Problem of Evil." *American Philosophical Quarterly*, 14 (April), pp. 109–117.

———. 1985. "Alvin Plantinga on the Problem of Evil." In Tomberlin and van Inwagen (1985).

Albritton, Rogers. 1957. "Present Truth and Future Contingency." *Philosophical Review*, 66 (January), 1–28.

Alston, William P. 1985. "Divine Foreknowledge and Alternative Conceptions of Human Freedom." *International Journal for Philosophy of Religion*, 18, 19–32.

———. 1986. "Does God Have Beliefs?" *Religious Studies*, 22 (September/December), 287–306.

Aquinas, St. Thomas. *Summa Theologiae*, I, Q. 10, 14, and 25.

———. *Summa Contra Gentiles*, Chap. 65.

Augustine. *On the Free Choice of the Will*.

———. *The City of God*, Book V.

Basinger, David. 1984. "Divine Omniscience and Human Freedom: A 'Middle Knowledge' Perspective." *Faith and Philosophy*, 1 (July), 291–302.

———. 1986. "Middle Knowledge and Classical Christian Thought." *Religious Studies*, 22 (September/December), 407–422.

———. 1987. "Middle Knowledge and Human Freedom: Some Clarifications." *Faith and Philosophy*, 4 (July), 330–336.

Basinger, David, and Basinger, Randall. 1986. *Predestination and Free Will: Four Views of Divine Sovereignty and Human Freedom*. Downers Grove, Ill.: Intervarsity Press.

Bennett, Jonathan. 1984. "Counterfactuals and Temporal Dependence." *Philosophical Review*, 93 (January), 57–91.

Boethius. *The Consolation of Philosophy*.

Burrell, David B. 1984. "God's Eternity." *Faith and Philosophy*, 1 (October), 389–406.

Cahn, Steven M. 1967. *Fate, Logic, and Time*. New Haven, Conn.: Yale University Press.

Castaneda, Hector-Neri. 1976. "Omniscience and Idexical Reference." *Journal of Philosophy*, 64 (April), 203–209.

Chapman, T. 1982. *Time: A Philosophical Analysis.* Dordrecht, Holland: D. Reidel.

Cicero. *De Fato.*

———. *De Divinitatis.*

Clark, David W. 1978. "Ockham on Human and Divine Freedom." *Franciscan Studies*, 38, 122–160.

Cook, Monte. 1982. "Tips for Time Travel." In *Philosophers Look at Science Fiction*, ed. by Nicholas D. Smith. Chicago: Nelson-Hall.

Cook, Robert R. 1987. "God, Time and Freedom." *Religious Studies*, 23 (March), 81–94.

Craig, William Lane. 1985. "Was Aquinas a B-Theorist of Time?" *New Scholasticism* 59 (Autumn), 475–483.

———. 1986. "Temporal Necessity: Hard Facts/Soft Facts." *International Journal for Philosophy of Religion*, 20, 65–91.

———. 1987a. "Divine Foreknowledge and Newcomb's Paradox." *Philosophia*, 17 (October), 331–350.

———. 1987b. *The Only Wise God.* Grand Rapids, Mich.: Baker.

———. 1988a. "Tachyons, Time Travel, and Divine Omniscience." *Journal of Philosophy*, 85 (March), 135–150.

———. 1988b. *The Problem of Divine Foreknowledge and Future Contingents from Aristotle to Suarez.* Leiden: E. J. Brill.

Davies, Martin. 1983. "Boethius and Others on Divine Foreknowledge." *Pacific Philosophical Quarterly*, 64 (October), 313–329.

Davis, Charles C., and McKim, Vaughn R. 1976. "Temporal Modalities and the Future." *Notre Dame Journal of Symbolic Logic*, 17 (April), 233–238.

Davis, Stephen T. 1979. "Divine Omniscience and Human Freedom." *Religious Studies*, 15 (September), 303–316.

———. 1983. *Logic and the Nature of God.* Grand Rapids, Mich.: Eerdmans.

Dummett, Michael. 1964. "Bringing About the Past." *Philosophical Review*, 73, 338–359; reprinted in Gale (1968), 252–274.

Dwyer, Larry. 1975. "Time Travel and Changing the Past." *Philosophical Studies*, 27 (May), 341–350.

Earman, John. 1976. "Causation: A Matter of Life and Death." *Journal of Philosophy*, 73 (January), 5–25.

Edidin, Aron, and Normore, Calvin. 1982. "Ockham on Prophecy." *International Journal for Philosophy of Religion*, 13, 179–189.

Edwards, Jonathan. *Freedom of the Will* (1745).

Ehring, Douglas. 1982. "Causal Asymmetry." *Journal of Philosophy*, 79 (December), 761–774.

Factor, R. Lance. 1978. "Newcomb's Paradox and Omniscience." *International Journal for Philosophy of Religion*, 9, 30–40.

Fischer, John Martin. 1982. "Responsibility and Control." *Journal of Philosophy*, 79 (January), 24–40.

———. 1983a. "Incompatibilism." *Philosophical Studies*, 43 (January), 127–137.

———. 1983b. "Freedom and Foreknowledge." *Philosophical Review*, 92 (January), 67–79.

———. 1984. "Power Over the Past." *Pacific Philosophical Quarterly*, 65 (October), 335–350.

———. 1985. "Ockhamism." *Philosophical Review*, 94 (January), 81–100.

———. 1986a. "Hard-Type Soft Facts." *Philosophical Review*, 95 (October), 591–601.

———. 1986b. "Pike's Ockhamism." *Analysis*, 46 (January), 57–63.

———. 1988. "Freedom and Actuality." In Morris (1988).

———. 1989. *God, Foreknowledge, and Freedom.* (ed.) Stanford, Calif.: Stanford University Press.

Fitzgerald, Paul. 1970. "Tachyons, Backwards Causation, and Freedom." In *Boston Studies in the Philosophy of Science VIII*, ed. by Roger C. Buck and Robert S. Cohen. Dordrecht, Holland: D. Reidel.

———. 1974. "On Retrocausality." *Philosophia*, 4 (October), 513–551.

———. 1985. "Stump and Kretzmann on Time and Eternity." *Journal of Philosophy*, 82 (May), 260–269.

Flint, Thomas. 1983. "The Problem of Divine Freedom." *American Philosophical Quarterly*, 20 (July), 255–264.

Flint, Thomas P., and Freddoso, Alfred J. "Maximal Power." In Freddoso (1983).

Frankfurt, Harry G. 1969. "Alternate Possibilities and Moral Responsibility." *Journal of Philosophy*, 66 (December), 829–839.

———. 1971. "Freedom of the Will and the Concept of a Person." *Journal of Philosophy*, 68 (January), 5–20.

Freddoso, Alfred J. 1982a. "Accidental Necessity and Power over the Past." *Pacific Philosophical Quarterly*, 63 (January), 54–68.

———. 1982b. "Accidental Necessity and Logical Determinism." *Journal of Philosophy*, 80 (May), 257–278.

———. 1983. *The Existence and Nature of God.* (ed.) Notre Dame, Ind.: University of Notre Dame Press.

———. 1988a. "Introduction." In Molina (1988).

Gale, Richard M. (ed.) 1968. *The Philosophy of Time.* Atlantic Highlands, N.J.: Humanities Press.

Geach, Peter T. 1969. *God and the Soul.* London: Routledge and Kegan Paul.

———. 1977. *Providence and Evil.* Cambridge: Cambridge University Press.

Ginet, Carl. 1980. "The Conditional Analysis of Freedom." In *Time and Cause: Essays Presented to Richard Taylor*, ed. by Peter van Inwagen. Dordrecht, Holland: D. Reidel.

———. 1983. "In Defense of Incompatibilism." *Philosophical Studies*, 44 (November), 391–400.

Haack, S. 1974. "On a Theological Argument for Fatalism." *Philosophical Quarterly*, 24 (April), 156–159.

Hasker, William. 1983. "Concerning the Intelligibility of 'God is Timeless'." *New Scholasticism*, 57 (Spring), 170–195.

———. 1985. "Foreknowledge and Necessity." *Faith and Philosophy*, 2 (April), 121–157.

———. 1987. "The Hardness of the Past: A Reply to Reichenbach." *Faith and Philosophy*, 4 (July), 337–342.

———. 1988. "Hard Facts and Theological Fatalism." *Nous*, 22 (September), 419–436.

———. 1989. *God, Time, and Knowledge*. Ithaca, N.Y.: Cornell University Press.

Heinaman, Robert. 1986. "Incompatibilism Without the Principle of Alternative Possibilities." *Australasian Journal of Philosophy*, 64, 266–276.

Helm, P. 1974a. "Divine Foreknowledge and Facts." *Canadian Journal of Philosophy*, 4 (December), 305–315.

———. 1974b. "On Theological Fatalism Again." *Philosophical Quarterly*, 24 (October), 360–362.

———. 1975a. "Fatalism Once More." *Philosophical Quarterly*, 25 (October), 289–296.

———. 1975b. "Timelessness and Foreknowledge." *Mind*, 84 (October), 516–527.

Hoffman, Joshua. 1979. "Pike on Possible Worlds, Divine Foreknowledge and Human Freedom." *Philosophical Review*, 88 (July), 433–442.

Hoffman, Joshua, and Rosenkrantz, Gary. 1980. "On Divine Foreknowledge and Human Freedom." *Philosophical Studies*, 37 (April), 289–296.

———. 1984. "Hard and Soft Facts." *Philosophical Review*, 93 (July), 419–435.

Holt, Dennis. 1981. "Timelessness and the Metaphysics of Temporal Existence." *American Philosophical Quarterly*, 18, 149–156.

Horwich, Paul. 1975. "On Some Alleged Paradoxes of Time Travel." *Journal of Philosophy*, 72 (August), 432–444.

Kenny, Anthony, ed. 1969a. *Aquinas: A Collection of Critical Essays*. Notre Dame, Ind.: University of Notre Dame Press.

———. 1969b. "Divine Foreknowledge and Human Freedom." In Kenny (1969a).

———. 1979. *The God of the Philosophers*. Oxford: Oxford University Press.

Kneale, William. 1960–1961. "Time and Eternity in Theology." *Proceedings of the Aristotelian Society*, 61, 87–108.

Kretzmann, Norman. 1966. "Omniscience and Immutability." *Journal of Philosophy*, 63 (July), 409–421.

Kvanvig, Jonathan. 1986. *The Possibility of an All-Knowing God*. New York: St. Martin's Press.

Lewis, David. 1973. *Counterfactuals*. Cambridge, Mass.: Harvard University Press.

———. 1976. "The Paradoxes of Time Travel." *American Philosophical Quarterly*, 13 (April), 145–152.

———. 1979. "Counterfactual Dependence and Time's Arrow." *Nous*, 13 (November), 455–476.

Locke, John. *An Essay Concerning Human Understanding*.

Lonergan, Bernard. 1971. *Grace and Freedom*. London: Darton, Longman, and Todd; New York: Herder and Herder.

Lorizan, Andros. 1986. *The Reality of Time*. Brookfield, Vt.: Gower.

Lucas, J. R. 1970. *The Freedom of the Will*. Oxford: Oxford University Press.

———. 1989. *The Future*. Cambridge, Mass.: Blackwell.

Lukasiewicz, Jan. 1967a. "On Determinism." In McCall (1967).

Mackie, J. L. 1955. "Evil and Omnipotence." *Mind*, 64 (April), 200–212.

———. 1966. "The Direction of Causation." *Philosophical Review*, 75 (October), 441–456.

Mann, William. 1985. "Epistemology Supernaturalized." *Faith and Philosophy*, 2 (October), 436–456.

Maritain, Jacques. 1966. *God and the Permission of Evil*. (Aquinas Lecture), trans. by Joseph W. Evans. Milwaukee: Marquette University Press.

Mavrodes, George. 1976. "Aristotelian Necessity and Freedom." In *Midwest Studies in Philosophy 1*, ed. by Peter French, Theodore E. Uehling, Jr., and Howard Wettstein. Minneapolis: University of Minnesota Press.

———. 1983. "Vestigial Modalities." *Analysis*, 43 (March), 91–94.

———. 1984. "Is the Past Unpreventable?" *Faith and Philosophy*, 1 (April), 131–146.

Mayo, Bernard. 1962. "The Open Future." *Mind* 71; reprinted in Gale (1968), 275–291.

McArthur, Robert P. 1974. "Factuality and Modality in the Future Tense." *Nous*, 8 (September), 283–288.

McCall, Storrs. 1976. "Objective Time Flow." *Philosophy of Science*, 43 (September), 337–362.

Molina, Luis de. 1988. *On Divine Foreknowledge* (*Part IV of the Concordia*.), trans. and introd. by Alfred J Freddoso. Ithaca, N.Y.: Cornell University Press.

Nerlich, Graham. 1979. "How to Make Things Have Happened." *Canadian Journal of Philosophy*, 9 (March), 1–22.

Newton-Smith, W. H. 1980. *The Structure of Time*. London: Routledge and Kegan Paul.

Normore, Calvin. 1982. "Future Contingents." In *Cambridge History of Later Medieval Philosophy*, ed. by Norman Kretzmann, Anthony Kenny, and Jan Pinborg. Cambridge: Cambridge University Press.

———. 1985. "Divine Omniscience, Omnipotence, and Future Contingents: An Overview." In Rudavsky (1985a).

Nozick, Robert. 1970. "Newcomb's Problem and Two Principles of Choice." In *Essays in Honor of Carl G. Hempel*. ed. by Nicholas Rescher. Dordrecht, Holland: D. Reidel.

Ockham, William. 1969. *Predestination, God's Foreknowledge and Future Contingents*. trans. by Marilyn McCord Adams and Norman Kretzmann. Indianapolis: Hackett.

———. 1980. *Ockham's Theory of Propositions: Part II of the Summa Logicae*, trans. by Alfred J. Freddoso and Henry Schuurman. Notre Dame, Ind.: University of Notre Dame Press.

Pike, Nelson. 1965. "Divine Omniscience and Voluntary Action." *Philosophical Review*, 74 (January), 27–46.

———. 1966. "Of God and Freedom: A Rejoinder." *Philosophical Review*, 75 (July), 369–379.

———. 1969. "Omnipotence and God's Ability to Sin." *American Philosophical Quarterly*, 6 (July), 208–216.

———. 1970. *God and Timelessness*. London: Routledge and Kegan Paul.

———. 1977. "Divine Foreknowledge, Human Freedom and Possible Worlds." *Philosophical Review*, 86 (April), 209–216.

———. 1984. "Fischer on Freedom and Foreknowledge." *Philosophical Review*, 93 (October), 599–614.

Pinnock, Clark H. 1986. "God Limits His Knowledge." In Basinger and Basinger (1986).

Plantinga, Alvin. 1973. "Which Worlds Could God Have Created?" *Journal of Philosophy*, 70 (October), 539–555.

———. 1974a. *God, Freedom and Evil*. New York: Harper and Row.

———. 1974c. *The Nature of Necessity*. Oxford: Oxford University Press.

———. 1980. "Does God Have a Nature?" *Aquinas Lecture*. Milwaukee: Marquette University Press.

———. 1986. "On Ockham's Way Out." *FP*, 3 (July), 235–269.

Prior, Arthur. 1957. *Time and Modality*. Oxford: Oxford University Press.

———. 1959. "Thank Goodness That's Over." *Philosophy*, 34 (January), 12–17.

———. 1962. "The Formalities of Omniscience." *Philosophy*, 37 (April), 114–129.

———. 1967. *Past, Present, and Future*. Oxford: Oxford University Press.

———. 1968. "On the Logic of Ending Time." In *Papers on Time and Tense*. Oxford: Oxford University Press.

Purtill, Richard. 1974. "Foreknowledge and Fatalism." *Religious Studies*, 10 (September), 319–324.

Quinn, Philip L. 1978. "Divine Foreknowledge and Divine Freedom." *International Journal for Philosophy of Religion*, 9, 219–240.

———. 1985. "Plantinga on Freedom and Foreknowledge." In Tomberlin and van Inwagen (1985).

Reichenbach, Bruce. 1984. "Omniscience and Deliberation." *International Journal for Philosophy of Religion*, 16, 225–236.

———. 1986. "God Limits His Power." In Basinger and Basinger (1986).

———. 1987. "Hasker on Omniscience." *Faith and Philosophy*, 4 (January), 86–92.

Rosenthal, David M. 1976. "The Necessity of Foreknowledge." *Midwest Studies in Philosophy 1*, ed. by Peter French, Theodore E. Uehling, Jr., and Howard Wettstein. Minneapolis: University of Minnesota Press.

Ross, James. 1983. "Creation II." In Freddoso (1983).

Rowe, William L. 1964. "Augustine on Foreknowledge and Free Will." *Review of Metaphysics*, 18 (December), 356–363.

———. 1978. *Philosophy of Religion*. Belmont, Calif.: Wadsworth.

———. 1980. "On Divine Foreknowledge and Human Freedom: A Reply." *Philosophical Studies*, 37 (May), 429–430.

Rudavsky, Tamar, ed. 1985. *Divine Omniscience and Omnipotence in Medieval Philosophy*. Dordrecht, Holland: D. Reidel.

Runzo, Joseph. 1981. "Omniscience and Freedom for Evil." *International Journal for Philosophy of Religion*, 12, #3, 131–147.

Saunders, John Turk. 1958. "Sea Fight Tomorrow?" *Philosophical Review*, 67 (July), 367–378.

———. 1965. "Fatalism and Ordinary Language." *Journal of Philosophy*, 62 (April), 211–222.

———. 1966. "Of God and Freedom." *Philosophical Review*, 75 (April), 219–225.

———. 1968. "The Temptations of 'Powerlessness.'" *American Philosophical Quarterly*, 5 (April), 100–108.

Schlesinger, George N. 1980. *Aspects of Time*. Indianapolis: Hackett.

Slote, Michael. 1982. "Selective Necessity and the Free-Will Problem." *Journal of Philosophy*, 79 (January), 5–24.

Smith, Quentin. 1985. "On the Beginning of Time." *Nous*, 19 (December), 579–584.

Sorabji, Richard. 1980. *Necessity, Cause, and Blame: Perspectives on Aristotle's Theory*. Ithaca, N.Y.: Cornell University Press.

Stalnaker, Robert. 1968. "A Theory of Conditionals." In *Studies in Logical Theory*, ed. by Nicholas Rescher. Oxford: Oxford University Press.

Steuer, Axel D. 1983. "The Freedom of God and Human Freedom." *Scottish Journal of Theology*, 36, 163–180.

Streveler, Paul A. 1973. "The Problems of Future Contingents." *New Scholasticism*, 47 (Spring), 233–247.

Stump, Eleonore, and Kretzmann, Norman. 1981. "Eternity." *Journal of Philosophy*, 78 (August), 429–458.

———. 1987. "Atemporal Duration: A Reply to Fitzgerald." *Journal of Philosophy*, 84 (April), 214–219.

Suarez, Francisco. *De Divina Gratia*.

———. *De Scientia Quam Deus Habet de Futuria Contingentibus*.

———. *Opera Omina*.

Swinburne, Richard. 1977. *The Coherence of Theism*. Oxford: Oxford University Press.

Talbott, Thomas B. 1986. "On Divine Foreknowledge and Bringing About the Past." *Philosophy and Phenomenological Research*, 46 (March), 455–469.

Taliaferro, Charles. 1985. "Divine Cognitive Power." *International Journal for Philosophy of Religion*, 18, #3, 133–140.

Taylor, Richard. 1957. "The Problem of Future Contingency." *Philosophical Review*, 66 (January), 1–28.

———. 1962. "Fatalism." *Philosophical Review*, 71 (January), 56–66.

———. 1964. "Deliberation and Foreknowledge." *American Philosophical Quarterly*, 1 (January), 73–80.

Thomason, Richard. 1970. "Indeterminist Time and Truth-Value Gaps." *Theoria*, 36 (November), 264–281.

Tomberlin, James, and van Inwagen, Peter, eds. 1985. *Alvin Plantinga*. Dordrecht, Holland: D. Reidel. *Profiles*, Vol. 5.

van Inwagen, Peter. 1983. *An Essay on Free Will*. Oxford: Clarendon Press.

Walls, J. L. 1987. "A Fable of Foreknowledge and Freedom." *Philosophy*, 62 (January), 67–75.

Waterlow, Sarah. 1974. "Backward Causation and Continuing." *Mind*, 83 (July), 372–387.

Whitrow, G. J. 1980. *The Natural Philosophy of Time*. Oxford: Clarendon Press.

Widerker, D., and Zemach, E. M. 1987. "Facts, Freedom and Foreknowledge." *Religious Studies*, 23 (March), 19–28.

Wierenga, Edward. 1989. *The Nature of God: An Inquiry into Divine Attribute*. Ithaca, N.Y.: Cornell University Press.

Williams, C. J. F. "True Tomorrow, Never True Today." *Philosophical Quarterly*, 28 (October), 285–299.

Wippel, John F. 1985. "Divine Knowledge, Divine Power and Human Freedom in Thomas Aquinas and Henry of Ghent." In Rudavsky.

Wolterstorff, Nicholas. 1982. "God Everlasting." In *God and the Good*, ed. by Clifton J. Orlebeke and Lewis B. Smedes. Grand Rapids, Mich.: Eerdmans. Reprinted in *Contemporary Philosophy of Religion*, ed. by Steven M. Cahn and David Shatz. Oxford: Oxford University Press.

Zagzebski, Linda. 1985. "Divine Foreknowledge and Human Free Will." *Religious Studies*, 21 (September), 279–298.

———. 1990. "What if the Impossible Had Been Actual?". In *Christian Theism and the Problems of Philosophy*, ed. by Michael Beaty. Notre Dame, Ind.: University of Notre Dame Press.

Index